JESUS IS DEAD

Jesus is Dead

Robert M. Price

2007
American Atheist Press
Cranford, New Jersey

Published April 2007 by American Atheist Press
ISBN-10: 1-57884-000-7
ISBN-13: 978-1-57884-000-7

American Atheist Press
P. O. Box 5733
Parsippany, NJ 07054-6733
Voice: (908) 276-7300
FAX: (908) 276-7402

www.atheists.org

Library of Congress Cataloging-in-Publication Data

Price, Robert M., 1954-
  Jesus is dead / Robert M. Price.
      p. cm.
  ISBN-13: 978-1-57884-000-7
  ISBN-10: 1-57884-000-7
  1. Jesus Christ--Resurrection. 2. Christianity--Controversial
literature. 3. Jesus Christ--Historicity. I. Title.

BT482.P75 2007
232.5--dc22
                          2007008294

Printed in the United States of America

This book is dedicated to
August Berkshire,
An Atheist more Christ-like than Christians

CONTENTS

Introduction

There's no shame in it. Everybody dies. Even great historical figures. Even Jesus. No one will deny that – at least if one believes there *was* an historical Jesus in the first place – but that's another can of worms! The issue is, did he *stay* dead? Everybody else does. Why should Jesus be an exception? But the Christian claim is that Jehovah *did* make an exception in his case — handing him over to the Grim Reaper, yes, but then snatching him back before his corpse was scarcely cool. How does one evaluate such a claim? Insofar as its proponents urge it upon us as a datum of history, we must evaluate the resurrection creed in historical terms. And the verdict I must then return is the title of this book. It is not quite so simple, but I do not want to obfuscate the issue with a haze of religious sentimentality as many do.

In the present collection I have assembled some of my best writing and thinking on the resurrection (and in a couple of cases, closely related issues). "Easter Fictions" was the opening statement in a debate I had at Colorado State University with Dr. Craig Blomberg. The next two, "What Can We Know of the Historical Jesus?" and "Must Jesus Have Risen?" are condensed versions of two chapters from my book *Beyond Born Again* (out of print at the moment). I have found these versions useful in debates with my pal and sparring partner Greg Boyd at UCLA and other venues. I wrote "Night of the Living Savior" for the 2005 Atheist Alliance conference in Los Angeles. "Was Jesus John the Baptist Risen from the Dead?" was a Jesus Seminar paper that nearly convinced even the late, great Robert Funk. "How Secure Is the New Testament Witness?" began as a long answer to a question by my friend Fred Lykes.

"Templars and the Tomb of Jesus" grew out of research I did for another book, *The Da Vinci Fraud: Why the Truth is Stranger than Fiction* (Prometheus Books). There turned out to be too many related books to survey in that context, but they invited comment anyway, and this seems the place for those comments. I analyzed another bit of pseudo-evidence about Jesus, *The Talmud of Jmmanuel*, for a course I teach on Modern Gospels. Fundamentalists are not the only pseudo-scholars requiring refutation. I don't accept the dictum that "the only heresy is orthodoxy." No, there are plenty of crazy views out there in need of refutation. Why not just ignore them? Why not welcome them as allies in the struggle against reigning orthodoxy? For a very simple reason. If we are offering a credible, viable, even compelling alternative to orthodox beliefs about the Bible, it is important that we be equally impatient with other inadequate treatments of the Bible and Christian origins.

If we welcome any old attack on the traditional creeds, we are embodying the caricature (at least I *hope* it's a caricature) drawn of us by our foes, namely that we dislike Christianity just because it's Christianity, not because we are really interested in the facts. Well, I *am* interested in the facts, and I must demonstrate that I am impartial in my scrutiny. I do not target fundamentalist apologetics because I have a vendetta against fundamentalism. Rather, as a biblical scholar, I attack any and all views insofar as they misuse and manipulate the Bible. A Homer scholar would feel the same concern to respond to all fanatical appropriations of the *Iliad* and the *Odyssey* (that is, if there were any). Besides, it seems to me that a fundamentalist who relishes a demolition of *Holy Blood, Holy Grail* may have a harder time laughing it off when the same critical criteria are then applied to his own favorite axe-grinders. What is sauce for Michael Baigent is sauce for William Lane Craig. When I sit down to review a book, I take the opportunity to write something of an essay not only on the book itself but on the wider questions addressed in it. Some of these reviews, I am vain enough to think, feature valuable ideas tucked away here and there. I would like to recirculate them here for something of a wider reading. I have several times been asked to review and critique Internet essays by various apologists, and I have shaped up and polished some of these comments for this book, too. Several major issues central to the resurrection and the origins of Christianity come up for consideration, and I think I have made some interesting points. Here's your chance to consider them.

I conclude the book with another opening statement, "Christ a Fiction," this one for a debate with John Rankin, a fine fellow whom I debated at the Unitarian Church of Montclair.

I guess I ought to apologize for the occasional sarcasm scattered through these pages. There is a limit to the degree that I can show politeness without being a hypocrite. You see, I don't want to make an outrageous proposition sound like it deserves any respect by speaking of it respectfully. I don't want to get sucked into that trap.

My fellow Atheists, my fellow Bible-lovers, let me commend the humble search for truth, for which, unless we live in a cosmic madhouse, no one will be damned.

Robert M. Price
May 2, 2006

Easter Fictions

Enter and Exit the Apologist

For some dozen years I was a born-again Christian. I did quite a lot of personal witnessing, and eventually I studied apologetics as an aid to evangelism. I knew I could not argue anyone into the kingdom of God, but if I were well prepared, I hoped I might help unbelievers get past certain questions that were keeping them from faith. How could I expect them to accept Christ as their savior if it were an open question whether Christ even existed? And so on. I was active in InterVarsity Christian Fellowship, where I devoured the works of many Christian apologists, most of them centering upon New Testament issues, mainly the historical Jesus. I read everything I could get my hands on by John Warwick Montgomery (*History and Christianity,* 1964), F. F. Bruce (*The New Testament Documents: Are They Reliable?* 1960), J. N. D. Anderson, *Christianity: The Witness of History,* 1969) and *The Evidence for the Resurrection,* 1966), Edwin M. Yamauchi, *Jesus, Zoroaster, Buddha, Socrates, Muhammad,* 1972), Frank Morison, *Who Moved the Stone?* 1930), Ralph P. Martin (*Mark: Evangelist and Theologian,* 1972), I. Howard Marshall (*Luke: Historian and Theologian,* 1970), Josh McDowell (*Evidence That Demands a Verdict,* 1972, and *More Evidence That Demands a* Verdict, 1975), and others.

These writers compose a mixed bag. Bruce, Martin, and Marshall were all genuine New Testament scholars, but they were half-apologists — what James Barr (in his amazingly insightful book, *Fundamentalism*, 1976) called "maximal conservatives." They functioned within a certain ecclesiastical-academic world in which the traditional seemed always the most plausible. Any theory outside of certain parameters just could not seem worthwhile to them. Thus, while seeming to employ critical arguments and axioms, they always, in virtually every case, arrived at "safe" conclusions comfortable for orthodoxy. Anderson and Montgomery, though very well read in history and theology, were primarily legal scholars, and they disdained what seemed to them the excessively skeptical procedures of professional New Testament specialists. This put them in the odd position of claiming, precisely as outsiders to the field, to know better than the insiders, a stance that comes in quite handy in apologetics, as when a chiropractor praises himself as being "independent of the medical establishment." Morison and McDowell were just hacks, Morison a very imaginative one, McDowell a jack-of-all-trades who mainly amassed research done by students and organized it into syllabi of paragraph-length notes and quotes. Reading the works of all these men, I learned much — some of it valid.

As years went by and I augmented what I read from them with my own research, I came to be amazed again and again to discover major items of relevant information, even whole aspects of crucial questions, that I would never have been aware of had I rested satisfied with my old guiding lights. I could not imagine they could have been ignorant of many cases and parallels that simply shattered their arguments. As I eventually read the works of the critics and skeptics whom the apologists and maximal conservatives so eloquently refuted, I realized their arguments had not been treated fairly or representatively.

Upon my college graduation, I enrolled at Gordon-Conwell Theological Seminary, where I had the privilege of studying with evangelical New Testament scholars David M. Scholer (*A Basic Bibliographic Guide for New Testament Exegesis,* 1973; *Nag Hammadi Bibliography, 1948-1969*; *Nag Hammadi Bibliography, 1970-1994* [both 1997], *Women in Ministry,* 1987), Gordon D. Fee (commentaries on the Corinthian, Philippian, and Pastoral Epistles; *Gospel and Spirit,* 1991; *Paul, the Spirit, and the People of God,* 1996), Andrew T. Lincoln (commentaries on Ephesians and John), and J. Ramsey Michaels (*Servant and Son: Jesus in Parable and Gospel,* 1982, commentaries on Revelation, John, and 1 Peter). These men were all quite conservative, though in some ways progressive, and all genuine scholars.

I recall the last course I took at Gordon-Conwell, an exciting, high-level seminar taught by all four of these professors, called "New Testament Canon and Hermeneutics." As I weighed their sophisticated and fine-tuned reasonings, I remember being impressed with what a fragile mind-game it all was. Even as believers in the supernatural, they were all too cognizant of the great distance that lay between the first century and our own, and the conceptual bridges they sought to build dwarfed the Bridge over the River Kwai. It was such a house of cards, such a stretch getting from the supposedly inspired and authoritative texts of the apostles to theological assertions or ethics of today, that I realized a sophisticated evangelicalism was in one sense a contradiction in terms. The learned professors wanted badly to preach the Bible with the note of authority they were accustomed to from their church backgrounds. But they knew it was not so simple, and as a result their efforts were aimed at working their way back to simplicity by a complex and twisted path. Just as the maximal conservative New Testament historian really wishes the Higher Criticism did not exist and essentially spends his time trying to turn the clock back and neutralize the results of real criticism, so does the evangelical hermeneut try to justify with appeals to Wittgenstein and Polanyi the simplistic stance which criticism properly renders impossible.

You know by now that these studies wound up having the last result I ever would have anticipated. I came to the end of my evangelical faith, abandoning belief in the authority of the Bible and the resurrection of Jesus. How did this happen? It all comes down to this: I learned from evangelical Christianity a love for the exegesis of scripture above all things. I learned what I still believe: that it is an intellectual sin to fudge the meaning of the text, to stretch it to mean what you want it to mean. Thus I forswore the harmonizations used by apologists to keep the Bible sounding inerrant and authoritative. I concluded that my faith must in the end be sacrificed to keep myself honest with the text. Otherwise, if I twisted the text for the sake of my faith, what could my faith possibly be worth?

Literature, not History

It is for the sake of understanding the New Testament as accurately as I can that I have learned to read the gospel resurrection accounts as the products of legend and of creative redaction by the gospel writers. I love these texts. I do not mean to attack them, only to get them straight in my mind, to apprehend them as accurately and realistically as I can. To believe, as I used to, that they are historical reportage now seems to me an implausible way of reading them. It is a reading in the service of a dogmatic agenda, one I used to hold myself. My conclusion has nothing to do with any so-called "naturalistic presuppositions," for I hold none. I gladly acknowledge that there must be far more things in heaven and earth than are dreamt of in my philosophy.

Apologists often admit that the gospel resurrection narratives seem to contradict one another. They go on to suggest possible ways in which all the details might be salvaged, combined in some great, synoptic mosaic. But these efforts strike me as no more plausible than Harold Lindsell's attempts to have Peter deny Jesus six times. Worse, they miss the point. The contradictions are not flies in the ointment; they are clues to a mystery. They do not so much spoil the evidence of the texts; instead, they are crucial evidence for understanding the texts. As Warfield might have said, they are *indicia*, pointers to the fictive character of the texts. Here's what I mean.

Mark 16:1–8, the earliest version of the Easter story, features the discovery of the empty tomb and the interpretive words of a young man, perhaps an angel. He announces that the absence of the body means that Jesus has risen. His words anticipate an appearance of Jesus, but none is offered. In the oldest and best manuscripts, Mark's gospel ends right there. (Some time later, used to reading the fuller accounts of Matthew and Luke, which extend beyond the empty tomb, some scribe added Mark 16:9–20, in which Jesus does appear to this and that disciple after all. Independently, someone else supplied yet a different, much shorter, ending for Mark's gospel.)

By itself, as Charles Talbert has shown, the empty tomb story looks so much like other ancient 'apotheosis' narratives, *e.g.*, of Apollonius, Empedocles, Romulus, Hercules, *etc.*, that it seems to me special pleading to insist that Mark's is however not one more of these legends but rather a report of historical fact. Here is another:

> Heracles sent Licymnius and Iolaus to Delphi to ask Apollo what he should do about the sickness [caused by the poison his wife had put on his shirt, thinking it was a love charm].

The god replied through an oracle that Heracles should be brought along with his armor to Oete and that a giant pyre should be prepared. The god stated that what followed should be up to Zeus. When Iolaus and his companions had carried out these commands, they withdrew to a distance to see what would happen. Heracles, given up hope for himself, went to the pyre and asked everyone coming up to him to light it. No one dared to obey him except Philoctetes. Having received the gift of Heracles' bow in return for this service, he lit the pyre. Immediately lightning bolts fell all around, and the entire pyre was consumed in flames. After this, Iolaus and his companions came to collect the bones, but they did not find a single bone. They supposed that Heracles in accordance with the oracle had passed from men to the gods. (Diodorus Siculus, *Library of History* 4:38:4–5).

Matthew and Luke, both using Mark as their basis, jump off the diving board provided by Mark 16:1–8, but they jump in different directions. Especially since each evangelist's continuation bears ample marks of that writer's distinctive style and vocabulary, the most natural inference would be that each is making it up as he goes along. Similarly, various writers have tried their hand at finishing Dickens's fragment *The Mystery of Edwin Drood*. No one would take a second author's attempt to continue the abrupt work of the first to be historical fact. The very nature of the enterprise shows the whole to be fiction. Matthew and Luke are, so to speak, each taking a crack at finishing *Edwin Drood*. They are writing fiction.

Matthew has altered Mark's unseemly ending so that the fleeing women obey the charge of the angel at the tomb. And he adds a sudden appearance of the Risen Jesus to the same women. But this Jesus merely repeats the charge the angel gave them, which implies that the Jesus episode is Matthew's doubling of Mark's young man episode. I think it likely that in this way Matthew sought to clear up the ambiguity left by Mark's description of the "young man" — who was he? An angel? Or Jesus himself? Matthew decided to cover both bases, so he divides the scene between an angel and Jesus, having them both bear essentially the same tidings.

The appearance on the Galilean hilltop (Matthew 28:16*ff*) is scarcely a story at all, but the barest narrative frame for a Matthean speech, betrayed by his distinctive vocabulary, "to disciple," "till the consummation of the age." Jesus, risen or not, can scarcely have given such a forthright 'Great Commission,' or the uproar over Peter's visit to Cornelius is simply impossible to explain. Here we see two passages in direct conflict. In Acts chapter 10 (repeated almost verbatim in chapter 11!) we read how Simon Peter is unwilling to preach the gospel to 'unclean' Gentiles, apparently because it would entail sharing meals with them, and that would present the risk of accepting non-kosher food. In a vision, the Holy Spirit assures him that henceforth all foods are kosher, and immediately he receives messengers from a Roman centurion, Cornelius, inviting Peter to come and preach in his home. Forewarned by the vision, he agrees to go. As he preaches, the Spirit fills all present, and even the Gentiles begin to speak in tongues, God himself endorsing the reality of their faith. Word of this gets back to Jerusalem, and the elders there call Peter on the carpet: what on earth can he have been thinking, preaching to Gentiles? He relates the story, and they, too, are convinced. A new chapter of Christian expansion thus opens. Now somebody please explain how any of this would have been either possible or necessary if the parting words of the resurrected Son of God had been: "Go and make disciples of all nations, baptizing them in the name of the Father and of the Son and of the Holy Spirit" (Matthew 28:19) ?

If Jesus had given such marching orders to his disciples, whence Peter's initial reluctance? Whence that of the Jerusalem elders? And why should Luke have needed to tell the story in Acts to convince readers? It is obvious that Luke's story of Peter's vision and Matthew's story of Jesus issuing the Great Commission are independent attempts to do the same thing: to win ancient Christians over to supporting the Gentile Mission. We err in viewing either episode as history. Matthew 28 is not a report of what Jesus said to his disciples; surely it makes much better sense as a send-off by Matthew himself to those for whom he compiled the gospel, his missionaries to the Gentiles. It is they who know they must take this digest of teaching and relay it to the nations.

The business about the guards at the tomb is pure comedy: imagine them trying to get anyone to believe they knew the disciples stole the body when by their own account they were asleep at the time! Not even Sergeant Schultz on *Hogan's Heroes* would resort to such an excuse! And if Jesus had actually exited the tomb despite a cordon of armed soldiers, is it in any way possible to imagine that any other accounts of the event would have omitted it? Were Mark, Luke, and John just economizing on ink? Was this 'detail' unworthy of their notice? You just are asking not to be taken seriously if you say, "Oh, it happened all right; the other writers just didn't happen to include it!" Let us rather account for the distinctiveness of Matthew's version by admitting that he embroidered and embellished his story, as he did also at the crucifixion account, where the death of Jesus prompts a mass resurrection of the saints who then appear in Jerusalem, all unnoticed by any other gospel.

What has Luke done, faced with Mark's seemingly washed-out bridge? He, too, has the women obey the angel — or rather the two men. Mark and Matthew had only one each. Again, let us not emulate the O. J. Simpson defense team, the Clinton spin-doctors, by suggesting that there were actually two men or angels but that Matthew just didn't happen to see one because the other was fatter and in front of him, or one was on a coffee break when Mark got there. Let's be honest with the text. There weren't 'actually' two, with Matthew and Mark choosing only one to mention. No, the truth is that Luke decided the story would read better if there were two heavenly spokesmen, just like the two men he has talking with Jesus at the Transfiguration and again with the Twelve at the ascension. Remember, the same author has the ascension itself occur on Easter Day in his gospel and forty days later in Acts. He simply cannot have been trying to report history in the first place. Luke was not an incompetent historian; he was a very competent creative writer!

Why does Luke's speech of the two men at the tomb differ from that in Mark? Mark had the man say, "Go to Galilee; there you will see him, as he told you." Luke has changed this to "Remember how *when he was in Galilee* he told you the Son of Man must be delivered into the hands of men," *etc*. Luke wants salvation history to proceed from Jerusalem; thus his appearances happen in and around Jerusalem. He has simply lopped off the Galilean appearance Mark implied but neglected to narrate. He has the men at the tomb say what he knows no one actually said on that morning. It is not a question of that.

This is a writer creatively rewriting a story. He has decided, for the sake of his story's flow, to exclude Galilean appearances, and it is to obscure Luke's theological agenda for apologists to pretend to harmonize him with Matthew by intercalating Matthew 28 in between Luke 24 and Acts 1. I am interested in what Matthew said, and in what Luke said. I am not interested in replacing them with some composite *Life of Christ in Stereo*.

The wonderful story of Jesus appearing to the disciples on the Road to Emmaus (Luke 24:13-32), again, belongs to a certain legendary subgenre, that of the pious who 'entertain angels unaware.' One could point to Zeus and Hermes visiting Baucis and Philemon and various others, but the closest is a story, recorded four centuries before Luke, from the healing shrine of Asclepius at Epidaurus. A woman named Sostrata journeys to the holy site to be delivered of a dangerously long pregnancy. There she expects to have a dream of the savior who will tell her what to do. But nothing happens. Disappointed, she and her companions head for home again. Along the way they are joined by a mysterious stranger who asks the cause of their grief. Hearing her story, he bids them lay her stretcher down, and he cures her of what turns out to be a false pregnancy. Then he reveals his identity as Asclepius himself and is gone. It is not impossible that Luke borrowed the story, but that is not my point. The Emmaus story is recognizable as another tale of the same type. Why should we insist that the one is a legend but the other is historical?

The sudden appearance (Luke 24:36*ff*) of the Risen Jesus among the dumbfounded disciples provides some of the favorite ammunition for apologists. In this episode, Jesus suddenly pops into the midst of a meeting of the Eleven and others. Everyone thinks he is a ghost, but he shows his hands and feet to prove he is flesh and bones. Many remaining unconvinced, he eats some fish they have cooked to prove his corporality.

We are told that the resurrection appearances must not have been subjective hallucinations because, in stories like this one, those who saw him were initially skeptical and had to be convinced despite their doubts. But this is to assume we are reading a direct transcript of a scene that actually happened and are trying to decide if it represents a hallucination or something else. If it represents a genuine event in the lives of the disciples, then it cannot have been a hallucination: wishful thinking produces hallucinations, and wishful thinking is hardly compatible with doubt.

But this approach strategically ignores the fact that such skepticism is a stock feature of miracle stories in general. The skepticism of the bystanders occurs again and again as a device to increase the suspense, to heighten the odds against which the wonder will seem all the greater. "How are we to feed all these people?" "Master, do you not care if we perish?" "She is not dead but sleepeth, and they laughed him to scorn." Asclepius restored the sight of a blind man who had an empty eye socket, despite the skeptical jeering of the crowd. Another man with a withered hand himself doubted the god could cure him, but he did, and Asclepius told him he must henceforth bear the nickname "Incredulous." The key is to see that the skepticism is simply a narrative device. The key to what? To understanding the text as what it is, not what it is not. It is literary, not historical.

As for John, he has put his own spin on the story of Jesus appearing amid the disciples in order to conform it to his private story of the spear-thrust. His Doubting Thomas story is cut from the same legendary cloth as its counterpart in Philostratus' *Life of Apollonius of Tyana*:

> The young man in question... would on no account allow the immortality of the soul, and said, "I myself, gentlemen, have done nothing now for nine months but pray to Apollonius that he would reveal to me the truth about the soul; but he is so utterly dead that he will not appear to me in response to my entreaties, nor give me any reason to consider him immortal." Such were the young man's words on that occasion, but on the fifth day following, after discussing the same subject, he fell asleep where he was talking with them, and... on a sudden, like one possessed, he leaped up, still in a half sleep, streaming with perspiration, and cried out, "I believe thee." And when those who were present asked him what was the matter; "Do you not see," said he, "Apollonius the sage, how that he is present with us and is listening to our discussion, and is reciting wondrous verses about the soul?" "But where is he?" they asked, "For we cannot see him anywhere, although we would rather do so than possess all the blessings

of mankind." And the youth replied: "It would seem that he is come to converse with myself alone concerning the tenets which I would not believe." (*Life of Apollonius of Tyana* 8:31). Conybeare trans., Loeb Ed, Vol. II. pp. 403, 404.

The miraculous catch of fish story (not even a resurrection story in Luke 5) seems to be borrowed from a Pythagoras story in which the exact number of the netted fish actually made some difference.

At that time he was going from Sybaris to Krotona. At the shore, he stood with men fishing with nets; they were still hauling the nets weighed down (with fish) from the depths. He said he knew the number of fish that they had hauled in. The men agreed to do what he ordered, if the number of fish was as he said. He ordered the fish to be set free, living, after they were counted accurately. What is more astonishing, in the time they were out of the water being counted, none of the fish died while he stood there. He paid them the price of the fish and went to Krotona. They announced the deed everywhere, having learned his name from some children. (Iamblichus, *Life of Pythagoras,* 36, 60*f*)

What does all this give us? My point is not to 'debunk' the resurrection narratives as false witnesses, uncovering fatal inconsistencies between them. Like the false witnesses at the trial of Jesus: "their testimony did not agree." No, I have tried to show how the inconsistencies form a discernible pattern: that of various creative authors reworking a common draft to gain different effects. Not bad witnesses, but good storytellers. Not on the witness stand, but around the campfire. And the parallels with other ancient stories indicate what genre the stories belong to: they are religious legends. Not a bad thing. Not unless you want them to be something else: historical reports. I don't want them to be one or the other. I just want to understand the texts, and I think I do.

Did Jesus rise from the dead? That wouldn't be a bad thing either. But given the nature of our sources, there is no particular reason to think so.

How Secure Is the
New Testament Witness?

The Gospels: Whose Witness?

From Sunday School classes on up to seminary classes the opinion prevails that the gospels represent the witness of the original disciples or apostles of Jesus who saw what he did and heard what he said and would have taken considerable trouble to keep the developing Jesus tradition pure — especially including the gospel texts that crystallized it. But such a working hypothesis, beloved of apologists, is simply untenable. In *a priori* terms (asking what *would have* happened) as well as in *a posteriori* terms (looking at the texts), the belief in gospel accuracy fails.

To begin with, the whole thing is circular to a degree seldom even envisioned by apologists. They don't even seem to realize the need to deal with the relevant point: do we even know there *was* an original 'college of apostles'? This may seem hypercritical to ask, but I believe that reaction is simply a function of a mindset that has little patience for searching questions and wants to get on with defending a traditional view which it cannot help seeing as more reasonable — whether or not it is. But it is a live question as to whether there was such an apostolic band, or whether this list of characters is a fiction. In the latter case it might be that the list of twelve represents a reading back into the ministry of Jesus of a group only subsequently constituted as such by a shared resurrection vision (an appearance or an hallucination, I leave to you to decide). These men may have actually been among the associates of Jesus even though he had never chosen a circle of twelve. (The story of Jesus choosing them seems to me clearly to be based on that in Exodus 18 in which Moses chooses the seventy elders at the behest of Jethro, and thus a fiction.)

Or they may not have been associates of Jesus at all, owing their leadership role to other factors entirely. For instance, they may have been chosen as leaders of a Jewish-Christian faction, standing for the number of the twelve tribes, just as the Qumran sect had a council of twelve. And then, at some later time, they may have been fictively retrojected into the time of Jesus to increase their clout.

Or, as Robert Eisenman suggests in his *James the Brother of Jesus*, they may be fictional replications (more than one of each) of an earlier leadership group that survives alongside them in Galatians and to some extent in Acts — the Pillars or the Heirs (*Desposunoi*), the 'brethren of the Lord.' These, in turn, were eventually understood to be literal, fleshly siblings of Jesus, but they were also understood in Gnostic (and maybe other) circles as *spiritual brethren* of Jesus. Eisenman opts for a physical, dynastic understanding, which is perhaps the most plausible option. At any rate, their ranks included James the Just (also represented as Salih, 'the Just,' in the Koran, as well as, I would add, Silas in Acts), Judas Thomas, Simeon bar-Cleophas, and Joses. I think, however, his presence in Mark 6:3 is a scribal slip or alteration, misplacing the name of Jesus' father Joseph and replacing a fourth brother named John (reflected in the Catholic belief that James and John bar Zebedee were Jesus' 'cousins' and in Luke's nativity story that makes Jesus the cousin of another John, the Baptist.

On Eisenman's theory (though the details are my inferences), *James bar Zebedee* and *James 'of Alphaeus'* (meaning 'the substitute'!) are both transformations of James the Just, Brother of the Lord. *Simon Peter* and *Simon Zelotes* would be versions of Simeon-bar-Cleophas, the brother of Jesus who succeeded James as bishop (*mebaqqr*) of Jerusalem. *Judas Thomas* became *Judas Iscariot* ('the False One,' reflecting later doctrinal disputes), '*Judas not Iscariot,*' *Bar-Tholomew*, *Thaddaeus/Addai*, as well as *Thamoud* and *Hud* in the Koran. *Andrew* the brother of Simon Peter reflects the *Son of Man* (*aner*), brother of Simon bar-Cleophas. *Matthew* is a broad pun on *mathetes*, 'disciple.' *Lebbaeus* is another form of *Oblias*, 'the Bulwark,' title of James the Just. *Philip* has been misplaced from the list of seven Deacons. *John bar Zebedee* represents the Pillar John, Jesus' brother instead of the misplaced Joses.

The scarcity of information about these men in the New Testament is startling and more than a little suggestive of the possibility that they represent an artificial construction. Every single instance of Peter, James, or John taking the stage looks like one of the Buddhist tales of Ananda where the disciple is simply a straight man for the Master. This idea is reinforced by the fact that when one of them momentarily surfaces to say something, he is simply an artificial mouthpiece for the group. And notice, it is only James, John, and Peter, the same names, though supposedly not entirely the same characters, as the Pillars of Galatians, implying these have been chosen for fifteen minutes of fame on account of the lingering memory of their original identity as Jesus' brethren.

Thus we have no reason at all to believe there would have been a group of apostolic censors riding herd on early Christians, keeping them straight about what Jesus said and did. Instead, it seems to me we have reason to expect that the early Christian leaders would have had ample cause to fabricate sayings and ascribe them to Jesus. They would have needed to assert their own credentials and to negate those of their rivals. This is surely why Mark's gospel repeatedly trounces both the Twelve and the Heirs. Mark must have been like Marcion, the early second-century theologian who championed Paul as the only genuine apostle.

Marcion believed that the Twelve had completely bungled the task assigned to them, failing to understand that Jesus was the Son and revealer of a hitherto-unknown God who was now offering the human race adoption as his children. As creations of the Old Testament Jehovah, humanity slaved under the repressive laws of a vengeful deity, but the loving Father of Jesus offered forgiveness and salvation. Marcion believed Jesus had recruited Paul because Peter and the others had failed to grasp Jesus' point: they were confusing the two deities as well as the two religions. Marcion's theory is certainly plausible historically and psychologically. It is by no means uncommon for even the most ardent followers of a reformer to balk at the more radical of his teachings and to readjust the new faith to the old as soon as they get the chance. That is just what happened, *e.g.*, with Martin Luther, who wanted to relegate several New Testament books (James, Jude, Hebrews, Revelation) to an appendix in his new Bible. His followers just couldn't go the whole way with him. It didn't take Wesleyans long to bury their teacher's radical doctrine of Christian perfectionism, either.

Well, Mark seems to have had a similar disdain for both the major Jewish leadership cliques. This is why he portrays James and John as shameless self-promoters, asking for first dibs on the best seats next to Jesus in his messianic reign (Mark 10:35–40). This has to be why he chopped up and rewrote an earlier story (derived by some creative Christian from Exodus 18) in Mark 3:20–21, 25, 31–35.

In Exodus chapter 18, the Israelites have crossed the sea and, free of Egyptian harassment, they are settling down to a peaceful nomadic existence. They depend heavily upon Moses as a divine oracle to settle their disputes and to make new laws to guide them in their new existence. Moses is busy all day, every day. One day someone announces that his father-in-law Jethro has arrived with Moses' wife Zippora and their two young sons. Will Moses see them? He hastens to greet them warmly. Jethro eventually notices the burden of work occupying Moses 24/7, and he ventures a bit of advice: why not appoint a body of lower court elders to hear cases and apply Moses' rules, leaving only the most serious cases for his personal attention? Moses sees the wisdom in this, and he sees to organizing a system of lower courts to share his work.

Now someone thought this would make a good story applied to Jesus. As it must originally have read, Jesus' mother and siblings pay him a visit, concerned that, as they have heard, Jesus is constantly mobbed, with no time to grab a meal. They arrive, someone announces them, and Jesus readily defers to them as Moses did, happily taking their advice, which issues in the appointment of the Twelve. Thus the Heirs and the Twelve are both honored, albeit in a way that gently gives precedence to the Heirs, since, without them, there would be no Twelve Apostles.

The transparent parallel to the Mosaic original marks the whole story as a fiction right off the bat. But then Mark has transformed it, removing it even further from historical reality, by placing the choosing of the Twelve (Mark 3:13–19a), with no stated motivation, just *before* the introduction of Jesus' kin into the story — and when they get there, he rebuffs them! Not only that, their journey to Jesus has been made into the mission of a modern family trying to take a cultist son or daughter in hand to deliver him to a deprogrammer! They come to take Jesus away, concluding that he is insane (Mark 3:21). The artificiality of the present arrangement is obvious from the fact that the appointment of the Twelve to share Jesus' workload seems to have been without result, since Jesus is still swamped after his relatives get there.

Like Marcion, Mark must have preferred Paul. He seems to have Paul in view in another episode, Mark 9:38–40. This story is patently rewritten from another version of the appointment of Moses' assistants, this time Numbers 11. This time, it is God himself who tells Moses to appoint seventy elders to share the burden. Moses takes them out of the camp, and the Spirit descends upon them, lending them a share of Moses' own oracular authority. However, two of the seventy could not make it on time. "Now two remained in the camp, one named Eldad, the other Medad, and the spirit rested upon them... and so they prophesied in the camp. And a young man ran and told Moses, 'Eldad and Medad are prophesying in the camp!' And Joshua son of Nun, Moses servant, one of his elite, said, 'My lord Moses, forbid them!' But Moses said to him, 'Are you jealous for my sake? Would that all Jehovah's people were prophets, that Jehovah would put his spirit upon them!' " (Numbers 11:26–30).

Here is Mark's version: "John said to him, 'Teacher, we saw a man casting out demons in your name, and we forbad him, for he was not following us.' But Jesus said to him, 'Do not forbid him, for no one who does a miracle in my name will soon be speaking evil of me.' " Why repaint Jesus' face over Moses' in this picture? Simply in order to rebut a common distaste for some notable someone doing miracles in Jesus' name — someone who was perceived to be "working the Twelve's side of the street." Who could Mark have been thinking of? Surely Paul. He was claiming Jesus' approval for Paul, as if before the latter had come on the scene.

By the same token, however, the evangelist Matthew omits this scene from Mark when composing his own gospel, and he substitutes for it Matthew 5:17, 19: "Do not think I have come to abolish the Torah and the Prophets; I have come not to abolish scripture but to fulfill it... Therefore anyone who relaxes the least of these commandments and teaches other to do so shall be ranked least in the kingdom of heaven." Matthew is dealing with a rival Christian viewpoint, because he does not say,

"Don't *accuse me* of *abolishing* the Torah,' as an enemy might be imagined saying, but rather, "Do not think *I came to abolish* the Torah" — language suggesting a Christian interpretation of the mission of Jesus.

What *had* God sent him to do? A non-Christian detractor would never have said this, but a rival Christian might — someone with the belief that Christ's mission was to bring the law to an end, with the result that Christians need no longer obey it. Does that sound like anyone we know? Of course, this is the Pauline gospel. And we know just as clearly that Matthew did not espouse it. It is already clear he expected Christians to keep every last provision of the Torah, and at the end of the gospel he has Jesus say to the missionaries (the original audience for the book) to go to the nations, *i.e.*, the Gentiles, and to instruct them in everything Jesus has commanded in the gospel. That obviously intends the Sermon on the Mount, including the commandment not to let the least commandment of the Torah slip. In other words, Matthew preaches the very gospel Paul in Galatians condemns! And thus it is no surprise that Matthew puts a condemnation of Paul into his gospel where Mark had Jesus praise Paul.

Paul is also certainly in Matthew's mind in Matthew 7:21–23: "Not everyone who says to me, 'Lord, Lord' will enter into the kingdom of heaven, but he who does the will of my Father who is in heaven. On that day, many will say to me, 'Lord, Lord, did we not prophesy in your name, and cast out demons in your name, and do many miracles in your name?' And then I will declare to them, 'I never chose you; depart from me, you workers of lawlessness!' " The 'many' are the multitudes of Pauline Christians among the Gentiles, shocked to find at this late date that they have backed the wrong horse. Jesus does not reject them for sinful habits and hypocrisy, of which he says nothing. These are people who expect to receive his approbation! What can they have done wrong? They did not keep the Torah: "you workers of lawlessness." And, literally, the text says, "I never knew you," but often in the Bible, *to know* denotes 'to choose,' as in Genesis 18:17–19, where God says that, of all living on the earth, he has "known," *i.e.*, chosen, Abraham to bequeath his covenant to future generations. Thus Matthew summarily rejects all the talk about Paul having been chosen from his mother's womb to bring the gospel to the Gentiles (Galatians 1:15–16). Jesus never knew – *chose* – him. Matthew composed 5:17 and 19 to embellish verse 18, which already stood as a saying of Jesus in the Q source of sayings, which he shared with Luke, where it also appears (Luke 16:17). So, again, Matthew has added sayings of Jesus in order to discredit a rival Christian teacher.

By contrast, Matthew's favorite was Peter, which is why he adds material to the story of Peter's confessing Jesus' messianic office. "Blessed are you, Simon bar-Jonah! For flesh and blood have not revealed this to you, but my Father in heaven. And so I say you are 'Peter' [*a rock*], and on this rock I will erect my church. And the gates of Hades shall not withstand its assault. Behold, I entrust you with the keys of the kingdom, so that whatever command you bind upon men will be considered bound in heaven, and whatever sins you loose men from on earth shall be considered loosed in heaven" (Matthew 16:17–19). Mark and Luke have pretty much the same story up to this point. In both Mark 8:27–30 and Luke 9:18–22 Peter confesses Jesus' messiahship, but this investiture of Simon Peter as the fountainhead of the Papacy is conspicuous by its absence. Did both Mark and Luke just happen to omit it? Running short on ink maybe? Of course, Matthew has added it to reinforce the dignity of the authorities he venerated.

Matthew, unlike Mark's nameless predecessor who tended to elevate the Heirs above the Twelve in his story of the choosing of the Twelve, seems to have preferred the Twelve to the Heirs, as he does not omit Jesus' rebuff to the relatives (Matthew 12:46–50).

John the evangelist goes out of his way to make sure the reader understands Jesus' brothers were not in sympathy with him in John 7:2–7, where they dare him to go to Jerusalem for public relations reasons, knowing he is wanted by the authorities there. And when on the cross, Jesus commits his aging mother into the care of one of the Twelve, conspicuously it is not one of his brothers (John 19:25–27). That is almost as much as saying outright that Jesus wants his disciples to be in charge of the church, not his relatives.

None of this should be very surprising, since such succession disputes are common in new religions. Muslims had to line up behind either the Companions of the Prophet (the first three Caliphs, Muhammad's disciples Abu-bekr, Umar, and Uthman) or the Pillars, as his relatives were also called: Khadijah, Fatima, and Ali. The former became the Sunnis, the latter the Shia. After Joseph Smith went on to glory, the Mormon Church divided over whether to follow the Quorum of the Twelve Apostles Smith had named or his son, Joseph Smith, Junior. The former became the Church of Jesus Christ of Latter-day Saints, while the latter became the Reorganized Church of Jesus Christ of Latter-day Saints. Should the followers of the Honorable Elijah Muhammad follow his chief evangelist, Reverend Louis Farrakhan, or his son, Warith Deen Muhammad? The former became the Nation of Islam, the latter the American Muslim Mission. And in several of these cases partisans forged more than one saying or letter from the founder to secure their favorite contender's claim. The same would likely have happened in the case of Jesus and the earliest disciples. Looking at the evidence of the sayings, it seems that it did.

Dead and Can't Blow the Gaff

The question now arises, what exactly are the Twelve supposed to have to do with the four gospels? There are two claims often made. One is that advanced by Harald Riesenfeld (Professor of New Testament at the University of Uppsala, Sweden, author of *The Gospel Tradition*, 1970) and Birger Gerhardsson (*Memory and Manuscript: Oral and Written Transmission in Rabbinic Judaism and Early Christianity,* 1961) that, since the gospels stem from the circle of twelve disciples, they must be accurate because these men must have followed the rabbinical practices of strict memorization and transmission of their Master's sayings. This, again, is hopelessly circular, even if for the sake of argument we were to grant that there was such a circle of close disciples. For we just do not know where the gospel materials came from! *If* they stem from a circle of stenographer disciples who memorized everything for posterity, then, fine — the gospels can be trusted.

But that is a big if! That is precisely what we do *not* know! And this is where internal evidence – the phenomena of the texts themselves – comes in.

There are so many variations and contradictions between sayings, not to mention stories, of Jesus that surely the most natural explanation is that of the form critics: Jesus traditions arose as needed in this and that quarter of the early church — the coinages of anonymous prophets and catechists. Did Jesus prohibit preaching to Samaritans and Gentiles or not? Did he say no longer to fast, temporarily to leave off fasting, or to fast? Was there one pretext for divorce or none? Is the Kingdom to be heralded by apocalyptic signs or not? Did he proclaim his messiahship or keep it a secret? As reporter Harry Reasoner once commented, at the end of a Christmas edition of *Sixty Minutes*: "It seems that, like beauty, Jesus Christ is in the eye of the beholder." If the texts are anything to go by, no one held the copyright on 'Jesus.'

The other claim is even more futile, namely, the apostles must have corroborated the gospels (even if they did not write them) before they circulated far and wide. There is no reason to assume that the gospels were written before the destruction of Jerusalem, headquarters of the apostles according to Luke.

John A. T. Robinson, the feisty bishop of Woolwich who caused so much controversy on both sides of the Atlantic in 1963 with his book *Honest to God* (in which he advocated a synthesis of Rudolf Bultmann, Paul Tillich, and Dietrich Bonhoeffer) was a walking contradiction. He loved to twit his various publics by combining radical theological views with conservative criticism. He was a masterful and critical interpreter of the New Testament, and yet he tried, in his astonishing *Redating the New Testament*, to lasso all twenty-seven New Testament writings and pull them kicking and screaming back before 70 CE. He argued that none of them absolutely demanded a post-70 date since none of them explicitly mention the fall of Jerusalem. This is special pleading, since the gospels, at least, *do* mention the Fall of Jerusalem in the only appropriate way: as if Jesus had predicted it. Conservative (*e.g.*, evangelical pietist) scholars always reply that such a view of gospel prophecy is just the unbelief of skeptics. Why *couldn't* a guy predict the future, whether Jesus Christ, or, let's say, Nostradamus? Just because you find a predictive prophecy that came true included in a writing needn't prove the text was written after the event, does it?

Well, no. But consider the fact that no scholar ever takes such an approach to dating, say 4 Ezra, 2 Baruch, or 1 Enoch, refusing to acknowledge the chief trope of apocalyptic: the thin veiling of the author's past as the narrator's future. They are all books of *faux*-predictions *written after the fact*, and we can tell when each was written by locating where along the time-line the 'predictions' veer off the track. That means, as all agree, that here the author has stopped disguising history as prophecy and is entering blue skies, making genuine predictions which, alas, do not come true. Conservatives never protest that to date *these* books in this manner represents "naturalistic skepticism" about genuine prophetic prediction.

Robinson, like fundamentalists, demands special exemption for passage after passage. Revelation 11:13 says, "And at that hour there was a great earthquake, and a tenth of the city fell; seven thousand people were killed in the earthquake." Where? It was "the great city which is allegorically called Sodom and Egypt, where their Lord was crucified" (11:8), namely Jerusalem.

Mark 13:14–23 gives a deadline for the destruction of the Jerusalem temple: "But when you see the desolating sacrilege set up where it ought not to be (let the reader understand), then let those who are in Judea flee to the mountains... From the fig tree learn its lesson: as soon as its branch becomes tender and puts forth leaves, you know that summer is near. So also, when you see these things taking place, you know that he is near, at the very gates. Truly I say to you, this generation will not pass away before all these things take place." That would be 70 CE, if not a bit earlier. Luke 21:20 is an even clearer version of the same prediction: "But when you see Jerusalem surrounded by armies, then know that its desolation has come near."

John 4:21 ("The hour is coming when neither on this mountain [*Gerizim*] nor in Jerusalem will you worship the Father.") clearly looks back on the destruction of the Mt. Zion temple of Jerusalem, which has become as defunct as the old Samaritan temple on Mt. Gerizim.

Acts 6:14 ("We have heard him say Jesus of Nazareth will destroy this place and will change the customs Moses gave us.") reflects Jewish *vs*. Christian debate as to whether the destruction of Jerusalem in 70 CE was divine punishment for the Jewish rejection of Jesus.

1 Thessalonians 2:14–16 ("For you, brethren, became imitators of the churches of God in Christ Jesus which are in Judea; for you suffered the same things from your own countrymen as they did from the Jews, who killed both the Lord Jesus and the prophets, and drove us out, and displease God and oppose all men by hindering us from speaking to the Gentiles that they may be saved — so as always to fill up the measure of their sins. But God's wrath has come upon them at last!"). But then Paul did not write it. Can't Robinson take a hint? Or rather, a whole series of them? The New Testament writings *do* look back on the fall of Jerusalem and therefore date from a later time.

In *The Theology of Acts in its Historical Setting* J. C. O'Neill (late Professor of New Testament Language, Literature and Theology at New College, Edinburgh University) demonstrates that many factors in that book fit in with, not merely a post-70 date, but even a date in the second century. Thus there is just no inherent likelihood that any of the original apostles would have survived the tumultuous events of 70 CE, the devastating war with Rome that ravaged Galilee and resulted in the siege, starvation, and fall of Jerusalem at Roman hands. They just wouldn't have been around to stamp any of the gospels with their *Imprimatur*. That is a wish-fulfillment fantasy of apologists.

Character Witnesses — or Just Characters?

Appeal is also made to various persons whose testimonies allegedly underlie the gospels. These individuals seem to sit so close to the narrated events that, *provided the events happened at all, and that these characters were the source of the narrator's 'knowledge' of these events*, we would have good grounds for confidence in the narratives. I have just indicated the multiple difficulties besetting this grossly circular claim. Do we have any reason to believe there were such people and that, if there were, they reported their experiences to the gospel authors?

For instance, the women who discovered the empty tomb: are we sure there even *were* such women? It is not at all implausible that Jesus, like all gurus ancient and modern, attracted a circle of smitten, usually middle-aged, female admirers. But then, on the other hand, the only actual stories we possess starring these women characters bear a striking resemblance to the passion, burial, and resurrection narratives of other Hellenistic redeemer gods!

Mary Magdalene, Salome, Joanna, *et al.*, bear a startling resemblance to Isis and Nephthys who mourn for the betrayed and slain Osiris, search for his body, and anoint it, raising him from the dead. They bear more than a passing resemblance, too, to Cybele who discovered the body of her beloved Attis and resurrected him. And let's not forget Ishtar Shalmith ('the Shulammite') who, as the Song of Solomon knew, had descended into Sheol to recover the slain Tammuz. And there was Athena who found the remains of Dionysus Zagreus and besought Zeus on his behalf, occasioning his rebirth. Aphrodite similarly found the gored corpse of Adonis and raised him to new life. Not to mention Anath who sought Baal, found his death site, the field of blood, and rescued him from the Netherworld.

Let's take an inventory, shall we? The *only* story in the gospels that features the women is the one in which they seek the tomb of the slain savior, leading to his resurrection. And this story exactly parallels the stories of women devotees seeking the bodies of the other slain saviors who rise from the dead. I'd say it is at best a toss-up whether these women ever existed as anything but Christian counterparts to the women characters of the resurrection myths of neighboring religions, whence they were likely derived. And if we cannot even make it look all that likely that they existed, it is obviously moot to appeal to them as sources of information. One might as well appeal to the testimony of Cybele to argue that Attis rose from the dead.

The Emmaus disciples (Luke 24:13*ff*) who walk and talk with the risen Jesus without recognizing him – might be called to the stand as witnesses of the Risen Christ. Except for two damning criticisms.

First of all, the story sure looks an awful lot like biblical and classical myths in which gods travel among mortals *incognito* as a kind of *Candid Camera* stunt, to test their reactions. Yahweh's angels so visit Sodom, after visiting Abraham for the same reason. Zeus and Hermes visited palaces and hovels to determine whether mankind deserved destruction in a flood. They appeared to the pious old couple Baucis and Philemon, whose generosity caused them to be spared and made into pillars of Zeus's temple upon death.

A second critical point we might raise is that the Emmaus story greatly resembles a story of the fourth-century BCE, repeated long afterwards, in which a couple has journeyed far to the healing shrine of Asclepius, son of Apollo. Like other suppliants, they had expected a dream-appearance of the god who would relieve the woman of a prolonged pregnancy. But he had not appeared, and they were headed home depressed — until a mysterious stranger joined them and asked why they were so glum. Hearing the sad tale, he tells them to set down her stretcher, whereupon he heals her of what turns out to be tapeworms, not a pregnancy at all. Then he disappears. Sound familiar? What are the chances the Asclepius version is but a myth, while the Jesus version is true fact? Be careful! That is what we mean by special pleading!

But suppose we do take the story as a record of a strange encounter on the lonely Emmaus road? What kind of evidence for the resurrection does it provide? Very ambiguous evidence, if that, for the simple reason that the pair of disciples travels with Jesus for hours, apparently, *without recognizing him*! Oh, you can just cover up the problematical nature of this feature as Luke does, by simple authorial fiat: "They were prevented from recognizing him," but then you're just dealing with a literary composition, not reporting. Imagine if you read such a detail in a newspaper. What would you think? Funny business! The fundamentalist apologist is willing to swallow the problem only because he already wants to believe the text is inspired and inerrant. He is only interested in historical plausibility insofar as he needs it as an argument to rope you in. Where it is lacking he does not miss it.

No, if they spent all that time with the famous Jesus of Nazareth and only decided *after he was gone* that it had been he, then what we have is a case of wistful mistaken identity. Hugh J. Schonfield, notorious author of *The Passover Plot* (1965), saw this, and he was right. The story practically invites disbelief, as does the similar one in John 20:1–18, where Mary Magdalene does not recognize Jesus either. So does Matthew 28:17, which actually says, "And when they saw him, they worshipped him, but they doubted."

But, let's go the second mile. Suppose the story *does* stem from the breathless testimony of the Emmaus disciples, and suppose it is fairly represented in Luke 24, so that you are sure you have the authentic report of what they told the Eleven. Should you believe it? Would you believe such a thing if your friend told you he had seen a mutual friend, known to be dead, alive again? I think you would not. You would suddenly transform into the Enlightenment philosopher David Hume and rediscover the principles he enunciated in his famous essay "On Miracles." You would ask yourself, "Which is more probable? That Bill is alive again? Or that Stan is lying, or hallucinating, or deceived?" You would automatically assume Stan is not to be believed, though you cannot imagine he is consciously lying. *And this is only if you are quite sure Bill was dead.*

Once a parishioner told me that Alan Duke, our church's almost-resident street bum, had died during the harsh winter. A couple of weeks later, someone else told me he had seen Alan, alive if not well. It was easy to conclude that my first informant had been the victim of a false rumor, perhaps a case of mistaken identity. Another time, a friend was sitting outside a convenience store, growing increasingly feverish. He spotted his roommate and hailed him, but he received no acknowledgement back. When my friend returned home, his roommate denied having been there at the store. Well, it turned out that my friend Ralph was suffering hallucinations from a ruptured gall bladder poisoning his pancreas! He was rushed to the hospital and came out fine some weeks later. My mother was in the hospital under heavy drugs. She told me she had seen my father and my uncle, both long dead, come walking through her hospital room, wordlessly waving to her! Were my dad and Uncle Douglas raised from the dead? Or was it no coincidence she was drugged at the time? In short, if you heard your friend report that another was resurrected from the dead, you would not automatically believe him, and probably not at all. You would know that some neglected factor must be making the difference.

What Hath Hierapolis to Do with Higher Criticism?

Apologists prize the statement of Irenaeus (bishop of Lyons in Gaul, but hailing from Asia Minor), who wrote about 175 CE. He appeals to Papias, the famous bishop of Hierapolis, adjacent to the New Testament cities of Colosse and Laodicea in Asia Minor. Papias, a man with antiquarian tastes, had been a hearer of the apostle John, whom Irenaeus also considered the author of the Gospel of John. (He does not say that Papias knew anything about that gospel.) But as Eusebius of Caesarea, Constantine's court historian in the early-to-mid fourth century, pointed out, Irenaeus had failed to note that Papias mentioned the apostle John but says only that he had interviewed the Elder John, who would seem to be a personage of the next generation, someone who had himself ostensibly heard the teaching of some apostle. Most scholars feel Eusebius, who had come to disdain Papias' 'chiliasm' – his belief in a literal coming Millennium – was just trying to distance John the apostle from Papias and his doctrines. But the ambiguity in Papias' statement is quite real and plainly present in Irenaeus' quotation of Papias. By the way, numerous passages in Irenaeus have him attribute this or that theological or liturgical point to the tradition of the elders who heard the apostles. And the appeals are obviously fanciful, even anachronistic, demonstrating that for Irenaeus as well as for Eusebius, whatever they deemed true was to be provided an 'apostolic' pedigree after the fact. 'Apostolicity' was just a function of 'correct in my opinion.' There is no genuine historical claim here, whether about apostolic authorship of the gospels or anything else.

When Source Criticism Is Textual Criticism

We have what at least at first appears to be a rather different question on our hands when it comes to a different aspect of gospel reliability, namely that of textual soundness. Is it possible that, already by the early third century, when the first manuscripts appear, the gospels had suffered serious textual corruption — so early that it has forever undermined whatever the evangelists meant to write for us? It would not be surprising from one standpoint, in that it is the earliest extant texts which feature more flagrant scribal freedom, not the latest, possibly reflecting a scenario in which the texts came to seem sacrosanct only as time went on. At any rate, the further back one goes, the more extravagant the corruption. But is there a firewall back there somewhere?

What about gospel source criticism, specifically the question of Synoptic dependence? It looks to most scholars as if Matthew and Luke each used two major sources, namely the Gospel of Mark and the Q Source ('Q' for *Quelle*, German for 'source'), with the result that there is a great deal of overlap between Matthew, Mark, and Luke, which are therefore called the *Synoptic* gospels, "the gospels told from the same vantage-point." Does not this Mark/Q hypothesis (or any of the other Synoptic theories in principle) demand that we *do* have a very early 'core sample' of the earlier gospel in the use made of it by subsequent evangelists? Let's stick with the Mark/Q version for simplicity's sake.

Since we have two gospels, Matthew and Luke, that both used Mark, and they both seem to have used the same text, doesn't that mean the agreements between Matthew and Luke preserve a text of Mark that had already circulated pretty widely by the time the other two were written? (Of course, then you have to try to date all three Synoptics, and this is a hugely complex matter in its own right. Internal data lead me to posit a date of about 100 CE for Mark, and about 150 for both Matthew and Luke. Most scholars seem to adopt the earliest possible dates, probably for apologetical purposes. I don't know if that matters a great deal here, since we are in any case talking about relative dates of composition: how long it might have taken for the Markan original to have become significantly altered versus the window of time between Mark and his followers Matthew and Luke.)

I believe that, yes, the agreements between Mark and the other two *do* provide a helpful and important control. The relationship between them does not allow much time between the writing of Mark and a version of Mark much like our own being available to both later evangelists, perhaps widely separated geographically. But, for what it's worth, this fact cuts both ways. It becomes just as important to consider where Matthew and Luke *diverge from Mark in agreement with one another*. For a long time, proponents of the Mark/Q hypothesis have pointed to these "minor agreements" against Mark as evidence that Matthew and Luke both used an edition of Mark earlier than the canonical one.

Most of these agreements against Mark are in my opinion not that significant for our purposes, but one important one – as it bears on gospel Christology – would be the trial scene of Jesus. According to Mark 14:62 Jesus answers the Christological question forthrightly: "I am." By contrast, Matthew 26:64 has "You have said so," while Luke 22:70 has "You say that I am." It is hard to resist the suggestion that both Mathew and Luke were reading a text of Mark in which he gave an equivocal answer. In fact there actually are a couple of old copies of Mark that do have, though not in exactly the same words, something like "You say [so]." I would say we have not so much a simultaneous, independent redactional change by Matthew and Luke to make an originally clear answer ambiguous, as a scribal 'improvement' to an ambiguous Mark to make Jesus forthrightly confess what Christians would like him to have confessed. A textual corruption at an important point, I should say.

We also need to look for places where it appears that one of the later evangelists was not looking at the same version of Mark as the other. The prize example of this would be the 'Great Omission' of Mark 6:45–8:26 by Luke, though it appears reproduced in Matthew 14:22–16:12. Some scholars have long suggested that Luke's copy of Mark lacked the whole section, and this observation is especially interesting in that the omitted portion of Mark contains one of a pair of miracle story sequences in Mark.

We find two parallel chains of miracle stories in Mark. The first commences with a sea miracle: the stilling of the storm in Mark 4:35–41. Next comes a set of three healings: the demoniac with 'Legionnaire's Disease' (5:1–20), the hemorrhaging woman

(5:25–34), and Jairus' daughter (5:21–23, 35–43). Then there is a miraculous feeding (6:34–44). The second sequence has as its sea miracle the walking on water (6:45–51). Its three healings are those of the Bethsaida blind man (8:22–26), the Syro-Phoenician's daughter (7:24b–30), and the deaf-mute (7:32–37). Finally, a miraculous feeding (8:1–10).

How striking that Luke's Great Omission covers the second sequence! It might be that Luke saw the Markan duplication, decided he lacked space for redundancy, and cut the second sequence. But it may well be that Mark's gospel had been circulating with two alternate versions of the miracle chain, some copies with the one, others with the other, and Luke's copy of Mark had only the first. Matthew's copy of Mark would have been a version that included both — just to be on the safe side. That is standard scribal procedure after all.

One might also wonder if Matthew was using a copy of Mark that lacked the peculiar feature of 'sandwiching' stories together. For example, Mark has the healing of the bleeding woman and the raising of Jairus' daughter imbricated one within the other, but not Matthew. There, one is over before the second begins. Our copies of Mark have the anticlimactic scene of Jesus cursing the fig tree with no immediate result, then entering Jerusalem and merely looking around, then returning next morning when the fig tree is discovered to be withered, then proceeding back into the city, where he cleanses the temple. It all seems unnatural. Matthew, however, has the cursing of the fig tree, all at once and self-contained, then the Triumphal Entry and an immediate temple cleansing. One wonders if Matthew's versions are not original. It is elsewhere manifest that Matthew has copied and abridged Mark, so I am not suggesting Mark abridged Matthew. Rather, Matthew rewrote Mark, but a version of Mark that had not split up unitary episodes and enclosed them within one another. So, yes, to some extent, *the gospels may have begun to mutate and multiply even before they began to use one another*.

The Gospel According to John Rylands

Much has been made of the John Rylands Papyrus (𝔓52). It is a fragment from a codex (a bound book, not a scroll) and it contains the text of John 18:31–33 on one side and 37–38 on the other. Discovered in the sands of Egypt, it is now housed at the John Rylands Library in Manchester, England. The papyrus is widely held to anchor both the composition of the book in the first century, because of the paleography, and the authenticity of the text, since it matches our version so perfectly and so early. But this is over-simple. Paleography (the study and comparison of ancient handwriting styles, and dating manuscripts on that basis) makes the John Rylands Papyrus date from around 125 CE, with a range of about 50 years in either direction. But, as Alvin Padilla (Professor of New Testament at Gordon-Conwell Theological Seminary) has shown, there are altogether too few relevant writing samples to make such a judgment possible in this case. He speaks of "the circuitous nature of dating manuscripts according to text types," noting that it "is rather arbitrary since there simply aren't enough writing samples" from the envisioned period. "Since the John Rylands Papyrus is considered the oldest extant manuscript, it is used as the 'standard' for the time period." And that is obviously circular. So much for the attempt to rule out a mid-second-century date for the Gospel of John by appeal to this lone papyrus. It is, sorry to say, a weak reed.

Here is the whole of the text: "Pilate said to them, 'Take him yourselves and judge him by your own law.' The Jews said to him, 'It is not lawful for us to put any man to death.' This was spoken to fulfill the word which Jesus had spoken to show by what death he was to die. Pilate entered the praetorium again and called Jesus, and said to him, 'Are you the King of the Jews?' " and "Pilate said to him, 'Then you are a king?' Jesus said to him, 'You say that I am a king. For this I was born, and for this I have come into the world, to bear witness to the truth. Everyone who belongs to the truth hears my voice.' Pilate said to him, 'What is truth?' After he had said this he went out to the Jews again and told them, 'I find no crime in him.'"

I submit to you that this postage stamp of John does not vindicate the pure transmission of the entire document. The rest of this gospel *might* have looked just like our Gospel of John, but then again it might *not* have. Would it have contained the Appendix, chapter 21?

Consider the various theories meant to account for the many puzzling discontinuities and skips in the Fourth Gospel. Jesus leaves Judea in one chapter, only to be back there later in the same chapter with no recorded transition. He gives most of the Good Shepherd discourse in chapter 10:1–18, but seems to pick it back up months later without missing a beat in verse 25. The Last Supper discourse stretches from 13:31 to 14:31, when Jesus says it's time to leave. But then he resumes in 15:1 as if nothing happened. Scholars have surmised that some early copyist made a mess of the pages and reassembled them in the wrong order, or that scribes expanded the gospel, cramming in more text where it seemed to fit thematically, but without considering whether it made any sense as a narrative. Who knows? The John Rylands snippet just does not help resolve any of these questions of textual evolution. It does not tell us what version of the gospel it represents, so it remains difficult to date the gospel as a whole on the basis of it. It might even be a fragment of one of the underlying *sources* of the gospel.

By Your Words You Shall Be Acquitted; By Your Words You Shall Be Condemned.

Some have protested claims of wholesale textual degradation in the New Testament by appeal to the presence in the texts of all manner of consistent word and concept usage distinctive to each author and even to underlying source documents. Had the texts really been ravaged by haphazard alterations by many hands already before our earliest copies, it would not be possible to observe these authorial/redactional patterns. I agree completely. Furthermore, if one had to conclude the readings of any and all texts were random, none particularly likely to represent an author's or redactor's intent, one would have to dismiss a redaction-critical performance like that of Hans Conzelmann (Göttingen Professor of New Testament, author of the milestone work *The Theology of Saint Luke*) on Luke.

Conzelmann catalogued the numerous subtle word changes Luke made in Mark and showed they pointed in definite directions, tending, for instance, to tone down Mark's expectation of a soon-coming end of the age. He showed how Luke had schematized biblical history, with the ministry of Jesus as "the center of time," culminating the era of Israel and preparing for the church age to follow, chronicled in the Acts of the Apostles. The whole analysis is striking and compelling. Are we to dismiss it all as a series of exegetical hallucinations? I am not willing to do so. I don't think Conzelmann could have made the sense he made of both Mark and Luke if he was really studying a mass of random readings, not something approaching the original text.

However, let me note that it is the detection of sudden departures from these characteristic patterns that signals that the texts *have* suffered significant interpolations — much more so than conservatives seem willing to consider. We do not have total textual chaos, as we do very nearly in the cases of documents like the *Acts of Paul*. What we have are documents, which contain a number of significant patches and additions identifiable precisely by comparison with the authorial and redactional styles manifest elsewhere in them. Indeed, this is exactly how it is possible so neatly to slice up the Pentateuch into four component sources.

One illustrative New Testament example would be Acts 20:28: "Take heed to yourselves and to all the flock, in which the Holy Spirit has made you bishops, to feed the church of the Lord [or, of God] which he obtained with his own blood." The idea on display here – that the death of Jesus on the cross saves believers – so drastically contravenes Luke's studied avoidance of this theme elsewhere in his gospel and Acts (he even omits it from his Markan source), that we must severely doubt we are in possession of the original reading.

Luke went to the trouble of omitting the words "This is my blood of the covenant which is poured out for many" from Mark when composing his own version of the Last Supper. Mark also had Jesus say, "the son of man came not to serve but to be served, and to give his life as a ransom for many" (Mark 10:45). Significantly, Luke has substituted for that saying a subtly but crucially different version: "Who is greater: he who reclines at table, or he who serves? Is it not he who reclines at table? But I am among you as one who serves" (Luke 22:27). He has again omitted the ransom business. In Luke 24 and in Acts, where he several times has Jesus and the apostles preach the word of salvation, he makes it clear that one must believe in Jesus and be baptized in his name, but there is never any mention of his *death* as the means of salvation. For Luke it is simply a matter of fulfilled prophecy: Messiah's death was predicted, so Jesus had to die before he could reign (Luke 24:25–27; Acts 3:18; 13:26–28), but that is the extent of it. It is his *name* that saves (Luke 24:46–47; Acts 2:38; 3:16; 4.10–12), neither his blood nor his death. The presence of textual variations (some manuscripts have "the church of God" instead of "church of the Lord") confirms this suspicion.

Similarly, even if we had no manuscript evidence for the secondary character of both the woman taken in adultery pericope of John and the Longer Ending of Mark (the last twelve verses of Mark printed in the King James Version and in many modern translations as well), stylistic irregularities would be enough by themselves to reveal them as spurious text.

Voyage of the Beegle

In his great book *The Inspiration of Scripture* (1963), Dewey M. Beegle (a Free Methodist and New Testament Professor at the New York Theological Seminary) attacked B. B. Warfield's version of biblical inerrancy from many angles. He really let the old Princeton divine have it over the latter's claim that inerrancy, strictly speaking, applies only to the original autographs. Beegle replied, in effect, "*What* original autographs?" He reminded us how few, if any, biblical documents began in the form we now possess. Virtually all of them are patchwork quilts stitched together from many sources. Or else they have been heavily interpolated, or at least appear to have been. Whether you're talking about J, E, D and P, or 1, 2, and 3 Isaiah, Q, Mark, Ur-Markus, Proto-Luke, the Signs Source, the Johannine Discourse Source, the 'Little Scroll' underlying Revelation 11, or the Little Apocalypse underlying Mark 13 — or even the adulteress pericope and the Longer Ending of Mark: every biblical book looks like a flowing stream of tradition. The redactional 'correction' of these texts has only proceeded apace in modern times, even since Beegle's time.

Now, with a flood of loose and theologically slanted paraphrase versions flooding the Bible market from both the right and the left, the biblical writings continue to mutate. We must remind ourselves of the dictum of the pre-Socratic philosopher Heraclitus — "You cannot step twice into the same river." Given the fluidity of the biblical text, inerrancy just does not fit the Heraclitean reality of the situation.

What this means is that there is no firm line to be drawn between 'corruption' of the texts and the evolution of the same writings (and their oral sources) in the shadow period before they reached their 'canonical' form. Even if we do have Matthew's gospel, for example, in the latest form produced by the church at Antioch, we can still discern loose ends of previous editions. Should we try to excise later elements? For example, should we get rid of the Great Commission and go back to the original 'Not So Great Commission' of chapter 10? If not, then why chop the Longer Ending of Mark? Or the adulteress passage in John?

The only difference I can see is that the various additions entered the copying process each at a slightly later point. We have no copies of earlier versions of Matthew lacking the Great Commission, so it must have been added early enough for all copies of previous editions to have perished. Eusebius tells us he had seen with his own eyes pre-Nicene copies of Matthew in which the Commission's baptismal formula was "in my name," not the familiar Trinitarian version. We don't have such copies any more, perhaps because they perished in a Constantinian purge of manuscripts (which is surely why there are no manuscripts from before 200 CE). We do happen to have copies, very few, lacking the Longer Ending of Mark, though none of John without the equally secondary Johannine Appendix, chapter 21. Clear evidence of the changes remains, but unaltered texts do not remain, who knows why?

Terms like 'Ur-Markus,' 'Proto-Matthew,' 'Proto-Luke,' etc., remind us that there were quite likely earlier, 'transitional forms' of these evolving gospels, too. Each underwent significant amplification at some point or another. How is this different in principle from significant interpolations? They are merely two names for the same process. Thus the question is entirely moot as to whether the books of the Bible come to us more or less corrupted from the way they were 'first' written down.

Beegle was right: what counts as the first? It recedes into the mist of the untraceable past. Have people added miracle stories to hitherto-complete gospels? Or have they added miracle stories to the growing traditions from which the gospels were eventually composed? What difference does it make? Any 'original autograph' version one postulates is just an arbitrary line drawn in the shifting sand. But there is no reason to deny that the traditions-*cum*-texts evolved, and there is certainly no way to prove they didn't. The possibility that they did has proven a fruitful working hypothesis for explaining numerous problems in the text. Thus the suggestion of textual mutation is not intended as destructive in any way and will be perceived so only by those whose theology forces them to assume 'inerrant autographs' and 'eyewitness testimony.'

Can We Know the Jesus of History?

Evangelicals repudiate the notion that the gospels contain legendary or fictitious material about Jesus Christ. They want to be able to believe he did and said everything attributed to him there. They always use the same arguments, including the importance of the short time span between Jesus and the writing of the gospels, and the centrality of eyewitnesses in the formation of the gospel tradition. Such factors are said to make it unlikely if not impossible for the gospels to contain fabricated or legendary material.

Time Tunnel

Josh McDowell, a superstar apologist for evangelical Christianity, says: "One of the major criticisms against the form critics' idea of the oral tradition is that the period of oral tradition (as defined by the critics) is not long enough to have allowed the alterations in the tradition that the radical critics have alleged" (*More Evidence That Demands a Verdict*, 1975, p. 205).

Similarly, John Warwick Montgomery, the leading apologist of the 1960s and '70s and Professor of Theology at Trinity Evangelical Divinity School, concluded that "with the small time interval between Jesus' life and the Gospel records, the Church did not create a 'Christ of faith' " (*History and Christianity*, 1974, p. 37).

This "small time interval" would be about thirty or forty years! Apologists protest that this is not really a long period at all. A. H. McNeile (author of *An Introduction to the Study of the New Testament*, 2nd. Ed rev C. S. C. Williams, 1953, p. 54) states that "It is not unusual for men even of slight intellectual ability to recall and relate clearly important events occurring thirty-five years previously." But surely this is not the point. Form critics aren't suggesting simply that eyewitnesses forgot the details of what they saw. ("Eh, I forget, Peter, did Jesus walk on water, or was he water-skiing?") The question is whether *other people* spun out legendary material during the same period. Perhaps, as David Friedrich Strauss [1808–1874] suggested back in the nineteenth century, people who witnessed little or none of Jesus' activity formed legendary 'remembrances' to fill in the gaps in their knowledge (*The Life of Jesus Critically Examined*, 1972, p. 74).

If the apologists are right, records of similar religious figures written within a comparable time span should also be free of legendary embellishment. What do we find?

Gershom Scholem was the twentieth century's greatest historian of Jewish mysticism. His 1973 study of the seventeenth century messianic pretender Sabbatai Sevi (Z'vi) [1626–75] provides a good parallel here. Sevi was able to arouse apocalyptic fervor among Jews all over the Mediterranean during the 1660s. The movement suffered a serious setback when the messiah renounced Judaism and turned to Islam! But still it did not die away. The history of Sabbatai Sevi is more readily accessible to us than that of Jesus. Sabbatai Sevi lived much closer to our own era, and much more documentary evidence survives him. Here, too, according to the apologists, legends should have waited at least a couple of generations till they reared their heads. But Gershom Scholem speaks of "the sudden and almost explosive surge of miracle stories" concerning Sabbatai Sevi within weeks or even days of his public appearances. Listen to his description:

> "The... realm of imaginative legend... soon dominated the mental climate in Palestine [*while Sabbatai was there*]. The sway of imagination was strongly in evidence in the letters sent to Egypt and elsewhere and which, by the autumn of 1665 [*the same year*] had assumed the character of regular messianic propaganda in which fiction far outweighed the facts: [*e.g.*] the prophet was 'encompassed with a Fiery Cloud' and 'the voice of an angel was heard from the cloud' (Gershom Scholem, *Sabbatai Sevi: The Mystical Messiah*, 1973, pp. 252, 265).

Letters from December of the same year related that Sabbatai "command a Fire to be made in a publick place, in the presence of many beholders... and entered into the fire twice or thrice, without any hurt to his garments or to a hair on his head" (*Ibid.*, pp. 390, 535, 375, 605). Other letters tell of his raising the dead. He is said to have left his prison through locked and barred doors, which opened by themselves after his chains miraculously broke. He kills a group of highwaymen merely with the word of his mouth. Interestingly, the miracle stories often conformed to the patterns of contemporary saints' legends, just as Strauss theorized that the gospel miracle stories are frequently based on Old Testament tales of Moses, Elijah, and Elisha. Literary prototypes were ready to hand, so it needn't have taken long at all (Strauss, pp. 84–86).

The same thing happened to Jehudah the Hasid [d. 1217]. In his own lifetime, legends made him a great magician, though actually Jehudah staunchly opposed magic (Gershom Scholem, *Major Trends in Jewish Mysticism,* 1973, pp. 82, 99). Twentieth-century African prophet and martyr Simon Kimbangu became another 'living legend' against his own wishes. One group of his followers, the Ngunzists, spread his fame as the 'God of the blacks' or 'Christ of the blacks,' even while Kimbangu himself disavowed the role. Legends of Kimbangu's childhood, miracles, and prophetic visions began within his own generation (Vittorio Lanternari, *Religions of the Oppressed: A Study of Modern Messianic Cults,* 1965, pp. 25–26ff; G.C. Oosthuizen, *Post-Christianity in Africa,* 1968, p. 40; Marie-Louise Martin, *Kimbangu: An African Prophet and His Church,* 1976, pp. 73–75).

Faith-healer William Marrion Branham [1909–1965], a phenomenally successful Pentecostal healer, was held in high esteem by legions of his followers, many of whom believed him to be Jesus Christ returned or even a new incarnation of God. He, however, did not teach such notions. In fact, once on a visit to such a group of devotees in Latin America he explicitly denied any such wild claims, but his followers reasoned that he was just testing their faith! (C. Douglas Weaver, *The Healer-Prophet, William Marrion Branham: A Study of the Prophetic in American Pentecostalism,* 1987, p. 156)

Ed Sanders encountered a number of legends about Charlie Manson while researching his book *The Family.* On one particular bus trip in Death Valley, "several miracles were alleged to have been performed by Charles Manson." One story relates that "Charlie levitated the bus over a creek crag" (*The Family,* 1972, p. 133).

So it seems that an interval of thirty or forty years could indeed accommodate the intrusion of legendary materials into the gospel tradition.

I See Nothing, I Know Nothing

Apologists do not argue only from dates and time intervals. They also appeal to the role of eyewitnesses in the gospel tradition. Montgomery, like McDowell and others, employs what he calls the "external evidence" test: "as to the authors and primary historical value of the Gospel accounts, confirmation comes from independent written sources." He goes on to quote second-century bishops Papias and Irenaeus [c130–c200] to the effect that the gospels of Matthew and John were written by the disciples of those names, and that Mark was written from the preaching of Peter. But there is no reason to think so. Remember, Irenaeus also records how Jesus lived to the age of fifty to be crucified in the reign of Claudius Caesar! His source Papias also informs us how Judas Iscariot's head swelled up bigger than an ox-cart, and that he began urinating worms. Reliable sources?

If the author of so-called Matthew had been an original disciple, why would he have merely expanded Mark, itself a gospel not written by an eyewitness, instead of basing it on his own recollections? Nor can we be sure Papias even refers to the books we call Matthew and Mark. What he says of the first would apply just as well to the *Gospel According to the Hebrews*. And what he says about Mark recording the preaching of Peter would fit the apocryphal *Kerygmata Petrou* better.

But some apologists will accept a looser connection between the gospels and the eyewitnesses: the gospels, they say, are the result of a process of oral tradition. Some, like F. F. Bruce, actually seem to accept this idea; others, like Montgomery, seem only to be accepting this premise for the sake of argument. But in either case the objective is to show that the formation of any such oral or communal tradition was firmly under the control of eyewitnesses all the way, and thus did not admit of legendary embellishment. For example, F. F. Bruce writes: "it can have been by no means so easy as some writers seem to think to invent words and deeds of Jesus in those early years, when so many of his disciples were about, who could remember what had and had not happened." But what proof do we have that there were any disciples or apostles anywhere near the people who were writing gospels? It seems quite unlikely, given the fact that, even on the most conservative dating, the earliest gospel was written in the thick of the Jewish War, when Romans were devastating both Galilee and Jerusalem. The others would have been composed still later, after the war had carried off virtually all witnesses to Jesus.

Bruce's idea is that the apostles and other eyewitnesses would have seen to it that the rank-and-file believers did not let their fancy run wild in creating stories and sayings of Jesus. It seems to me that this argument rests on a rather anachronistic picture of the apostles' activity. They are imagined as a team of fact-checkers, ranging over Palestine, sniffing out legends and clamping the lid on any they discover. If the apostles declined to leave their preaching to wait on tables, I doubt if they had time for this sort of thing either. (Strauss pointed this out long ago in *The Life of Jesus Critically Examined*, p. 74, but what modern apologist even thinks he needs to read Strauss?)

Again, look at Sabbatai Sevi: we know that the chief apostle of his movement, Nathan of Gaza, repeatedly warned the faithful beforehand that the Messiah would do no miracles. But, as we have seen, miracle stories gushed forth without abatement (*Sabbatai Sevi*, p. 252).

Keep in mind the caution of Bollandist scholar Hippolyte Delehaye. He belongs to an order of specialists who study the many hagiographies of the Catholic tradition, and of these he is by no means uncritical. His comments directly apply to the saints' legends, but they seem equally appropriate to the study of the gospels. In discussing the sources and historicity of saints' legends, he remarks:

> The intellectual capacity of the multitude reveals itself on all sides as exceedingly limited, and it would be a mistake to assume that it usually submits itself to the influence of superior minds. On the contrary, the latter necessarily suffer loss from contact with the former, and it would be quite illogical to attribute a special value to a popular tradition because it had its origin amid surroundings in which persons

of solid merit were to be met with (*The Legends of the Saints,* 1961, pp. 16–17).

F. F. Bruce and John Warwick Montgomery go on to add a negative version of the eyewitness argument: what about *hostile* eyewitnesses who could have called the Christians' bluff? "Had there been any tendency to depart from the facts in any material respect, the possible presence of hostile witnesses in the audience would have served as a further corrective" (Bruce, *The New Testament Documents: Are They Reliable?,* 1972, p. 46). Bruce is not reckoning with the contagious fervor of apocalyptic movements; one hears what one wants to hear. In the case of Sabbatai Sevi, we know that "hostile witnesses" tried to keep things under control but to no avail. The rabbis of Constantinople announced that during Sevi's stay there "we have not beheld a single miracle or sign... only the noise of rumors and testimonies at second hand" (*Sabbatai Sevi,* p. 612). No one seemed to listen. Bruce also seems to forget how easily and thoroughly the early church suppressed and destroyed unwelcome 'heretical' writings. If hostile eyewitnesses *had* recorded their protests, what are the chances we would have known it?

In our own day we can find several parallel cases, none of which seem to accord with the apologists' claims about what would or would not have happened. You may recall the brief flurry of interest, during the great 'cult' hysteria of the 70s and early 80s, over the young Guru Maharaj Ji. He was a rotund little Buddha of a man, a boy really, who had a notorious preference for Baskin-Robbins ice cream. As it happened, he also had a preference for his secretary and married her, much against the Old-World wishes of his mother. She promptly booted the young godling off the throne of the universe and replaced him with his drab older brother. What, one might ask, was the reaction of the membership to this train of events? On a visit to Berkeley a year or so later, I saw them still handing out literature featuring the boy-god's grinning visage. I asked how this was still possible and was told that they refused to believe the whole debacle had happened. All was the same as far as they were concerned.

Or take the Rastafarians of Jamaica. They venerated Ethiopian Emperor Haile Selassie as God incarnate, despite his own puzzled reaction to this news. What became of their faith when the deposed emperor died? On a *Sixty Minutes* broadcast an intelligent-looking Jamaican journalist who was himself a Rastafarian said he believed Haile Selassie was still alive, his supposed death a "premature report" engendered by the unbelieving Western media.

In all such cases we have to ask if 'cognitive dissonance reduction' is involved. When one has so much at stake in a belief being true ("Lo, we have left everything to follow you" Mark 10:28), one simply cannot, psychologically speaking, afford to admit one was mistaken. Any fact may be denied or rationalized (Leon Festinger, Henry W. Riecken, and Stanley Schacter, *When Prophecy Fails: A Social and Psychological Study of a Modern Group that Predicted the Destruction of the World*). Finally one is impervious to the carping of 'hostile witnesses.'

The eyewitness argument is dubious in yet another respect. Evidence shows that the proximity of eyewitnesses to the events does not even guarantee the factuality of their own enthusiastic reports. Turning again to the Sabbatian movement, we note Scholem's description: "The transition from history to legend took place with extraordinary rapidity in what are practically eyewitness accounts. Already the earliest documents confuse dates and chronologies, and abound in legendary accounts of miracles" (*Sabbatai Sevi*, p. 215).

William Peter Blatty's *The Exorcist* was supposed to be based on an actual case. Henry Ansgar Kelly, himself a Roman Catholic priest, interviewed the priest who had conducted the rite. He freely confessed that all the supernatural effects had been added by rumormongers and scriptwriters. More important for our purposes, the exorcist (himself obviously no Bultmannian skeptic, given his profession) admitted that "he recognized a strong myth-making tendency even in himself. If he did not record the events of each session of exorcism as soon as possible after it occurred, he declared, he found the details changing in his mind, becoming more 'impressive' " (*The Devil, Demonology and Witchcraft: the Development of Christian Belief in Evil Spirits*, 1974, p. 95).

Studies have shown that eyewitness testimony is often remarkably unreliable, most especially when it is testimony of a surprising and remarkable event. The witness will have to reach for some familiar analogy or category (perhaps from myth or science fiction) in order to be able to comprehend the oddity at all. Psychologists have staged unusual events and then immediately interviewed the observers with wildly disparate – and one might add distinctly unharmonizable – results. And it may take only half an hour for recollections to begin to blur and metamorphose! After a series of experiments, Hall, McFeaters, and Loftus report that "Whatever the source, additional information is acquired and is often readily integrated with original memory for the event. Thus, both pre- or post-event information has in fact altered the content of what is recalled... Once created, the new memory can be as real and as vivid to the person as a memory acquired as the result of 'genuine' perception" ("Alterations in Recollections of Unusual and Unexpected Events," *Journal of Scientific Exploration*. Vol. 1, Sampler, 1987, p. 2).

For 'pre-event information' here we might read "prior messianic expectations." For 'post-event information' we might read "the early Christian preaching." In other words, memory altered in the light of the suggestions of faith. Far from supporting the apologists' position, the dynamics of eyewitness testimony would seem to point strongly in the direction of gospel-embellishment: the witnesses of Jesus saw a most remarkable man endowed with unusual gifts and proceeded to interpret him in categories drawn from Old Testament miracle tales and from Jewish apocalyptic and Hellenistic mythology. Once the gospel of a miracle-working savior began to be preached, it is no surprise if the eager memories of 'eyewitnesses' would begin to reflect that faith.

What Would Jesus Say?

Let us turn now to the related question of the tradition of the sayings of Jesus. Wouldn't special care have been taken to preserve Jesus' authentic sayings and to exclude bogus ones? Form critics suggest that sayings were created by the early Christians by the prophetic inspiration of the Spirit, and then were ascribed to Jesus. The idea is that it mattered little to them whether the saying came from the earthly or the exalted

Lord. Conservatives reject this suggestion. F. F. Bruce is typical here: "Indeed, the evidence is that the early Christians were careful to distinguish between sayings of Jesus and their own inferences or judgments. Paul, for example, when discussing the vexed questions of marriage and divorce in I Corinthians vii, is careful to make this distinction between his own advice on the subject and the Lord's decisive ruling: 'I, not the Lord,' and again, 'Not I, but the Lord'" (*New Testament Documents*, p. 46).

But surely one text (and the same one is invariably quoted when apologists argue this point) is not enough to indicate what the general practice was. Elsewhere Bruce himself recognizes the very ambiguity stressed by the form critics. Citing I Thessalonians 4:14–18, Bruce says "We cannot be sure whether Paul is quoting a [*word of Christ*] which had come down to him in the tradition... or one which was communicated by the risen Lord through a prophet" (*Paul and Jesus*, 1974, p. 70).

By ancient middle-eastern standards, it is not at all certain that faithful 'ministers of the word' would never dare let a 'phony' saying slip in. This might be the very thing they *should* do! Early Muslims handed down the *hadith*, or oral traditions of the Prophet Muhammad. How did they accomplish this? Robert D. Smith has this to say:

> Regarding the character of the transmitters of the traditions, especially during that vulnerable century when they were transmitted only by word of mouth and memory, two ancient Moslem authorities agree that "a holy man is nowhere more inclined to lie than in the matter of traditions." There are many venerated Moslems who actually are known to have succumbed to this temptation, some of them explicitly admitting that they did so. It is important to note, moreover, that in spite of the fact that these men were known as forgers, they were nevertheless revered as holy men because their lies were considered to be completely unobjectionable. It was a quasi-universal conviction that it was licit in the interest of encouraging virtue and submission to the law, to concoct and put into circulation sayings of the Prophet (*Comparative Miracles*, 1965, pp. 131–132).

Jan Vansina, a major field anthropologist and an expert in oral tradition, in his book *Oral Tradition as History*, comments:

"Historical truth is also a notion that is culture specific.... When G. Gossen reports that the Chamuleros (Maya Chiapas) believe that any coherent account about an event which has been retold several times is true the historian does not feel satisfied.... In many cultures truth is what is being faithfully repeated as content and has been certified as true by the ancestors. But sometimes truth does not include the notion that x and y really happened.... One cannot just assume that truth means faithful transmission of the content of a message. The historian must be on his guard; he cannot assume anything on this score, but must elucidate it for the culture he studies" (pp. 129–130).

So much for the arguments used vainly by apologists to try to choke off gospel criticism at its source. Really they are all attempts to get evangelical students and seminarians to "pay no attention to the man behind the curtain," because if they do, things will get complicated. It will no longer be so easy to claim one is parroting the teaching of Jesus, no longer so easy to claim a 'personal relationship' with a figure of history whose outlines are irreparably blurred in the mists of antiquity.

The task of the apologist is a quixotic quest. The locomotive of New Testament research will not stop for such a suicidal cow astride the tracks. I invite you instead to hop on board at the next stop. And then you can join in the exciting task of sifting the gospel traditions, recognizing the innumerable gospel contradictions and anachronisms no longer as troublesome flies in the dogmatic ointment but rather as valuable clues and levers for unlocking the mysteries of the texts.

The Future Disguises Itself
As the Past:
The Origin of the Resurrection

It is a commonplace in New Testament scholarship that the Messiahship of Jesus is strongly and clearly tied to his resurrection. Early preaching formulas preserved in Acts 2:36 and 13:33 as well as in Romans 1:3–4 are actually *adoptionistic* — having Jesus gain his Messiahship only as of the resurrection event. This would make Jesus a man who became God's 'son' only in an honorary sense, hence 'adopted' — albeit exalted to heavenly glory. Even where New Testament writers see Jesus as the Messiah already during his life, they preserve the resurrection-Messiahship link by their frequent citation of Psalm 110, an enthronement psalm. Equally clear is that Acts 3:19–21 preserves a tradition according to which the exalted Jesus was not yet the Messiah but only the Messiah-designate and would enter upon the Messianic office only at the *Parousia* (= apocalyptic Second Coming).

Waiting in the Wings

When we try to make sense of both of these early Christologies, here is what I think emerges: in view of the strong link between resurrection and Messianic enthronement, if Jesus was viewed as not yet the Messiah until the Parousia, then he equally must have been viewed as not yet resurrected *until* the Parousia! His resurrection was yet future and would coincide with that of all believers (as is said of the Messiah in 2 Esdras 7:29–32).

I suspect that the earliest Christians venerated Jesus as a martyr whose soul was exalted to heaven after his death, who would someday rise, at the general resurrection, to return as the Messiah. Until then he stood before or beside the throne of

Yahweh, even as Judas Maccabaeus had glimpsed the martyred high priest Onias III and Jeremiah pleading for Israel before Yahweh's throne (2 Maccabees 15:12–14). No doubt there were similar visions of the beatified martyr Jesus shortly after his death. At this stage of primitive Christian belief, Jesus was viewed as not yet enthroned as the Messiah, but only designated to be such at his return at the (soon-coming) end of the age. So argued the great New Testament scholar J. A. T. Robinson — Bishop of Woolwich and author of *Honest to God* (1963) in his 1956 essay "The Most Primitive Christology of All?" (in his collection *Twelve New Testament Essays*).

In Acts 3:19–21, Peter is made to describe Jesus not as Messiah but as Messiah-elect, Messiah designate, waiting for his investiture: "Repent therefore, and turn again, that your sins may be blotted out, that times of refreshing may come from the presence of the Lord, and that he may send the Christ appointed for you, Jesus, whom heaven must receive until the time for establishing all that God spoke by the mouth of his holy prophets from of old." Accordingly, the martyr Stephen sees him standing before Jehovah as an exalted martyr — not sitting as the enthroned Messiah (Acts 7:55). These are fragments of early tradition preserved by Luke in new contexts.

It is from this period that we get the image of Jesus interceding for his own before the divine throne. "Consequently he is able for all time to save those who draw near to God through him, since he always lives to make intercession for them" (Hebrews 7:25). "My little children, I am writing this to you so that you may not sin; but if any one does sin, we have an advocate with the Father, Jesus Christ the righteous" (1 John 2:1). "Is it Christ Jesus, who died, yes, who was raised from the dead, who is at the right hand of God, who indeed intercedes for us?" (Romans 8:34). From this period also stems the cry *Maranatha* ("Our Lord, come!"), which implies the plaintive longing for an absent Lord, not fellowship with a present, Risen One. Likewise, here we have the life-setting of Mark 2:20 ("The days will come, when the bridegroom is taken away from them, and then they will fast in that day."), a period of mourning for the absence of Jesus — instead of joyful celebration of his resurrection.

How did they move to the subsequent Christology whereby Jesus was already the resurrected Messiah? It is a case of *Realized Eschatology* (coping with the delay of the Parousia by reinterpreting it as somehow already having happened here and now). Many New Testament scholars believe that the Messianic interpretation of Jesus' earthly life and ministry was a reinterpretation prompted by the delay of the Parousia. As time went on, and there was no Messianic Coming of Jesus to experience, the gap was in some measure filled by the belief that he had already come as the Messiah. So the events of his earthly life were now in hindsight given new Messianic significance. Miracle-working became a Messianic work, though this is unprecedented in Judaism. His death became the preordained death of the Messiah, though no Jew had ever heard of such a thing — including Jesus.

I would carry this logic a significant step further. I suggest that the resurrection of Jesus itself was the first attempt to claim for the present (and recent past) a bit of the anticipated but ever-delayed Messianic glory. It was first believed that Jesus' resurrection, *i.e.*, his return as the Messiah, would begin the general resurrection of the End. To close the widening gap in some measure, Christians came to believe that he had already risen as the *avant-garde* of the resurrection, and that finally the End was close at hand for sure. It was a prop for failing, increasingly disillusioned faith.

Here is where I think the language of his resurrection as the "first-fruits" of the eschatological (end-time) resurrection comes in. The idea was to forge a link between Jesus' resurrection as an event of the recent past and the general resurrection to come, so that one must shortly follow the other. Hold out just a little longer!

Such a step is not only required to move my theory along toward its desired conclusion; it is quite possible and natural in the nature of the case. It is precisely the sort of thing that happens in moments of sectarian apocalyptic disappointment, as witness Festinger, Riecken, and Schachter, *When Prophecy Fails*, as in the cases of the Seventh Day Adventists and Jehovah's Witnesses. When each staked all on an apocalyptic deadline, and that deadline passed, they had to reduce cognitive dissonance by reinterpreting the great event along private or invisible or spiritualized lines — in short, some manner in which it might be said to have happened, yet without upheaving the external world (since in fact, alas, it *didn't* upheave the external world). What was to have been a matter of sight was now converted into a matter of faith.

So it (must have) happened in the recent past — it was not noticed at the time, not until a vision or a reexamination (reinterpretation) of scripture suggested to disciples who were slow of heart to believe, that they had missed it while it was happening in a way they did not expect.

If You Blink, You Might Miss It

For narrative purposes, the only way to present the spiritualization of the desired fulfillment, to have it occur in a way no one would notice but for the eye of faith, is to have it so occur and be — missed. Logically, the moment one conceives the idea of an invisible fulfillment, the only way it can be realized is by the assumption that it has happened already; otherwise, if it only might happen invisibly, in the future, how will you ever know when it happens? In the nature of the case there can be no visible sign! So to bring the notion from the realm of speculative possibility to that of faith appropriation, you have no other option than to take it as having happened already. This is the only available, viable form of 'facticity.'

In precisely this way, I am suggesting, the disillusioned early Christians at some point comforted themselves with the 'realization' that while they were waiting for Jesus to rise at the End-time resurrection as glorious Messiah, he had already done so! He already reigned (albeit from heaven, where he remained) as Messiah! Any further delay, then, was not a matter of such urgent concern. The main thing was already done.

We have at least one actual historical example of such a transformation of future expectation into legendary past. In 1919, a Papua, New Guinea prophet named Evara came forward with the prophecy that very soon tribal ancestors would return aboard a ghostly freighter, the steamer of the dead. They would bring to their living descendants great troves of Western goods like those enjoyed by the European colonizers and missionaries. It was the beginning of the 'Vailala Madness,' as it came to be called — involving one of the most important of the famous Cargo Cults of Melanesia studied by Peter Worsley in his *The Trumpet Shall Sound*. After numerous false alarms and disappointments, the movement petered out in 1931.

> But the effects of the Vailala Madness did not cease with the end of organized activity. The memory lived on in the minds of the villagers, and, as time passed, legends grew up... In 1934, people still firmly maintained the "belief that those first years of the Vailala Madness constituted a brief age of miracles." [F. E. Williams, "The Vailala Madness in Retrospect," in *Essays Presented to C. G. Seligman*. London: Routledge & Kegan Paul, 1934, p. 373.] The things which had been prophesied in 1919 were believed in 1934 to have actually taken place. It was recounted how, in that wonder time, "the ground shook and the trees swayed... flowers sprang up in a day, and the air was filled with their fragrance. The spirits of the dead came and went by night." [*ibid*.]...
>
> The steamer of the dead, moreover, actually had appeared. People had seen the vessel's wash, heard the noise of her engines, the rattle of the anchor-chain, and the splashing of her dinghy being lowered into the water and of the oars; similar noises were heard as it disappeared without ever having actually been seen. Others remembered obscurely seeing her large red funnel and three masts, and many saw her lights... Clouds often obscured a proper view of the vessel, though the inhabitants of villages unaffected by the Madness had greater difficulty in seeing the vessel than the faithful. [Worsley, pp. 90–91].

I think it not unlikely that the repeated frustrations of the early Christians led to a similar retrojection of their resurrection hope into the recent past. But then how did they determine precisely when in the recent past the resurrection (must have) occurred? By seeking a scriptural prophecy! Hosea 6:2 ("After two days he will revive us; on the third day he will raise us up, that we may live before him") became 1 Corinthians 15:4 ("and that he was buried, and that he rose again the third day according to the scriptures").

By the time the resurrection of Jesus became a Christian belief, the tomb was a moot point. At first no one denied the tomb was occupied. By the time they preached his resurrection the body was gone, lost to decay, and the emptiness of the tomb, entirely for natural reasons, was given new significance.

Lengthening Shadow of the Cross

What of the atoning death of Jesus? Following Sam K. Williams (*Jesus' Death as Saving Event: the Background and Origin of a Concept, 1975*) I think that it was only in connection with the Gentile Mission that his death was first seen as a sacrifice inaugurating a new covenant, not to supercede the original one for Jews, but rather to provide an atonement for Gentiles, a new covenant Yahweh was establishing with them alongside that with Jews.

Just as according to 4 Maccabees (6:26–30; 17:21–22) Yahweh had deigned to accept the faithful martyr-deaths of Eleazer and the seven brothers as an atonement for Israel, so he was now imagined to accept the steadfast death of the martyr Jesus as an atonement for those who had for centuries stood outside the sacrificial system of Israel and whose sins had been piling up toward a terrible judgment, now mercifully averted.

For Jewish believers in Jesus, Jesus was Messiah and soon-coming liberator; but for Gentiles he was an atoning savior, and by and large, Jewish Christians would have agreed Jesus was this — for Gentiles.

Note, for instance, how in Mark and Matthew the words of institution at the Lord's Supper make the blood of Jesus to be shed "for many," while Paul in 1 Corinthians 11 has it shed "for you." The Synoptic Gospels have him speaking to Jews, so it is not "for you," but rather for many others, *i.e.*, for the vast numbers of Gentiles. Paul is speaking to such Gentiles, so he changes it to "for you." The Synoptics have Jesus speaking to Jews about Gentiles, whereas Paul uses the same formula speaking to Gentiles.

The conception (already in 1 Corinthians) of the Eucharist as a sharing in the body and blood of Christ is a subsequent development in the Gentile Church on Hellenistic soil. I would further suggest that baptism in Christianity began not among the earliest Jewish Christians (the fanciful second-century

Book of Acts notwithstanding) but in the Hellenistic Jewish Christian mission to Gentiles. As it had been in Judaism, immersion was an initiation for proselytes — period. There was at first no reference to John the Baptist. In the tradition regarding him, in fact, we find a contrast between his mere water baptism and the Spirit baptism of the Coming One. This means that the Christian framers of this tradition did not baptize in water.

Note that in the most Jewish of the Gospels, Matthew, the command is to baptize "the nations" ('Gentiles') — with nothing whatever said of the baptism of the Twelve or the Jewish Christians for whom they stand. All Paul says of baptism is said to Gentile converts, who of course would have been baptized. (He himself may have been baptized, but this may be an exceptional case, just as his disregard of the dietary Laws was a prerogative of his being a missionary who must adapt himself to the Gentiles. "To those outside the Law I became as one outside the Law.")

When he says in Galatians 3:28 that all who have been baptized into Christ have put on Christ, and that there is now no more distinction between Jew and Gentile, he needn't mean that both Jews and Gentiles were baptized, but only that once Gentiles are baptized, Gentiles are no longer considered different from Jews in the eyes of Yahweh. After all, couldn't the same thing have been said of purely Jewish proselyte baptism?

On Hellenistic soil, however, baptism becomes far more than the original Jewish (then Jewish Christian) proselyte baptism. It rapidly takes on the contours of a Mystery cult initiation rite that confers salvation and a new nature by identifying the initiate with the fate of the Redeemed Redeemer, the dying and rising savior. It is at this point that Pauline 'Christ-Mysticism' becomes possible. My guess is that no Palestinian Christian ever thought of such a thing.

Even today, theology changes so rapidly that it is hard to keep up. One of the reasons it is hard to understand the earliest Christian beliefs, I think, is that they seemed to have changed even faster back then. We find them superimposed upon each other in the earliest documents, and in very thin layers hard to disengage from one another. But here is an attempt, however ham-fisted.

Must Jesus Have Risen?

Ihave no desire to overturn Christian faith. However, as I learned in InterVarsity Christian Fellowship, we must be honest with the evidence of the texts and not seek to secure faith on the basis of inadequate reasoning. My study of the gospels has convinced me that, while anything remains possible, there is no compelling reason to call upon the supernatural to explain the origin of either the Christian faith or the belief in Jesus' resurrection.

Mixed Signals

What suggests to many of us that the gospel resurrection accounts contain legendary embellishment? For one thing, there are the contradictions between the stories. They include the problem of which and how many women visited the tomb, and at what hour. Was it Mary Magdalene alone (John 20:1), or was she with others (Luke 24:1)? Did she or they see the man (Mark 16:5) or men (Luke 24:4) or angels (John 20:12) before (Luke 24:9; Matthew 28) or after (John 20:11–12) she or they had called on Peter and the others? Did the woman or women see Jesus at the tomb (Matthew 28:9-10; John 20:14) or not (Luke 24, Mark 16)? Was Jesus buried in a tomb that happened to be conveniently situated nearby (John 19:41–42), or in Joseph's own new tomb (Matthew 27:60) or just some unspecified tomb (Mark 15:46; Luke 23:53)? Did the risen Jesus (or his surrogate) tell his disciples to go to Galilee (Matthew 28:10; Mark 16:7) or to stay in Jerusalem (Luke 24:49)? And, if they were known facts, how on earth did the other gospel writers neglect to report what Matthew (28:2–4) tells of a shining angel swooping from the skies to roll the stone away, causing an earthquake and making posted guards faint dead away?

You will have heard attempts to harmonize these contradictions, but any such attempt is an implicit admission that the burden of proof is on this supposed 'evidence,' not on the one who doubts it. Harmonization means that, despite appearances, the texts still *might* be true, that is, if you treat them like jigsaw puzzle pieces.

One sometimes hears that the various contradictions are minor points such as one would expect in various accounts of the same car accident. But this is a damaging assessment of eyewitness testimony, admitting its inaccuracy. And besides, the texts are not independent. We can easily trace how Matthew, Luke, and John have rewritten Mark's earlier account, using literary imagination to fill in his gaps and improve his story.

Worse yet, the gospel accounts contradict an earlier conception of Jesus' resurrection found in 1 Corinthians 15. The chapter gives a bare list of names of some to whom Jesus appeared, but no real stories. However, it does go on to describe the resurrection body. Believers, it says, will one day have the same sort of immortal body. It will be a "spiritual body" (v. 44) — not a corruptible, natural body such as we have now, a body of "flesh and blood," whose frail materials can never inherit the kingdom of God (v. 50). Thus the resurrected Jesus had no "flesh and blood," but had instead "become a life-giving spirit" (v. 45). The gospel Easter stories presuppose the exact opposite: in Luke 24:39, Jesus extends his hands and says, "It is I myself. No spirit has flesh and bones as you see I have." In all the gospel accounts, he has a body of flesh and even open wounds that may be touched.

My point is this: if these stories embodied the historical memory of the risen Christ, how can the very different 1 Corinthians version ever have arisen? No one would speak in such dangerously equivocal terms like a "spiritual body" if the prior tradition had been of a solid, fleshly resurrection. But if the "spiritual body" version were the original, it is easy to see how a more concrete version would have arisen to replace it, in an attempt to fend off subjective Gnostic claims that made it hard to tell the difference between resurrection of the body and pagan-style immortality of the soul.

Some try to harmonize 1 Corinthians 15 with the gospels by saying that, by a "spiritual body," Paul refers to a physical body that can walk through walls as in Luke 24 and John 20 — if that is what Jesus does. Luke probably has in mind miraculous teleporting, 'rapturing,' which he also has happen with the unresurrected Philip in Acts 8:39-40. John may mean the same thing. At any rate, both stories simply have him appear. Neither says he walked through a closed door like Jacob Marley. Now that would be a *spiritual body*! But it's also just what Luke's risen Jesus says he is *not*, since he offers tangible flesh and bones for their inspection.

Legends Are Nobody's Fault

If the Easter stories of the gospels are not memory reports, what are they? Hoaxes? Apologists scoff at this: how could a world religion with high ideals be the product of a hoax? Of course, this is exactly what they think is true of Mormonism, a world religion in its own right. But hoaxing is not the only alternative. The gospel resurrection accounts make complete and natural sense as pious legends — and such legends were quite common in the ancient world.

Philosophers, kings, and other benefactors were often glorified by means of legend. Mythic heroes such as Hercules and Romulus were rewarded for their labors by apotheosis, being taken up into heaven and seated among the gods. Their ascension was in some cases supposedly seen by eyewitnesses or was at least evidenced by the entire absence of bodily remains. Not only were such legends circulating about mythic figures of the remote past; the same sort of tales were applied to historical and contemporary figures like Empedocles, Apollonius of Tyana, the Emperor Augustus, and the Cynic martyr Peregrinus.

The fact that no one could find so much as one of his bones in the funeral pyre convinced men that Hercules had been raised to Olympus. Aristaeus, son of Apollo, had been taken into heaven because, like the Old Testament Enoch, he was no more to be seen. Aeneas was known to have joined the gods because after a battle no trace of him could be found, the same evidence that convinced Elijah's disciples that their master had been taken into heaven. Romulus, first king of Rome, had been seen rising into the firmament, confirmed later by no one being able to find a scrap of his flesh or his armor.

In historical times, Empedocles got up from the table and did not return. His companions were unable to find him, and a heavenly voice explained he had ascended. Apollonius of Tyana entered a temple, the doors of which closed behind him, and heavenly voices sang, "Come up hither!" He was never seen on earth again, with one exception: a young 'Doubting Thomas' stubbornly refused to believe in the immortality of the soul. He said to his fellow disciples, "I, my friends, am completing the tenth month of praying to Apollonius to reveal to me the nature of the soul. But he is completely dead so as never to respond to my begging, nor will I believe he is not dead." But on the fifth day after that they were busy with these things and he suddenly fell into a deep sleep right where he had been talking. He, as if insane, suddenly leaped to his feet and cried out, "I believe you!" When those present asked him what was wrong, he said, "Do you not see Apollonius the sage, how he stands here among us, listening to the argument and singing wonderful verses concerning the soul? He came to discuss with me alone concerning the things which I would not believe" (*Life of Apollonius* 8:31).

Romulus, too, appeared to mourning Romans to reassure them, and to give a great commission for Roman might to conquer the world in his name.

Verisimilarly I Say unto You

Apologists like to point to the "vivid detail" in the gospel Easter stories as proof of eyewitness authorship. Their favorite passage is John 20:3–8, where Peter and the Beloved Disciple visit the empty tomb. But does vividness occur only in nonfiction reporting? Compare the same story with another scene from the first-century BCE novel by Chariton, *Chaireas and Callirhoe*. A comatose girl has been prematurely buried, but then rescued by grave robbers who happen to discover her waking up. They abscond with her. Her fiancé visits the tomb the next morning.

Chaireas was guarding and toward dawn he approached the tomb. When he came close, however, he found the stones moved away and the entrance open. He looked in and was shocked, seized by a great perplexity at what had happened. Rumor made an immediate report to the Syracusans about the miracle. All then ran to the tomb; no one dared to enter until Hermocrates ordered it. One was sent in, and he reported everything accurately. It seemed incredible — the dead girl was not there. [*When Chaireas*] searched the tomb he was able to find nothing. Many came in after him, disbelieving. Amazement seized everyone, and some said as they stood there: "The shroud has been stripped off, this is the work of grave robbers; but where is the body?" (*Chaireas and Callirhoe* 3:3).

I suggest that vivid descriptions of empty tombs, people hesitating to enter them and then noticing stripped-off grave clothes are not necessarily a mark of eyewitness testimony! Does anyone think the Lukan story of the Emmaus disciples (24:13–35) reads too much like vivid eyewitness reporting to be legendary? Compare it with a votive tablet posted in the healing shrine of the god Asclepius, son of Apollo, in Epidaurus, Greece, from the fourth century BCE:

Sostrata of Pherae had a false pregnancy. In fear and trembling she came in a litter and slept here. [*Asclepius was supposed to appear to the sleeping worshipper with a prescription*.] But she had no dream and started for home again. Then, near Curni, she dreamt that a man, comely in appearance, fell in with her and her companions; when he learned about their bad luck he bade them set down the litter on which they were carrying Sostrata; then he cut open her belly, removed an enormous quantity of worms — two full basins; then he stitched up her belly and made the woman well. Then Asclepius revealed his presence and bade her to send thank-offerings for the cure to Epidauros (votive tablet 2.25).

In both cases, disappointed pilgrims leave the holy city to return home and are met on the way by the Savior himself, unrecognized, who manifests the desired miracle after all, reveals himself and disappears! One is plainly legendary; why isn't the other?

Halluci-Notions

Apologists assure us that the resurrection appearances could not have been hallucinations. They claim that the apostles were too "hard-headed" and "prosaic" for this (J. N. D. Anderson, *The Evidence for the Resurrection,* 1974, p. 21). But just how "hard-headed" would we call someone who left his family and livelihood to join a wandering exorcist? How "prosaic" is a man who exclaims, "Lord, even the demons are subject to us in your name!" or "Do you want us to call down fire from heaven to consume them?"

J. N. D. Anderson contends that "Hallucinations are highly individualistic because their source is the subconscious mind of the recipient. No two persons will experience exactly the same phenomena. But the crowd of five hundred [1 Corinthians 15] claimed to have experienced the same 'hallucination,' at the same time and place" (*ibid.*). Of course, there is no evidence at all that 500 people even *claimed* to have experienced the same thing, let alone subjectively experienced the same thing. We have at best only a hear-say report. Even so, let us consider the phenomenon of group hallucination.

Collective hallucinations, as a matter of fact, are a well-known phenomenon discussed, for instance, in G. N. M. Tyrell's *Apparitions* and D. H. Rawcliffe's *The Psychology of the Occult.* Here is an example from the seventeenth century Messianic movement of Sabbatai Sevi, as Gershom Scholem describes it:

> The people of Smyrna saw miracles and heard prophecies, providing the best possible illustration of Renan's remark about the infectious character of visions. It is enough for one member of a group sharing the same beliefs to claim to have seen or heard a supernatural manifestation, and the others, too, will see or hear it. Hardly had the report arrived from Aleppo that Elijah had appeared in the Old Synagogue there, and Elijah walked the streets of Smyrna. Dozens, even hundreds, had seen him (*Sabbatai Sevi: The Mystical Messiah*, 1973, pp. 417, 446).

In a group hallucination not all participants necessarily see the very same thing. All that is needed is for each individual, prompted to see a familiar person's image, to see it as he or she imagines it. There is no telepathic link whereby all literally share the same vision. 1 Corinthians 15 does not tell us, "He was seen by more than five hundred brethren who all compared notes and found they had seen a man five feet, ten inches tall, wearing a white robe and a red cloak, hair parted in the middle, brown eyes, long beard, and nail-pierced hands, forearms at right angles to his body, and saying, 'My peace I leave thee'."

The most we may suppose – that is, if we are disposed to accept hearsay – is that they each saw what they took to be Jesus.

In fact, one ancient Christian document, the *Acts of Peter* offers us exactly such simultaneous *but non-matching* visions of the risen Christ.

> Peter said to them, "Tell us what you saw." And they said, "We saw an old man, who had such a presence as we cannot describe to you"; but others said, "We saw a growing lad"; and others said, "We saw a boy who gently touched our eyes, and so our eyes were opened." So Peter praised the Lord, saying, "God is greater than our thoughts, as we have learned from the aged widows, how they have seen the Lord in a variety of forms" (chapter 21).

But were the disciples in the proper mental state to experience hallucinations? Evangelical theologian and apologist Clark Pinnock thinks not: "all the factors favorable to the hallucination hypothesis are absent from the New Testament. The resurrection caught everyone off guard. The disciples were surprised and disbelieving for joy. They needed convincing themselves. Jesus did not come into an atmosphere of wishful thinking" (*Set Forth Your Case*, 1978, p. 97).

Once again, this argument is vitiated by its simply taking for granted that the resurrection accounts must be factually accurate, as if the only dispute were over supernatural versus natural explanations of them. The resurrection caught everyone off guard exactly as the apparition of Banquo's ghost caught Macbeth off guard. Indeed, contrary to Pinnock's assertion, if the resurrection accounts *are literary creations, the skepticism motif is quite natural, indeed inevitable.* Skepticism is almost always a component of a miracle story. It is a literary device that serves to heighten narrative tension and so make the miracle all the more climactic when it finally happens, a victory against all odds.

The temple of Asclepius contained all manner of fictitious testimonials of miracles, written as advertisements: One man whose fingers were paralyzed "disbelieved in the healings and sneered at the inscriptions." Yet in his mercy the god healed his hand, telling him that henceforth he should be called "Incredulous" (Epidauros votive tablet 1.3). One-eyed Ambrosia of Athens came to the shrine, her mind full of doubts: "as she walked around the temple of healings, she mocked some things as incredible and impossible, that the lame and the blind could be healed at only seeing a dream." But Asclepius healed her anyhow (1.4). Another man with an empty eye-socket came to be healed despite the skepticism of others, and the Savior gave him a brand new eye (1.9). In Philostratus' *Life of Apollonius of Tyana* 5:10, the sage identifies the cause of a plague as a poor blind beggar and tells the crowd to stone him. They are skeptical, but he persuades them, and what do you know? Under the heap of stones is a demon! Even so, the disciples' doubt depicted in the gospels is no proof of anything. It need be no more than simply a common literary device.

Seedbed of Failure

Another common argument is that only the resurrection of Jesus can explain the transformation of the disciples from a huddle of cringing cowards into a dynamic group of missionaries who turned the world upside down. Why didn't the Jesus movement die along with its founder?

Without dwelling on the simple fact that we really know nothing at all about the disciples before their supposed transformation and no trace of them as "missionaries who turned the world upside down" has ever been found, let's look briefly at some other cases of messianic disappointment.

In the 1660s, Sabbatai Sevi predicted he would convert the Ottoman sultan to Judaism. But when the sultan threatened to kill him if he didn't convert to Islam, he did! I think it would have to be admitted that the apostasy of the messiah would be fully as bitter a pill to swallow as the crucifixion of the messiah! What happened? There was a rash of after-the-fact rationalizations (scripture predicted the apostasy; the apostasy was a redemptive event; the apostasy didn't really happen, it was a phantom event, *etc.*) But the movement did not evaporate. It continued on for generations and may not be extinct even today. As Scholem explains, the hard core of the movement simply had lived with messianic excitement too intensely and for too long for mere external events to budge them.

The Millerite movement staked everything on the return of Christ occurring in 1843. Two different target dates fell through, but this did not spell the end of the Adventist faith. With a theological adjustment or two, the movement became what is known today as the Seventh-Day Adventist Church — still one of the fastest-growing missionary movements in the world. They simply decided that the anticipated judgment of Christ had been carried out in heaven, not on earth. Jehovah's Witnesses have used the same maneuver a number of times when their deadlines for the second coming have passed. They just decided that Christ had indeed commenced his messianic reign, only invisibly, from the heavens.

How can the obvious disconfirmation of religious hopes matter so little to believers? Social psychologists Festinger, Riecken, and Schachter devoted their great book *When Prophecy Fails* to this question. It dealt with the plight of a UFO sect that predicted a space invasion on a certain date and had to face the embarrassment when it failed to materialize. They explained that their own zeal, though unheeded by the public, convinced the aliens to grant a reprieve — sure, that's the ticket! Festinger theorized that in all these cases, the recovery was a matter of cognitive dissonance reduction, the process whereby the mind makes any sacrifice necessary to reconcile clashing realities, either by forsaking the debunked belief or embracing even the most outrageous rationalization. When a group or individual has staked everything on a belief and it seems to be destroyed by the facts, any reinterpretation of the inconvenient facts will do. The will to believe, especially when reinforced by one's fellow believers, makes any explanation seem plausible, however foolish it may look to outsiders. In order to increase the plausibility of their threatened belief, the believers will engage in a new surge of proselytizing: the more people they can get to believe in it, the truer it will seem! Thus, a drastic disconfirmation of its claims may be just what a new religious movement needs to get off the ground!

Empty Argument

Much is made of the 'empty tomb' argument. This argument is itself emptied of all force once we recognize the Markan empty tomb story as simply another apotheosis legend. The tomb is just part of the requisite narrative furniture. We just don't know what may have been done with the body of Jesus. Acts 13:29, the Gospel of Peter, and Justin Martyr all attest an alternate version of the story in which the enemies of Jesus buried his body. For all we know, the disciples didn't know where the body had been buried.

But what if the Sanhedrin knew? Why didn't they make short work of the resurrection preaching by producing the body? "Here's your messiah!" One crucial detail always seems to escape apologists at this point. According to the New Testament itself, the apostles only began to preach the resurrection *seven weeks after the crucifixion*! What good would it have done to produce an unrecognizable rotten corpse? Lazarus, we are told, had already started to reek after a mere four days. Producing the body of Jesus would have been pointless. Maybe they *did* exhume it, for all the good it did!

Could Jesus have risen from the dead? "With God all things are *possible*." But not everything is *probable*, and in this case there is certainly no need to invoke the supernatural. Christianity would look exactly the same, and the New Testament would read the same, even without a miraculous resurrection from the dead.

Night Of The Living Savior

Resurrecting the Rationalists

Anyone who has heard or read the arguments of evangelical apologists knows how they argue for the resurrection within a particular exegetical framework. They all strive to show that no other explanation fits the data so well as the conclusion that Jesus rose from the dead. The Wrong Tomb Theory won't cut it. The Swoon Theory won't do it. Each naturalistic theory always fails to account adequately for some crucial item of gospel evidence. The Swoon Theory can't justify the mighty majesty with which the Risen Jesus revealed himself. The Theft of the Body Theory can't get past the Roman guards, and so on. The apologists, in case you hadn't noticed, argue as if everyone on all sides of the argument took for granted the inerrant accuracy of the gospel Easter stories. And, though sometimes their debate opponents get sucked into this trap, it seems a very odd and arbitrary assumption for apologists to make. Why do they make it? It is a tradition they have inherited from their forbears in the eighteenth and nineteenth centuries. And their forbears were arguing against a species of skeptic that scarcely exists any more, an endangered species called *Protestant Rationalists*. David Friedrich Strauss [1808–74] argued against them, too. And that is how he came to be ridiculing the Swoon Theory in the very terms I alluded to a moment ago. For the Swoon Theory was itself originally a piece of apologetics *on behalf of* the inerrant text as the Rationalists understood it!

You see, the Rationalists had Deist leanings that inclined them to reject belief in miracles understood as violations of the order of nature — the *God-given* order of nature. Schleiermacher, the nineteenth-century "father of Liberal theology," was typical in his reasoning that it glorified God more to posit that he had preordained everything perfectly to begin with than to praise him for making mid-course corrections to get his favorites out of a jam, say, at the Red Sea. Protestant Rationalists, however, still held onto the literal accuracy of the biblical text wherever they could. They did not yet have a lively sense of myth and legend, much less biblical fiction. For them it was either "hoax or history," as it still is for evangelical apologists. Rationalist Christians argued against people like Hermann Samuel Reimarus [1694–1768] who *did* think the disciples of Jesus were money-grabbing con men, capitalizing on the reputation of their dead master.

So the Protestant Rationalists saw it as their task to defend the Bible, albeit rejecting belief in supernatural intervention. This strange hybrid agenda led to all those gospel interpretations we now laugh at, for example, that Jesus was not walking on the water but only walking on stepping-stones. Or that Jesus was not really multiplying loaves and fish for the crowds, but that his hidden Essene buddies in the cave behind him were secretly passing him more loaves as fast as he needed them. Or that Jesus appeared alive on Easter because he had been taken down from the cross still alive. You see how that works? They weren't trying to debunk the resurrection narratives. No, they were trying to vindicate them as accurate! And they imagined they had done so by showing how Jesus could indeed have been crucified, entombed, and seen alive again without resorting to superstitious claims of miracles!

The more traditional Protestant apologists, on the other hand, who still believed in miracles, the ones Strauss called the Orthodox, hated Rationalism and argued against its defenders precisely as premiere evangelical apologist William Lane Craig and his allies argue today. They had opponents who obliged them by taking for granted a large share of common ground: the inerrant accuracy of the gospel narratives. The orthodox apologists had pretty good luck arguing on those terms. But it is most important simply to grasp that these were the terms of the debate: a common and dogmatically derived belief in scriptural inerrancy. From there on in, it was basically a matter of competing interpretations, essentially no different from debates about the text between Calvinists, who thought scripture taught predestination, and Arminians, who read it as teaching free will.

Contemporary apologists such as William Lane Craig and company do not seem to realize their imagined opponents, the old-time Rationalists, are dead and gone. The last one, by my reckoning, was Hugh J. Schonfield, author of *The Passover Plot* (1963). Genuine New Testament critics, of whom Strauss was one of the first, realize that the gospel Easter stories are mixtures of fertility myths, common Mediterranean legends, and midrashic fiction, that is, rewritten versions of Old Testament passages, especially from Daniel. One need not agonize over whether, for instance, Joseph of Arimathea would have been allowed to take custody of the corpse of a state criminal. No, it seems more realistic to ask whether he, as a fictive character, is more likely based on King Priam or on Joseph the Genesis patriarch. To argue as Craig and company do seems to genuine gospel scholars like arguing that Daphne must really have turned into a tree to escape the lust of Apollo because there are no alternative accounts of the origin of the laurel tree.

It seems foolish to discount the Theft Theory by appeal to the Roman guards when they appear only in the late gospel Matthew and have patently been added as a bit of apologetics after the fact. It is a waste of time arguing that the disciples could not have hallucinated the appearances of Jesus because they were initially skeptical — once you realize that initial skepticism is merely a common literary device present in most miracle stories to highlight the greatness of the miracle.

Naturally apologists stand to make a good showing if they can beguile skeptics into accepting the basic terms of their argument: that the gospels are accurate in all respects but the punch line. And from there it is no big step to arguing that the punch line must be accurate, too. We must not fall into that trap. We need to challenge the factual character of the story up to that point, as genuine gospel critics do.

Slow of Heart to Believe All that the Prophets Have Said

Once one removes the blinders of dogmatic literalism, the demand that the Bible record only history and that anything else would be a hoax, many new possibilities for understanding the text emerge as from a locked and guarded tomb. Friends of the Bible will welcome such an advent, while its hypocritical enemies will still try their best to keep the tomb secure, the prisoner suffocating inside.

What I want to suggest next is that fundamentalists are (perhaps willfully) missing certain, I think, blatant signals in the texts themselves that their authors did not even want us to take them literally. Let us begin with Mark and his striking ending (*i.e.*, Mark 16:8 — the following verses having been tacked on by later scribes): a mysterious young man, perhaps an angel, tells the frightened women that Jesus is not in the tomb but has been raised. They are to report the news to the disciples, who must then go to Galilee to meet him. But the women do not say anything to anyone.

On the face of it, such an ending appears to be an imposture trying to explain the late emergence of the empty tomb story, why no one had ever heard it before. But deeper than this lies the fundamental question of how Mark himself came to know of the story, assuming it really happened. If we say the women did at length break their silence, like the spiritualist Fox sisters eventually confessing their toe-tapping hoax, we are simply calling the text of Mark wrong and self-contradictory, since it does say, "They said nothing to anyone, for they were afraid." We have no right to read the text as if it said, "They did tell someone finally, which is how I know." From what we have to go on, the story as Mark told it, we have to assume he means the women never divulged their secret. And that means the whole thing is Mark's invention. The definitive silence of the women is his fiat as the omniscient author.

In the same way, we might ask how Mark knew what Jesus said in prayer in the Garden of Gethsemane when Mark himself tells us explicitly that Jesus had excluded any hearers. And then we realize: he 'knew' it because he made it up, like lines in a play. In short, literalists have long been missing an overt clue, which the author took no trouble to disguise, of the fictive character of the whole enterprise.

So play-like, in fact, are the texts of the passion story that the Jesus-Myth advocate John MacKinnon Robertson [1856–1933] devoted a whole chapter of his treatise *Pagan Christs: Studies in Comparative Hierology* (1911) to what he called "The Gospel mystery play." According to Robertson, the Passion narratives are descriptions or transcripts of a play. That's how we know what it was the ladies never divulged — and what Jesus prayed while all the stenographers were sleeping!

On to Matthew, and on to Galilee

Matthew supplies the Galilee appearance Mark anticipated but blocked, causing us to envision the Risen Christ glancing repeatedly at his watch as he waits for the arrival of disciples who do not even know they are expected. Matthew decided to help the disciples make the appointment. In Matthew 28 they do arrive, and they receive Jesus' marching orders to go evangelize the world, teaching everyone to keep Jesus' commandments. The attentive reader will have observed that the original Twelve Disciples have already been told not to venture so far as Gentile or even Samaritan territory (Matthew 10:5). But these twelve are not in view in Matthew 28's 'Great Commission' at all.

> And Jesus came and said to them, "All authority in heaven and on earth has been given to me. Go therefore and make disciples of all nations, baptizing them in the name of the Father and of the Son and of the Holy Spirit, teaching them to observe all that I have commanded you; and lo, I am with you always, to the close of the age."

No, that scene is a send-off to the Antiochene missionaries for whom Matthew has composed this gospel as a missionary catechism manual. Again, this is no wild-eyed theory, but a reading of Matthew now taken for granted by critical scholars.

It is to these late-first, early-second-century preachers that Matthew vouchsafes the assurance that the Risen Christ will go with them on all their travels: "And behold, I am with you always, even to the close of the age." And that is the end of the gospel. There is no ascension, but also, of course, no sequel in which the Risen Jesus actually embarks with them on the road preaching. So what did Matthew mean in this send-off? Plainly, he intends the reader to understand that the literary depiction of the Risen One on the page fades imperceptibly into the readers' sense of being accompanied by the intangible Spirit of Christ though the coming years of evangelistic labor. As one often hears the view of radical New Testament scholar Rudolf Bultmann [1884–1976] summed up: "Jesus rose into the *kerygma*" (*kerygma* is Greek for 'preaching' and refers to the evangelistic preaching of the early church). And there is just no reason to think Matthew meant the reader to think the scene happened one day, just like that. Minus an ascension, it would not even make any sense.

... and Luke and John

Luke offers another story he cannot have hoped his readers would take as a literal piece of history. I am thinking of the Emmaus narrative (Luke 24:13–35). Cut from the same cloth as countless Greek and Hebrew tales in which ordinary mortals entertain immortals unawares, this story is unmistakably a piece of Eucharistic liturgy. The central focus of the story is the moment when the Risen Jesus is recognized in the breaking of bread, whereupon he vanishes into thin air! Can anyone miss the symbolic significance of this episode? Is it not obvious that the point is that one may seek and find the Risen Lord in the Eucharistic breaking of the bread, albeit invisibly? I should think one would have to be as dull-witted as the disciples who misunderstood Jesus' warning about the leaven of the Pharisees as a complaint that they had omitted to bring sandwiches along in the boat!

This means Luke simply cannot have intended us to take the story as literal history. He wrote as a creator and redactor of the sacred texts of his community. He knew, as the Rabbis knew, that his god had commanded the text of scripture to "be fruitful and multiply," not to fossilize. And one would have to say that the evangelist Luke admirably fulfilled his task as a "steward of the mysteries of God" (1 Corinthians 4:1).

Finally, John, too, winks so blatantly to the reader of his resurrection narrative that we cannot imagine he thought we would take it as straight factual reporting. In John 20, Jesus has appeared alive to his disciples, minus Thomas, who was apparently out picking up the pizza at the time. Thomas feels he has been made the butt of a prank when he hears from the other ten that he has just missed Jesus dropping in from beyond the grave. But he, too, receives a visit from the Risen Lord only days later, to quiet his doubts. And as the now quiescent Thomas bows before his Lord, Jesus says, ostensibly to him, but manifestly *to the reader*, "Do you believe because you have seen? Blessed are they who have *not* seen, and yet believe!" If this is not to be taken as an aside to the audience, there is no such device. And if it is a literary aside, then we are not dealing with historical reporting. We are not even supposed to be dealing with historical narrative.

But, one might reply, is not the blessed assurance offered the reader negated if the reader is supposed to understand that the story is a fiction, that Thomas did not necessarily behold the Risen Christ after all? No, of course not. After all, what is the entire point? That it is better to believe without seeing for oneself. To that point it is utterly irrelevant what an ancient man may or may not have seen.

The Name of the Game
Is Riding the Grave-y Train

I have warned against getting snookered by the games of apologists who want to cast us as those Dead White Males known as the Protestant Rationalists. I have warned not to allow oneself to be maneuvered into and confined within their home stadium where gospel accuracy is taken for granted. And yet it may prove fun to join them in that game so long as one knows the rules. After all, it is very difficult in the space of a public debate to persuade a fundamentalist opponent and audience to abandon their pre-critical assumptions and to adopt the axioms of the Higher Criticism instead. It is a whole different world of discourse, and the transition is too great. So it may be tactically helpful to challenge the apologists on their own ground. And to this end, I would next like to call attention to four neglected features of the gospels, taken literally, that afford powerful ammunition to the skeptic, proving in the process that Shakespeare was right: the devil can indeed quote scripture to suit his purposes.

We find the first and the second items in the same story, that of the visit of Mary Magdalene to the tomb in John chapter 20. "She turned around and beholds Jesus standing there, and did not know that it was Jesus. Jesus says to her, 'Woman, why are you weeping? Whom are you seeking?' Supposing him to be the gardener, she says to him, 'Sir, if you have carried him away, tell me where you have laid him, and I will take him away'. "

The second is like unto it. Look at Luke 24, the Emmaus story again. "And it came about that, while they were conversing and discussing, Jesus himself approached and began traveling with them. But their eyes were prevented from recognizing him" (Luke 24:15–16). And if anyone cares for the spurious Markan Appendix (Mark 16:9–20), look at Mark 16:12, "And after that, he appeared in a different form to two of them, while they were walking along on their way to the country."

The first point, which has certainly been noticed before, is the startling item that the Risen Jesus was not first recognized as such. This is enough by itself, I think, to sink the ship. As Schonfield argued, such details, multiply attested as we have seen, surely invite the conjecture that the individuals involved were *not* seeing Jesus at all but someone else altogether and only subsequently, grasping at straws, decided it must have been Jesus. It is an astonishing element for the evangelists to have left intact. Oh, you may offer theological harmonizations, such as that they failed to recognize him because he was beaten and bloodied by his recent ordeal to the point of disfigurement — but wouldn't that have made him all the *more* recognizable to those who had witnessed his Passion?

More recently, one scholar has suggested, along somewhat similar lines, that Luke 24's Emmaus story is depicting two disciples meeting up, after Jesus' death, with one of the charismatic itinerants who spoke in the name of the Son of Man and expected to be heeded as Christ himself. "Whoever hears you hears me," Jesus had told his apostles, and did not Paul remind the Galatians that in happier days they had "received me as an angel of God, as Jesus Christ himself" (Galatians 4:14)? In that case, it would not have been a case, strictly speaking, of 'mistaken identity' as of theological 'spiritual identification.' But either way, it wasn't an undead Jesus.

As I say, I am far from the first to point this out, but I call attention to it because I think critics have made surprisingly little use of the motif, which just seems to me to rend the apologetic veil right down the middle.

The second point is also familiar but unsung, and that is the possibility, again raised by the gospel itself, that the tomb of Jesus was empty not by anyone's devious design but simply because the stashing of the body in Joseph's tomb, intended, after all, for his own eventual use, was only temporary. It is depicted as entirely natural for Mary Magdalene to suppose the body has been taken elsewhere in the meantime. Why not? It might well have been disposed of, honorably or dishonorably, by some custodian unknown to the disciples. And that would be that. Again, I do not even think there *were* such scenes set at any empty tomb. But if one wants to play the apologists' game, this may be the best way to play it. Even on their own terms, they have a lot of explaining – *too much explaining* – to do.

Our third gospel surprise occurs in Mark's story (6:14– 19; 8:28) that the crowds (plus Herod Antipas) thought the miracle-working Jesus was none other than John the Baptist raised from the dead (not merely resuscitated temporarily, but eschatologically raised so that "miraculous powers are at work in him"). We might pause to note that this bit is enough to bring crashing down that specious argument upon which Church of England bishop and fundamentalist apologist N. T. Wright (*The Resurrection of the Son of God,* 2003) so heavily relies, namely that the notion of someone rising from the dead already in mundane history, before the general resurrection at the end of days, was unheard of in Jesus' milieu, so that Jesus must really have risen since no one had any precedent for expecting (or fabricating) it. But there it is. So much for N. T. *Wrong.*

To unfold the implications a bit more, can we not imagine – if John the Baptist's fate so closely paralleled that of Jesus (both having been arrested and finally executed by a Roman or pro-Roman tyrant, despite the tyrant's initial reluctance) – that Jesus' disciples would have been led to expect him to rise as current rumor proclaimed John had arisen? If they had trod such a path of suffering in common, why not the sequel?

Again, the very notion that many followed Jesus confident in their faith that they were witnessing resurrection appearances of the slain Baptizer seems to me a staggering notion! And so does the gospel admission that it was all a case of mistaken identity! The believers were wrong: it was the still-living Jesus, not a resurrected John, that they were seeing. Well, then, why were not those who swore to having seen a Risen Christ similarly mistaken? Maybe they were seeing Simon Magus, the

Samaritan mystagogue whom Acts 9:10 says was known as the 'Great Power.' Early Christian apologists cast him as Peter's life-long rival and as the father of all heresy. Simon is said actually to have claimed he had previously appeared among the Jews as the Son. Or maybe what they saw was any of the vast number of self-deifying prophets the second-century critic of Christianity Celsus tells us were swarming over Palestine and Syria:

> I am God or God's Son or a divine Spirit. I have come, for the destruction of the world is imminent. And because of your misdeeds, O mankind, you are about to perish. But I will save you. Soon you will see me ascend with heavenly power. Blessed is he who now worships me! Upon all others I will cast eternal fire, on all cities and countries. And those who do not recognize that they are being punished will repent and groan in vain. But those who believe in me I will protect forever. (Origen, *Contra Celsum* VII, 9)

Fourth and finally, there is the astonishing business in Matthew's Passion narrative about a mass resurrection of the local saints coinciding with the crucifixion of Jesus: "and the tombs were opened; and many bodies of the saints who had fallen asleep were raised; and coming out of the tombs after his resurrection they entered the holy city and appeared to many" (Mathew 27:52–53). This strange *Night of the Living Dead* scenario has baffled scholars and embarrassed even apologists, some of whom have wanted to strike out the passage as a later interpolation, just to get it off the table. For it certainly extends the line of defense: how many empty tombs do you want to have to argue for? I judge it a clumsy piece of narrative theology, trying to illustrate Jesus' resurrection as "the first fruits of them that sleep" (1 Corinthians 15:20), except that the Jerusalem saints are actually said to have been raised *before* Jesus, so maybe this does not work either!

But suppose we take the text to reflect historical fact, at least to the point of admitting that people did report sightings of returned deceased loved ones, righteous old Uncle Ezekiel or pious old Aunt Naomi. The implication is dangerous for the apologist, for surely it would mean that the reports of Jesus' *post-mortem* reappearances were merely part of an epidemic wave of visions of the local well known dead that weekend in Jerusalem and its environs. This, I should think, would considerably lessen the evidential value of the resurrection sightings, making them very likely just one aspect of a local religious mass hysteria.

So — are the gospel Easter stories even intended to be read as literal history? I doubt it very much, since the evangelists have seemingly left clues scattered around like colorful Easter eggs to tell us otherwise. But even if we take them as factual narratives, the stories seem to contain potent seeds of their own destruction — elements, some long-neglected, subverting the stories' own reports of Jesus rising from the dead.

Was Jesus John the Baptist Raised From the Dead?

There are several New Testament passages which over the years have struck me as being pregnant with implications far beyond those scholars usually, reckon with. These texts seem to me to be held in check by the conventional ways in which we read the documents in which they occur. They are "anomalous data" (Thomas S. Kuhn, *The Structure of Scientific Revolutions*) which somehow seem 'left over' in the context of the paradigms which seem to make such excellent sense of the rest of the text, but which leave these odd verses cold. I sometimes wonder where the chips would fall if we were to start with one of these strange verses, rather than finding some contrived way of tying it up as a loose end after we find a place to put everything else. What follows is an attempt to give one pair of such passages, Mark 6:14–15 and 8:27–28, their full weight, their full voice. Bear with me, then, in an admittedly far-fetched thought-experiment, which is all I claim for what follows.

Some Say...

Mark 6:14–15 recounts a range of popular options for understanding Jesus: Herod Antipas, who has seen to the execution of John the Baptist, hears of Jesus' miracles as well as rumors that the miracle-worker is really Elijah, as some say, or perhaps some other returned biblical prophet, or maybe even a resurrected John the Baptist. The scene prepares the reader for 8:27–28, the confession of Peter at Caesarea Philippi, where the same menu of options is repeated. Jesus asks the disciples what opinions the crowds have concerning him, a request that shows at least that he had not been teaching his own Messiahship, or that he was God's Son. If he had, why would his identity still be such an open question as he assumes it still is? Again, some say Elijah, others another prophet, and still others the risen John the Baptist. What about the disciples themselves? Who do they understand Jesus to be? Peter answers, "You are the Christ." This scene is a major turning point in the gospel. It introduces the progress toward the Passion. But before we take it as a signpost and hasten to follow in the direction it indicates, we ought to pause to recognize the implicit Christological polemic contained in Jesus' question and the answers it elicits.

No reader fails to grasp Mark's Christological point that whatever manner of messiah Jesus may be, he is not one whose ordained path circumvents the cross. Yes, of course, but there is more to it than this. The messianic path of Jesus is not contrasted merely with the cross-shunning sentiments of Peter's hero-worship. No, Mark has also opposed to Peter's 'correct' Christological estimate ("You are the Christ" — accurate as far as it goes, though Matthew and Luke will expand it) a menu of options he means the reader to dismiss.

Who do the crowds *imagine* Jesus to be? These opinions, reported second-hand by the disciples, are probably Christological opinions current in Mark's own day. There are individuals, parties, sects, communities of faith among Mark's contemporaries who view Jesus as the eschatological Elijah, anticipating someone else as messiah, or else in lieu of a messiah. Others see him as "the Prophet Jesus," while others make him the resurrected Baptist. The Gospel of Thomas, saying 13, retells the same story to serve its own purposes; Thomas substitutes competing Christologies current in his own milieu, namely the angel Christology familiar from various Jewish-Christian sources and the sage 'Christ'-ology of the earliest stratum of the Q document, which seems to have viewed Jesus as a Cynic-type wise man like Diogenes, not as a martyred Son of God.

My point is that there seem to have been actual groups of people who held these opinions about Jesus in the time the gospels were being written, and the gospels argue against them. One such belief was that Jesus was the resurrected John the Baptist. It is remarkable enough to know that some believed John had been resurrected; but what are the implications of an early belief that John rose from the dead — and then became known as Jesus?

It ought to be mentioned that some see in this passage a reference to reincarnation: If some thought Jesus to be Elijah, wouldn't that mean Elijah had been reincarnated, reborn as the infant Jesus and grown to manhood again? We have no need for that hypothesis. As many Jewish folklore anecdotes demonstrate, Jews believed that Elijah was frequently sent back from heaven to do a miraculous favor for this or that pious Jew. Remember, Elijah, according to 2 Kings 2, had not died but been taken up alive into heaven. Thus he could not have been reincarnated, because that belief entails the death of one body and the housing of the same soul in a new one. But Elijah was living bodily in the sky with God, and every once in a while he would return, just like his Muslim/Arab counterpart al-Qadr, the Evergreen One. Those who suggest some believed Jesus to be Elijah's reincarnation go on to say that, to make Jesus John risen from the dead would also imply Jesus was John's reincarnation, which would in turn imply John was an earlier figure than Jesus, not his contemporary. But none of these readjustments is necessary, especially since "risen from the dead" is phraseology characteristic of Jewish apocalyptic doctrine, not later kabbalistic transmigration teaching.

Jesus Before Easter?

Some scholars have suggested that the apparent cleavage between the pre-Easter Jesus and the Risen Christ is an optical illusion in the sense that even before the Passion and Resurrection Jesus is already depicted thoroughly transformed by and into the Christological image of the church's faith. The sayings attributed to Jesus seem for the most part to have arisen within the early Christian communities to address the needs of those communities.

It is not as if we have the historical Jesus up till the Passion, followed by the Christ of faith as of Easter morning. No, it is the voice of Christian wisdom and prophecy which speaks the sayings of the gospels. The situation of the canonical gospels is essentially no different from that of the Gnostic resurrection dialogues in this respect: all the teaching ascribed to Jesus is attributable to the early Christians, as Norman Perrin (*e.g.*, *What Is Redaction Criticism?*, Fortress, 1969, 74–79) and James M. Robinson ("On the *Gattung* of Mark (and John)," in

David G. Buttrick, ed., *Jesus and Man's Hope*, Vol. I, Pittsburgh Theological Seminary, 1970, 51–98) make clear.

My colleague Darrell J. Doughty even goes so far as to suggest that the whole of the Gospel of Mark's "pre-Easter" period is in fact identical with the post-Easter period, the result of a circular structure whereby the meeting of the disciples with Jesus on the shore of Galilee in Mark 1:16–17 is the fulfillment of the words of the angel in Mark 16:7 that they should meet him there.

If we are to take all this seriously, an obvious question presents itself: what of the original, historical, pre-Easter Jesus? He is not simply to be identified with the character of Jesus of Nazareth in the gospels. Has he been altogether lost from the gospel narrative then? Perhaps not. Let us for a brief moment think the unthinkable.

Suppose the figure of the pre-Easter Jesus is to be found under the alias of 'John the Baptist.' When we impose this outlandish paradigm onto the gospels, we get some interesting results. A number of things make new sense.

Thy Kingdom Come

First, let us consider the sequential progression from John's ministry of repentance and asceticism, from which Jesus' style notoriously differed. Historical Jesus scholars commonly say that Jesus discerned that some great corner had been turned. Something signaled that the anticipated kingdom had now arrived, and that fasting was no longer appropriate. And thus he broke with John's ministry of penitential preparation for the kingdom and began a ministry celebrating the kingdom's advent. Instead of fasting with the Pharisees (like John's disciples, Mark 2:18) he began feasting with the publicans. What could that momentous event have been? What could have signaled the shift of the eons? Nothing we see in the gospels, at least not on any straightforward or any traditional reading. Scholars just approach the texts taking for granted the Christological solution that, since Jesus was divine he knew the divine plan, so he happened to know the crucial page had been turned.

But suppose the transition was something quite specific, namely his own death and (supposed) resurrection. This would have signaled the disciples, not Jesus himself, that the corner had been turned. Had we listened to the great form-critical New Testament scholar Rudolf Bultmann, we would have remembered that the pericope must in any case refer to the practice of Christians, not that of Jesus himself, since the critics ask concerning *their* behavior, not his.

> Good Christian men, rejoice,
> With heart and soul and voice.
> He calls you one and calls you all
> To share his everlasting hall.
> He hath opened heaven's door,
> And man shall live forever more.

Thus the difference between John's mournful, fasting disciples and Jesus' feasting disciples is that between the same group before and after the Passion Week. 'John's' disciples are already fasting because the bridegroom has been taken away from them (Mark 2:19–20), but once he is restored unto them at the resurrection, they rejoice again. No more fasting.

In a Looking Glass Darkly

Mark 1:14 ("And after John had been delivered up, Jesus came into Galilee, preaching the gospel of God") has Jesus neatly replace John on the public stage, occasioning the popular opinion that Jesus' public advent signaled the miraculous return of John. Note the use of the Greek *paradidomi*, the same pregnant word used for the sacrificial delivering up of Jesus to death, whether by God (Romans 8:32) or by Judas Iscariot (Mark 3:19). Can the same 'delivering up,' *i.e.*, of the same man, be in view? To say that John was delivered up and that Jesus appeared in Galilee immediately afterward would be like saying that the historical Jesus was delivered up for our sins and that shortly thereafter the Christ of faith appeared on the scene.

Similarly, the Johannine statements (John 3:26, 4:1) about the baptism of Jesus eclipsing that of John would refer, on the present hypothesis, to the new situation after Easter, when the sect of the historical Jesus is being transformed, not without some resistance on the part of 'doubting Thomases,' into the cult of the Risen Christ. "Lord, teach us to pray as John taught his disciples" (Luke 11:1) means that a new prayer is needed for the time of fulfillment, which has dawned. Perhaps the old prayer contained the petition "Thy kingdom come," whereas the new replaced it with "Send thy Spirit upon us and sanctify us" (as some manuscripts of Luke's version of the prayer at 11:2 still read) *because the kingdom was believed now to have arrived*.

Scholars have remarked how, despite the strong difference between the religious styles of the two men, Jesus continues to identify himself with John, as when he counters the chief priests' question as to his authority by asking their estimate of John's authorization (Mark 11:28–30). What if the answer to the one is the answer also to the other — because Jesus and John are the same? The authority of the Christian preaching of the Risen One is as authoritative as one was willing to admit the ministry of the Baptist (*i.e.*, his own earthly ministry) was. Of course the present narrative setting of the question and counter-question is anachronistic, as is most of the gospel material. We may suggest that the original context of the passage was in debate between post-Easter disciples of John ('Jesus'), believers in the Risen Baptist, on the one hand, and disciples of John who remained suspicious about this strange new proclamation on the other. What credentials did the new preaching have in its favor? The response? What credentials did the original ministry of the Baptist have? It was faith in either case, wasn't it?

So too the taunts "John came neither eating nor drinking, and you say, 'He is a demoniac.' The Son of Man came eating and drinking, and you say, 'Look, a glutton and a drunk' " (Matthew 11:16–19). Traditionally this is supposed to mean that people found a reason not to repent at the preaching of either man. John was too holier-than-thou for some, while Jesus seemed not to adhere to the parsimonious stereotype in the eyes of others. Finding an excuse to discount the messengers, that generation evaded coming to grips with their common message. But is that really the most natural reading of the text? The "damned if you do, damned if you don't" logic would fit best if the two styles characterized *the same figure in successive phases.* "Okay, first I tried this and you wouldn't have it; so then I tried doing what you said, but you didn't like that either!"

Twin Resurrections

Note, too, the strange similarity between Mark's report that some believed Jesus was John raised from the dead, accounting for the miraculous powers at work in him, and the resurrection formula of Romans 1:3–4, which has Jesus designated Son of God by miraculous power by virtue of the resurrection of the dead! Note the parallel:

Romans 1:4 Jesus	Mark 6:14 John the Baptist
Declared Son of God	
• by power	Powers are at work in him.
• by his resurrection from the dead	He has been raised from the dead

Perhaps this strange similarity denotes an even stranger identity, a dim recollection of the fact that Jesus was the same as John, that he had taken on the name/epithet *Jesus* – 'savior' – only after the resurrection. Compare two archaic hymn-fragments, the Johannine prologue (John 1:1–7ff) and the Kenosis (divine self-emptying) hymn (Philippians 2:6–11). It is striking that the first text names no figure other than John the Baptist, and that in portentous theological terms: "There came into being a man sent from God, named John." As all recognize, the subsequent denigration of John as merely a witness to the light but most certainly not the light itself, is a theological correction akin to that found in Matthew 11:11b ("Of all those born of women no one has arisen greater than John the Baptist... yet, I tell you that the least in the kingdom of heaven is greater than he"). Bultmann saw that the Johannine prologue hymn must originally have been all about the Baptist, not Jesus.

Now look at Philippians 2:6–11:

...who, though he was in the form of God,
did not count equality with God a thing to be grasped,
but emptied himself,
taking the form of a servant,
being born in the likeness of men.
And being found in human form he humbled himself
and became obedient unto death,
even death on a cross.
Therefore God has highly exalted him
and bestowed on him the name which is above every name,
that at the name of Jesus every knee should bow,
in heaven and on earth and under the earth,
and every tongue confess that Jesus Christ is Lord,
to the glory of God the Father.

You will note that the redeemer figure is named *only at the end,* where we learn that he received the honorific name 'Jesus' only upon his *post-mortem* exaltation — something which radical Christ-Myth theorist Paul-Louis Couchoud pointed out long ago ("The Historicity of Jesus: A Reply to Alfred Loisy," *Hibbert Journal*, XXXVI, 2, 205–206). (Loisy was quite the radical New Testament scholar himself, but he stopped short of denying the existence of a historical Jesus.) Note that according to the synthetic parallelism, "at the name of Jesus every knee should bow" matches "and every tongue confess that Jesus Christ is Lord" — implying that "bowing the knee to" equals "confessing the lordship of." The object of both is "Jesus."

This may seem to belabor the obvious except that it requires that the great name Yahweh gave him at the exaltation was not *Kyrios* ('Lord') as harmonizing exegesis tells us, but rather *Jesus*. The hymn means to say not that a man already named Jesus was then given the title 'Lord,' but that a hitherto-unnamed hero was then given the honorific name *Jesus*.

Couchoud remarks, "The God-man does not receive the name Jesus till after his crucifixion. That alone, in my judgment, is fatal to the historicity of Jesus." Unless, of course, he had borne some other name previously, as Peter had formerly been called Simon. What had *Jesus'* name been previously? "His name is John" (Luke 1:63). The identification of the pre-exaltation hero as John the Baptist would satisfy the problem Couchoud left open — had the hero been nameless before his exaltation?

Couchoud was implying that the earlier version of the bestowal of the name *Jesus* had the naming take place as part of the *post-mortem* exaltation of this figure. Only subsequently was the bestowal of the name associated with the earthly life of Jesus, namely at his conception (Matthew 1:21; Luke 1:31). We can easily fit Couchoud's hypothesis into the speculations of mainstream scholarship. The great Roman Catholic New Testament critic (who, it is safe to say, would have, in an earlier day, been excommunicated if not burnt at the stake!) Raymond E. Brown points out how "The same combined ideas that early Christian preaching had once applied to the resurrection (*i.e.*, a divine proclamation, the begetting of God's Son, the agency of the Holy Spirit), and which Mark had applied to the baptism, are now applied to the conception of Jesus in the words of an angel's message to Joseph and to Mary (respectively, in Matthew and in Luke). And once the conception of Jesus has become the Christological moment, the revelation of who Jesus is begins to be proclaimed to an audience who come and worship (the magi, the shepherds), while others react with hostility (Herod in Matthew; those who contradict the sign in Luke 2:34). And thus three infancy stories have become truly an infancy gospel" (*The Birth of the Messiah*, 31).

Brown might have included the observation by Ernst Käsemann (one of Bultmann's star pupils) that the confessions of Jesus' identity by the demons are retrojections of the acclamations of those under the earth mentioned in Philippians 2:10–11. The retrojection of the same motif into the infancy story is, as Brown implies, the demonic persecution of the baby king by Herod the Great, who thus acknowledges the true Messiahship of his rival. The granting of the glorious savior-name *Jesus* is part of this package. It, too, would have found a place at the end of the savior's earthly life and been retrojected, along with the rest of the package, into the infancy. Once this happened, the identity of John and 'Jesus' would have been severed and forever obscured.

Luke contains completely parallel accounts of the miraculous nativity of both figures, so close that even ancient scribes seem to have confused whether Zechariah was talking about the infant John or the infant Jesus (what is the reference to "the horn of salvation in the house of David" doing in a hymn about the Levitical John the Baptist?), and equally whether it was Elizabeth or Mary who sings the *Magnificat* (some ancient manuscripts of Luke 1:46 have "And Elizabeth said," while others read, "And she said.").

Splitting the Difference

More telling still is the parallel between the martyrdoms of Jesus and John, for both are put to death by a strangely reluctant profane tyrant — Jesus by Pontius Pilate, and John by Herod Antipas. But wait a moment! As Loisy pointed out, Luke, like the *Gospel of Peter*, seems to have known a version of the Jesus martyrdom in which it was Herod Antipas who condemned Jesus to death! (He has harmonized it with Mark only with difficulty, having Antipas first desirous of killing Jesus, then acquitting him, but nonetheless remanding him to Pilate!) Perhaps this is because they were the same!

How on earth could the single figure have been bifurcated? Simple: there remained a dour, penitential sect devoted to the martyred John that continued to anticipate the coming of the kingdom with (ascetic) observance (Luke 17:20), while another group of John's disciples came to believe he had been raised from the dead, as the firstfruits, ushering in the kingdom, albeit invisibly. These bestowed on John the title *Yeshua'* – Aramaic for 'savior' – for he had saved his people from their sins. In time this became a name, just as 'Iscariot' and 'Peter' did, finally supplanting the original name — except among those who had never embraced the title and Christology of 'Jesus.' Thus in time people began to imagine that John and Jesus had been two different contemporary figures, though the rivalry between them was vaguely recalled. On the basis of it, *e.g.*, Mandaeans rejected Jesus as a false messiah, though they did not deem John, their prophet, the true messiah! (This honor they reserved for Enosh-Uthra, a heavenly angel.) On the other hand, the first Christians were those who wondered in their hearts whether John himself were perhaps the Christ (Luke 3:15) and decided he was. He was the *Jesus*, the *Christ*.

A notorious problem text in Acts is the introduction of Apollos, who is confusingly said to have preached accurately the things concerning Jesus, yet knowing only the baptism of John. Priscilla and Aquila then set him straight in some unspecified way (Acts 18:24–28). All sorts of reconstructions have been advanced, many of them making Apollos a kind of half-Christian. How could he have correctly understood Jesus and yet known only John's baptism, when the main point about Jesus, at least with respect to John, was that he superseded John and made his baptism superfluous? But what if Luke's source preserves the fossil recollection that to know accurately the things about Jesus was precisely to know the baptism of John, since 'Jesus' was none other than the resurrected John? (I owe this suggestion to my colleague Arthur Dewey of the Jesus Seminar.)

Narrative Mitosis

Is the whole thing utterly implausible? If an historical analogy would help, recall the theory of the great nineteenth-century Tübingen University scholar F. C. Baur that Simon Magus, the mystagogue and magician who had bedazzled Samaria before Peter got there, was a bifurcated 'evil twin' of the Apostle Paul. Simon Magus was at first a caricature of Paul understood as a usurping opponent of Simon Peter, a false pretender to apostleship who sought to purchase the recognition by the Pillars by means of the collection made among the Gentile churches (compare Acts 8:18–24 with Galatians 2:7–10).

> But on the contrary, when they saw that I had been entrusted with the gospel to the uncircumcised, just as Peter had been entrusted with the gospel to the circumcised (for he who worked through Peter for the mission to the circumcised worked through me also for the Gentiles), and when they perceived the grace that was given to me, James and Cephas and John, who were reputed to be pillars, gave to me and Barnabas the right hand of fellowship, that we should go to the Gentiles and they to the circumcised; only they would have us remember the poor, which very thing I was eager to do. (Galatians 2:7–10)

> Now when Simon saw that the Spirit was given through the laying on of the apostles' hands, he offered them money, saying, "Give me also this power, that any one on whom I lay my hands may receive the Holy Spirit." But Peter said to him, "Your silver perish with you, because you thought you could obtain the gift of God with money! You have neither part nor lot in this matter, for your heart is not right before God. Repent therefore of this wickedness of yours, and pray to the Lord that, if possible, the intent of your heart may be forgiven you. For I see that you are in the gall of bitterness and in the bond of iniquity." And Simon answered, "Pray for me to the Lord, that nothing of what you have said may come upon me." (Acts 8:18–24)

As time went by, Simon Magus was imagined to be a separate figure from Paul. Later anti-Paulinists no longer got the joke, so to speak, while the whole idea would have been lost on Paulinists from the start. Especially once Petrine and Pauline factions become Catholicized and harmonized with one another, the connection between Paul and Simon Magus was utterly severed, and the two separate characters were established. Suppose something similar happened in the case of Jesus and John the Baptist, only in this case neither one was a caricature. The Baptist was simply the remembered 'historical Jesus,' while 'Jesus the Christ' was John the Baptist believed resurrected and made both *Jesus* (*i.e.*, 'Savior') and *Messiah*.

To translate the scenario envisioned here into more traditional terms, it is as if some admirers of the pre-Easter Jesus had later heard of a resurrected 'Christ' and not known to connect this figure with their Jesus. They might have thought that this new *Christos* they heard so much about was someone entirely distinct from their late, lamented master Jesus. In fact, a development something like this did take place in the case of 'Separationist' Gnostics who decided that the human Jesus had so tenuous a connection to the Christ that they might curse the former and bless the latter. 1 Corinthians 12:3 mentions such Jesuphobes: "Therefore I want you to understand that no one speaking by the Spirit of God ever says 'Jesus be cursed!' and no one can say 'Jesus is Lord' except by the Holy Spirit."

In his *Catena Fragmenta* (a collection of his quotes from lost works), the third-century Alexandrian theologian Origen explained the reference: "There is a certain sect which does not admit a convert unless he pronounces anathemas on Jesus," namely the Ophites. (Today's equivalent might be, say, a faction of New Agers who were so zealous to stress that Judy Zebra Knight was merely the passive channeler for the Atlantean warlord Ramtha that they went off the deep end and cursed Judy so as more highly to exalt the far more important Ramtha. I know of no such group, but I sure wouldn't object to such a practice, and I don't even believe in Ramtha!)

Needless to say, it would only have been once the single original character had been doubled, and the Risen Savior historicized, that Jesus could be read back into the pre-Easter history alongside John the Baptist, and once this happens we have the bizarre spectacle of Jesus appearing at John's baptism, only in another sense it is no longer so problematical: naturally he is there! Where else would he be?

Matthew's version (3:14) puts the problem in its most acute form but also provides a hint of the solution. "I need to be baptized by you! And do you come to me?" Most scholars think that the Fourth Gospel's depiction of Jesus having a baptismal ministry alongside John's is a piece of symbolic anachronism in which early Christian baptism is retrojected into the time of Jesus and John, as if to show the superiority of the Christian sect to John's. So far so good. What I am suggesting is that not only is the picture of Jesus baptizing alongside John an anachronistic retrojection; the whole idea of Jesus and John as distinct contemporaries is merely another facet of the same retrojection!

The Fourth Gospel has Simon, Andrew, and the Beloved Disciple already disciples of John the Baptist before they become followers of Jesus. Do they abandon the first master to follow a new one? Not if the point is that they are following the same master before and after Easter. Even on the conventional reading we can well imagine Peter being called a disciple of Jesus before Easter and an apostle of Christ afterward, and we can just as easily imagine someone hearing both and imagining Peter had transferred allegiances somewhere along the line.

Shall We Look for Another?

Finally, consider a passage from the Q Document, believed by most scholars to be the source of the material Matthew and Luke share with one another, but did not derive from Mark. The imprisoned John sends his messengers to ask Jesus whether he may not be the "Coming One" John's preaching had anticipated (Matthew 11:2–6/Luke 7:18–20, 22–23). John's question (actually Jesus hears it from the disciples themselves) "Or should we wait for another?" implies that the attribution of the question to John is secondary, just as in all the gospel pericopes wherein Jesus is asked why his disciples flout this or that pious custom (Mark 2:18, 24). As the form critic Rudolf Bultmann asked, why not *ask Jesus* why he fails to eat with hands washed (Mark 7:5), why he himself gleans on the Sabbath (Mark 2:24), if it is really Jesus himself who is in view? But it is not. He serves as a figurehead for his community, whose prerogatives are actually at stake. In just the same way it is not John's uncertainty of Jesus as the Coming One that this Q pericope presupposes, but rather that of his disciples, bereft following his martyrdom. Can they accept the Risen One preached by Christians as the return of their master?

Albert Schweitzer [1875–1965] (*The Mystery of the Kingdom of God*) understood the same passage along somewhat similar lines in that he had Jesus and John applying the same eschatological role each to the other. The Baptist sends his messengers to ask whether Jesus may be the Coming One. Jesus sends the same messengers to John and tells the crowd that John is himself the Coming One, Elijah (Matthew 11:10/Luke 7:27). The scene can be read as a *doublette*: Jesus = John, so the two sendings of the Baptist disciples are the same. And these "sent ones" are apostles bearing the tidings of the Coming One who has arrived: call him Jesus or call him John, it is all the same.

Finally, if the case set forth here is judged plausible, it would provide the answer to a thorny question aimed at the Christ Myth Theory — nowadays dismissed out of hand by apologists and even some skeptics but still beloved by many freethinkers. It is easy to show that, at least in its most famous form, the testimony of Josephus to Jesus is a Christian interpolation. I have argued (*The Incredible Shrinking Son of Man*, pp. 103–104) that Josephus' passage on John the Baptist is likely also an interpolation, partly because of the seemingly Christian anxiety in the passage to reinterpret John's baptism as a token of repentance and not as absolving sin in its own right, sacramentally. It seems unlikely Josephus would care about that, much less think his readers would. But the case is by no means as strong as it is for the *Testimonium Flavianum*, the Jesus passage.

Let us grant for the sake of argument that the John passage in Josephus is authentic, and it thus secures John's existence as an historical character. Then we would have to ask, with the apologists, is it really likely that Jesus was not a historical figure but John the Baptist was? That is exactly the implication if John the Baptist was the original 'Jesus,' and if the gospel Jesus is a figment of faith in the resurrected John. Only now it makes sense. That John should be a historical figure and Jesus a myth makes plenty of sense once you understand the relationship between the two figures as I have sketched it here.

Much Learning Hath Driven Thee Mad

What are we to conclude from this brief essay? That the historical Jesus was John the Baptist? We might consider it a possibility, though I doubt many readers will be able even to go so far as that. What most will conclude is that the author of this book is perhaps a bit too clever for his own good, that all he has shown, whatever he may have intended, is that New Testament scholarship has become a game where, using various exegetical moves, certain arguments or types of arguments, reasoning in unanticipated directions from accepted axioms, one may make a more or less plausible-sounding case for almost any notion. If the present chapter be deemed a bit of sophistry, then at least allow it to have demonstrated that virtually all exegetical scholarship is engaged in the same type of endeavor. It is all a matter of what test-paradigms, theoretical tools, and methodologies one will bring to bear on the texts. It is almost like dropping sticks on the open page of the I Ching and seeing what oracle you can construe from the pithy but enigmatic signifiers ranged there. As Stanley Fish says (*Is There a Text in This Class?*), meaning is not so much what we receive from the text as it is what we read into it. Or, better, also *à la* Fish, meaning is determined by the ways we read the text.

Or to borrow from Seymour Chatman (*Story and Discourse*), it is a matter both of the form of the content and of the content of the form. As to the former, what we seem to find in the texts will have been shaped by the type of tools, the grinding of the lenses we used to find that meaning. The form of the cookie that emerges from the exegetical oven will be determined by the shape of the cookie-cutter we use. As to the latter, the methodologies we choose to employ are themselves functions of certain assumptions as to how texts work, how they mean, and what sort of things they may tell us. In short, the New Testament texts are like a constantly shifting kaleidoscope, and the application of our methods is the twisting of the tube. The results may be quite spectacular, fascinating, intriguing, or entertaining. But the next twist will yield something else, and we may not judge it more 'true' or 'accurate' than the one before. None can carry any particular conviction. The history of the succession of regnant paradigms/theoretical frameworks in New Testament scholarship ought to have made that clear long before now.

The Templars and the Tomb of Jesus

The Teabing Hypothesis

The Priory of Sion hoax was made popular twenty years ago through a long and tedious pseudo-documentary tome called *Holy Blood, Holy Grail* by Michael Baigent, Richard Leigh, and Henry Lincoln. It has been given new and much wider currency in these last days in the best-selling pages of Dan Brown's novel *The Da Vinci Code*. (Brown's scholarly character Lee Teabing is a scrambled version of the names of Baigent and Leigh.) But between these two books many others have appeared, each arguing a related and equally speculative case, all of them involving in some manner Jesus and the Knights Templar. All argue that the Templar Knights undertook a top-secret mission to retrieve the legendary treasure of Solomon's Temple and succeeded beyond their wildest dreams. Baigent, Leigh, and Lincoln say that, besides a hoard of gold, the Templars found a cache of documents telling the real story of the Holy Grail, *i.e.*, the royal bloodline of Jesus. Possession of these moneys and of the highly volatile secret of Jesus and his queen Mary Magdalene enabled the Templars and Priory of Sion to bribe and blackmail their way to unchallenged prominence for centuries, all the while protecting the descendants of Jesus and Mary among the Merovingian dynasty. In turn, the Merovingian heirs, notably Crusader Godfrey de Bouillon, mindful of the messianic destiny implied in their very DNA, sought to regain their lost glory, finally establishing the short-lived Crusader Kingdom of Jerusalem.

Despite their indefatigable research, motivated no doubt by true scholarly zeal, these authors seem unacquainted with inductive historical method. They proceed instead, as they themselves recount the evolution of their hypothesis, more in a novelistic fashion, just like their recent disciple Dan Brown. That is, Baigent, Leigh, and Lincoln constantly connect the dots of data provided by medieval chronicles, *etc.*, linking them with one speculation after another: "What if A were really B?" "What if B were really C?" "It is not impossible that..." "If so-and-so were the case, this would certainly explain that and that." These are the flashes of imaginative inspiration that allow fiction writers like Dan Brown to trace out intriguing plots. It is essentially a creative enterprise, not one of historical reconstruction. It seems the authors of *Holy Blood, Holy Grail* concocted more than anything else a novel much like that of Brown, and, like him, they managed to convince themselves that it was really true. Admittedly, had the Templars discovered proof that Jesus and the Magdalene were husband and wife, messianic king and queen, and threatened to reveal it, this might account for their considerable clout. But what are the chances that this *is* the explanation? It is a shot in the dark, seeking to explain one unknown by a bigger one. We are familiar with this logic from tabloid theories that space aliens built the pyramids. Or that we may explain the Big Bang by positing that God lit the fuse.

The Knights Who Say...

Who were the Templar Knights? They were a monastic order, the Poor Knights of the Temple of Solomon, founded between 1110 and 1120. Their sworn duty was to protect Christian pilgrims on their way to and from Jerusalem. Over the years, as ascetic and admired religious groups tend to do, they acquired considerable fortunes and clout, eventually founding the practice of modern banking, as they used their vast funds to bail out the crowned heads of Europe. Finally, in 1308, Philip the Fair, King of France, subjected the Templars to a ruthless inquisition, stripping them of their moneys, the real object of his covetous lust.

What was the pretext of the persecution? The Templars were declared the vilest of heretics. Were they? It is difficult to tell, precisely as in the case of the so-called witches persecuted in Europe. We can never know the degree to which tortured wretches eagerly signed any crazy-sounding confession shoved in front of them. As the witches confessed under duress to having sex with the devil himself, describing the great size and unnatural coldness of his Satanic majesty's phallus, so did the beleaguered Templar Knights confess to blasphemies including the worship of a goat-headed demon statue called Baphomet and kissing its anus, as well as ritual homosexuality, trampling the cross, and eliciting oracles from a still-living severed head!

Actually, 'Baphomet' is – *contra* Baigent and company – almost surely an Old French spelling of 'Mahomet' or 'Muhammad.' This in turn means the accusations against the Templars reflect not actual Gnosticism or even diabolism, but garbled French beliefs about Islam. In just the same way, the medieval *Song of Roland* (verses 2580-2591) imagines Muslims as worshipping idols and devils including Mohammed, Termagant, and Apollo.

The Templars became lionized in folklore and in esotericist belief as adepts who guarded heretical secret doctrines which they had discovered, perhaps in the form of rediscovered manuscripts, while resident in Jerusalem. Baigent, Leigh, Lincoln, and Brown, echoing groundless speculations of various nineteenth-century eccentrics (including Joseph Hammer, *The Mystery of Baphomet Revealed*), link the Templars with the French Cathars (or Albigensians) wiped out in the Albigensian Crusade – another Catholic-backed persecution — in 1209. These Cathars were Gnostics who had rediscovered or reinvented something like ancient Manichean Gnosticism. Legend claimed that during the Catholic siege of the Cathar mountain fortress of Montsalvat, a few Cathars escaped with the group's great treasure, perhaps the Grail itself. But any link between the Cathars and the Templars is, again, part of the latter-day syncretism of modern occultists trying to cobble together an appearance of antiquity for their own inventions. There is no basis in fact or evidence. Only dots to be connected.

Such 'historiography' too often amounts to the reasoning of protagonists in horror movies: "But every legend has a basis in fact!" Not this one. It is rather simply part and parcel with the spurious lore of the Masons. And yet it is absolutely integral to the various Templar hypotheses. And this means the Templar castle is built on sinking sand. Our authors, both Baigent, Leigh, and Lincoln and their many followers, follow in the footsteps of conventional Mason-Templar pseudo-lore in positing an underground stream of esoteric knowledge passed on, ultimately, from the ancient Gnostics and Essenes. And it has always been irresistible to speculate whether Jesus and/or John the Baptist may have been connected with the Essenes and/or Dead Sea Scrolls community.

Teabing *versus* Thiering

Another advocate of the Templar Jesus scenario, Laurence Gardner (*Bloodline of the Holy Grail*, 1996), cleverly appropriates the work of Dr. Barbara Thiering in order to gain new plausibility for this connection. Dr. Thiering has advanced a controversial theory about Jesus, which does happen to parallel two cardinal features of the Templar hypothesis. The first of these is that Jesus, a messiah-designate of the Qumran Essenes, did marry Mary Magdalene and beget an heir, also born to royal pretensions. The second is that Jesus survived crucifixion thanks to Essene allies. Neither of these suggestions is either new or intrinsically unlikely. Dr. Thiering is well aware of the need to buttress such claims with evidence, and she has provided it in the form of a complex body of work which subjects the gospels to the same sort of *pesher* (decoding) exegesis used by the Qumran scribes on their own scriptures. Her unique mastery of the textual, hermeneutical, and calendrical lore involved has left her a voice crying in the wilderness, as none of her critics so far seem to be in a position to evaluate her theories competently, either positively or negatively. Suffice it to say that Dr. Thiering's reconstruction of the cult-political connections of Jesus would come in very handy for the Templar hypothesis. But Dr. Thiering vociferously repudiates the connection, pointing out in some detail how Gardner selectively misrepresents her work, and then gratuitously extends it. If Gardner even understands why Thiering says what she does, he does not attempt to explain where he derives the rest of his 'insights' on the connections between Jesus, Magdalene, and the Essenes.

Raccoon Revelations

Similar themes are pursued in a 1996 work by Lynn Picknett and Clive Prince, *The Templar Revelation: Secret Guardians of the True Identity of Christ*. Baigent, Lincoln, and Leigh were led a merry chase by a group of spurious sources called the *Priory Documents,* or the *Secret Dossier*, a mass of nonsense concocted by a modern ultra-rightist political group who appropriated the name of the medieval Priory of Sion. Picknett and Prince are writing in the wake of these texts having been royally debunked, but the authors are largely undaunted. In the manner of all polemicists boxing with one arm tied behind them, they plead that bad evidence might as well be treated as good anyway. They argue cleverly, if not convincingly, that the (modern) Priory of Sion must be up to something to go to all the trouble of faking those documents! The Priory claims to have some sort of shocking information that could blow the lid off Christianity. So maybe they do! So there is a secret to hunt down after all! And so what if the Priory of Sion that exists today is not the same as the one that was connected to the Templars many centuries ago? There might still be some sort of underground connection — or something.

The next step in the argument is to try to forge a link between the Templars and the Cathars. The authors have to content themselves (and, they hope, the reader) with the mere possibility that, given certain coincidences in time and place, and the circumstantial 'evidence' of common interests, the Knights Templar might have been linked with the Cathars. These common interests include, paramountly, an interest in John the Baptist and Mary Magdalene. They start spreading out the push pins across the map and come to the conclusion that there was a significant overlap in France between Templar-related sites, centers of devotion to Mary Magdalene in local village churches, and the presence of Black Madonna statues, which some scholars hypothesize may have originally represented Isis or some synonymous pagan goddess. They will soon be drawing the net closed with the conclusion that the Templars worshipped Mary Magdalene as Isis and, along with the Alchemists (whom Picknett and Prince gratuitously interpret as Tantric sex-mystics), preserved the rites of *hieros gamos*, the archaic nature-renewing intercourse ritual performed by the faithful in the roles of the god and goddess. But who was the Horny, ah, Horned God? That is still more complicated.

A deep dive into the Time Tunnel takes Picknett and Prince back into the first century and Christian origins. Here they make clever use of the work of mainstream scholars like Burton L. Mack and C. H. Dodd (whom they persistently misspell as *Dodds*, unlike whoever compiled their bibliography), employing them as hammers to chip loose the New Testament from traditional Christian conceptions. They try to soften the reader up with the ideas that Galilee may not have been strictly Jewish, and that Jesus may not have been a Jew, nor John the Baptist for that matter. They invoke the Gnostic Nag Hammadi texts, discovered in Egypt in 1945, to show how early Christianity was much more diverse than scholars had traditionally supposed (a valid enough observation), and that it was likely Gnostic.

Our authors maintain that Mary Magdalene corresponds to the Egyptian Isis in so many respects that Mary pretty much becomes the Christian version of Isis, with Jesus as her consort Osiris. The mythological parallels here are numerous and significant. Much of the discussion is derived from Barbara G. Walker's endlessly fascinating tome, *The Women's Encyclopedia of Myths and Secrets*. Though no longer taken seriously by mainstream scholars, even critical ones, the identification of Jesus with Osiris and of Mary Magdalene with Isis is, I think, a strong and finally even a persuasive theory. Most who have argued it, like Walker, understand that the natural implication is that Jesus as a dying-and-rising god, raised by his divine consort, is nonhistorical. If there was a historical Jesus, this myth was soon applied to him. That would be Bultmann's view, for instance.

But, with Walker, Gilbert Murray, and others, we might go the whole way and understand Jesus and the Magdalene simply as a local variant of the old myth, and that they were eventually made into the fictitious Jesus and Mary Magdalene of the gospels. But this Picknett and Prince do not do. They insist on historicizing the myth. They believe that the historical Jesus and Mary Magdalene regarded themselves as somehow being the incarnations of Osiris and Isis. This seems to me a fundamental misstep. Not only does it beget a reconstruction of the intentions of Jesus that is grotesque in its extravagance, it fundamentally misses a crucial feature of myths as Rene Girard (*Violence and the Sacred: The Scapegoat*) explains them. Girard knows that, *e.g.*, the Oedipus myth does not record a genuine historical case of scapegoating, but that it is a sacred story embodying and presupposing the *kind* of thing that used to happen in the ancient world.

Their historical Jesus is composed of equal parts of Hugh J. Schonfield's Jesus as 'scheming messiah' (*The Passover Plot*) and Morton Smith's *Jesus the Magician.*

From Schonfield they have learned that 'Jesus the Nazorean' denoted not 'Jesus from the town of Nazareth,' but rather 'Jesus of the Nazorean sect,' and that 'Nazoreans' meant 'Keepers of the Secrets,' related to today's Mandaeans. This gives us a sectarian and Gnostic Jesus. From Schonfield they also derive the notion that Jesus did believe himself to be the Messiah, or at least planned to be accepted as such, orchestrating even his own crucifixion, which he planned to survive.

From Smith, our authors borrow the notion that Jesus must have been a sorcerer. Not only is he depicted as driving out demons and healing with spit, mud, and imitative gestures, the stock in trade of magicians as described in Hellenistic Egyptian magic handbooks; he received his powers and divine sonship by the descent of a familiar spirit in the form of a bird, as the Egyptians did. Some early Christians, as well as Jewish and Gentile critics of Christianity, regarded Jesus as a magician, and so Smith judges that he was. It is not an implausible position.

Picknett and Prince add to the mix the belief of Talmudic Jews and of Celsus that Jesus learned magic in Egypt. They note, too, the occurrence of old Egyptian cosmology in the Coptic Gnostic texts like the *Pistis Sophia*, where the Gnostic revealer Jesus speaks of descending into Amente, the Egyptian netherworld. Add to this that the *Egyptian Book of the Dead* already contains the central Gnostic theme of preparing those about to die with the esoteric knowledge they will need to escape damnation, and you come up with a plausible case for Jesus and Christianity being not Jewish but Egyptian and magical in origin. Other scholars have argued for an Egyptian Gnostic origin for Christianity, and though no longer fashionable, the theory is well worth considering seriously. The great (really, the only) merit of The Templar Revelation is to make some of these notions current again.

What was Jesus' own personal mission? Picknett and Prince take seriously what the Talmud said about Jesus being crucified for attempting to introduce alien gods (a familiar charge aimed at Socrates, too). They believe Jesus was essentially an initiated priest of the Isis religion who had experienced orgasmic deification in a ritual of union with Mary Magdalene, a temple 'prostitute' (what I like to call *a priestitute*). He felt it incumbent upon him to restore to Israel its original gods, the Egyptian pantheon, particularly the worship of Isis, whose local avatar Anath had long been worshipped in the Temple. To gain public support he had to prove himself (or pretend to be, the authors are not sure) the Davidic Messiah, a notion more familiar to them. Then, once in a position of power and respect, he would lead them to believe in himself as Osiris and in Mary as Isis.

Blue Plate Special

As if this brilliant but implausible scenario were not artificial enough, Picknett and Prince next set their sites on John the Baptist. They are eager to relate the theory of David Friedrich Strauss (though they trace it back no further than Emil Kraeling [b. 1892] and C. H. 'Dodds' [1884–1973] who never claimed originality on the point) that John never endorsed Jesus, that Jesus had once been an apprentice with John, that Jesus withdrew and formed a rival sect, and that most of what the gospels say about John is Christian propaganda intended to co-opt the figurehead of a competing sect.

So far, so good. They go farther and take seriously the reports of the Pseudo-Clementine *Homilies* 2:23–24 that Jesus was not the only famous disciple of John, but that his colleagues included Simon Magus and Dositheus the Samaritan. The *Homilies* tell how Simon was John's chosen successor, but that Dositheus usurped his position. Pinckett and Prince posit that Jesus, too, was part of the jockeying. They read the Jesus/John split as particularly bitter and even suggest that Jesus had John killed! You see, Salome, a female disciple mentioned in the gospels, must have been the same as Salome the daughter of Herodias. (In fact, virtually every other woman one met in first-century Palestine was named Salome!) Neither woman especially wanted the Baptist dead. His imprisonment had done all the damage control that could be done for Herodias' reputation. No, it was Jesus who put her up to having his rival decapitated!

Remember the strange passage (Mark 6:14–16) where, haunted by his guilty conscience, Herod hears of Jesus' miracles and fears it is the return of John the Baptist to haunt him? Our authors ask in what sense Jesus could have been imagined to be John "raised from the dead" so that "powers are at work in him." And they adopt Morton Smith's theory (fanciful in my opinion) that Jesus was believed, *à la* current magical technique, to be channeling the powerful spirit of the deceased John. The power of a murdered man's soul was great, the magicians thought — especially if you possessed some relic of his corpse. Well, what do you suppose happened to John's head after the authorities granted the rest of the body to his disciples for burial (Mark 6:29)? Jesus must have procured it from his agent Salome and kept it for use as a magical talisman. What a coincidence, then, that the Templars were said to have possessed a severed head that spoke oracles to them! Guess who it must have been?

The followers of John must have surmised or discovered what happened, and this would explain the inveterate hatred of the Mandaeans (descendants of the ancient sect of John, as Bultmann contended) for Jesus. In a revealing admission, Picknett and Prince confess that there is a millennium-long gap between the ancient sects of Jesus and John on the one hand and the (apparently interchangeable) Templars, Masons, Cathars, Leonardo, and Priory of Sion on the other. But their guess, obviously, is that all these groups learned and passed down the secret that our authors think they have pieced together.

But why are they writing, so to speak, with bated breath? What's the big deal? The mere revelation of such an alternate account of Christian origins would have no real effect beyond the pond-ripples of titillation among readers of sensational books like those we are discussing here. Why on earth would one more such dime-novel hypothesis shake the foundations of the church? Picknett and Prince suggest that maybe the Priory of Sion has some definitive proof like the skull of John the Baptist or the bones of Mary Magdalene. How such bio-trash would prove anything to anybody remains to be explained. What is the Vatican supposed to do? Check the dental records of the Baptist? Compare the DNA of the Magdalene?

And as for the great gap, which is to say, the lack of any evidence of a historical transmission or dissemination of these ideas, can we offer a better explanation than *The Templar Revelation*? As it happens, we can. Ioan P. Couliano, in his book *The Tree of Gnosis*, argued how it is much less problematical to suggest that, since the human brain is much the same from generation to generation, from century to century, whenever it is faced with similar challenges and similar data, the brain of whatever century will produce the same range of solutions. Thus Gnosticism as a 'theodicy' – finding a way to exculpate the deity for the existence of evil – can be expected to resurface, independently, again and again through the ages.

We don't need to picture some cleric discovering some dusty old parchments and reading some blasphemous gospel, which then acts as a match to spark a rediscovery of Gnosticism. No, we can just count on the inventive mind to put the pieces together again and again. If the world is infested with evil, and if God is good, how can he have created this world? Faced with this difficulty, some minds will always come to posit: "Perhaps it wasn't God who made the world! Maybe some disobedient subordinates did it!" *Voilà* — a Gnostic theodicy is reborn.

The same is true when it comes to certain tantalizing biblical puzzles. Was something going on between Jesus and Mary Magdalene? You don't have to read the *Gospel of Philip* to suspect so. Martin Luther thought so. So did Garner Ted Armstrong, and numerous others, who apparently all came up with the idea from their own reading of the scriptures. Likewise, Pentecostal healer William Marrion Branham and the Rev. Sun Myung Moon both came up with the theory that Eve was sexually seduced and impregnated by the Serpent in

Eden. Neither knew of the other's interpretation, nor that some of the ancient rabbis thought the same thing.

No, it is just that "inquiring minds want to know," and, given the same set of data, some of the same answers are going to come up again and again. So if the Cathars had doctrines similar to the Nag Hammadi texts, that hardly means they must have read them there. Not that it couldn't have happened! For instance, we know that Anan ben David in the twelfth century stumbled upon copies of some of the Dead Sea Scrolls, and from these he got some ideas for the Kara'ite sect which he founded, an anti-rabbinic Jewish sect. But we can say so because there is surviving direct evidence. Picknett and Prince admit that this sort of direct evidence is lacking for their case.

This is all immensely ingenious. But it is not ingenious in the manner of historical reconstruction. It is rather ingenious in the manner of Richard L. Tierney who, in his Sword-&-Sorcery tales of Simon of Gitta (a fictionalized Simon Magus, based on the old Paul Newman movie *The Silver Chalice*) weaves together neglected and anomalous details from the gospels and other early Christian literature with material from H. P. Lovecraft's Cthulhu Mythos and Robert E. Howard's fictive Hyborian Age. The correspondences are so striking as Tierney connects the dots that the result has a beguiling narrative seductiveness. Picknett and Prince are, alas, doing the same thing. They should have taken their research and made it into a novel. They didn't.

Skeleton Key

Another adjunct to the Templar Jesus canon is *The Hiram Key: Pharaohs, Freemasons and the Discovery of the Secret Scrolls of Jesus* (1997) by two Freemasons, Christopher Knight (which ought to be a pen name if it isn't!) and Robert Lomas. The first is an advertising executive, the second an electrical engineer. This book is crackpot scholarship, giving the impression of a hoax, though it is the authors who are the victims of it. Again, *The Hiram Key* reads much like a novel, the doughty researchers sharing each and every new astonishing discovery as their dreams came true and their hypotheses seemed to take palpable form in the air before them. No reader of Dan Brown's *Da Vinci Code* can avoid seeing the similarity of adventuring authors Knight and Lomas to Brown's scholarly protagonist. But the real similarity is between Knight/Lomas and Brown himself. As with all these Look-what-we-discovered! books, what we are reading is something midway between a report of research and an adventure novel. One suspects that without the fictionalizing frame, the 'revelations' of books like *The Hiram Key* would not sound nearly as impressive as they probably do to the unschooled readers who buy them.

Knight and Lomas, as Masons and as inquisitive fellows, found that, no matter how superficial Freemasonry may appear, even to its members, there may yet be more to it than meets the eye. Like the earnest Catholic sitting in the pew who wonders why the priest races through the mass by rote, his mind obviously on other matters, Knight and Lomas began to wonder what some of the strange chants, not in English, were supposed to mean. Where did the Masonic names and stories come from? How far back did their traditions go? And they noticed how little inclined their brethren were to pursue such questions. So they embarked on a Grail-quest of their own.

The trouble with the result is that, assuming there would be something substantial to find, they at length cooked up something substantial and claim to have found it. The subtitle of the book, promising rediscovered Nazorean scrolls containing the Q document, *etc.*, is a perfect cameo of the whole. It is only a tease; our authors merely surmise that such a trove of texts resides within the vault of Roselyn Chapel in Scotland — exactly as Geraldo Rivera was so sure he had located the lost treasure of Al Capone in what tuned out to be an empty concrete bunker.

In this exercise in Masonic apologetics, the authors go about as far back as one could hope to go to find the roots of anything: ancient Sumer and Akkad. They cannot help seeing Freemasonry prefigured in the sacred geometry of the Ziggurats, the artificial step pyramids the Babylonians erected on the plain of Shinar to simulate the mountaintop high places where, in their original mountainous homeland, they used to worship their gods. But then the Flood intervened, wiping away most of civilization.

Never fear, hardy Sumerians reestablished civilization elsewhere, including Egypt, where new Pyramids arose. In the Egyptian concept of Maat, which Knight and Lomas understand as implying a sure foundation of virtues balanced in an architectonic manner, they cannot help but see the central insight of today's Masonic moral catechism. This is nearly enough, our authors imagine, to claim direct succession from the mysteries of the Egyptian pharaohs. And this is a tendency observable throughout their work. They discover "amazing parallels" to this or that piece of Masonic symbolism (*e.g.*, the wide use in temples of two pillars, the Boaz and Jachin of Solomon's temple, prefigured in Sumer and Egypt) and jump to the conclusion that the Masons got it from ancient, arcane sources — when it was readily available in the Bible all the time.

Knight and Lomas are like Dorothy, seeking Oz afar off when it was in her own back yard, when they embark on the quest for the true identity of Hiram Abif, the martyr hero of Masonic myth. They wind up identifying him with a minor Pharaoh, a client king of the interloping Hyksos dynasty, one Seqenenre Tao. They disdain the obvious truth that Hiram "Abif," pious architect of Solomon's temple, must have been intended as King Hiram of Tyre, period. Hiram supplied the materials and plans for the temple according to the Bible, but Masonic ritual splits him into two Hirams so as to be able to kill one of them off as a Masonic martyr. Hiram of Tyre did not so die, so they had to make from him a second Hiram. *Hiram Abif* is like 'Judas not Iscariot' (John 14:22), an artificial attempt to distance one version of the same character from another. Nor does it bother Knight and Lomas to derive *Abif* from the French word for 'lost,' on the basis of which they go on to treat 'Hiram Abif' as code for 'lost king,' referring to the obscure Seqenenre Tao.

The case made by Knight and Lomas reminds one of the modern theory of physics whereby what appears to be solid matter is actually mostly empty space with a mere scattering of material particles. Like Superman, our authors leap vast chasms of evidence in a single bound. As *Bible Questionnaire* radio host Walter Bjork used to say, "Every theory has holes in it, but this one is practically all hole."

But at crucial points Knight and Lomas try to fill in some of the holes, albeit with square pegs. There is a sleight-of-hand trick going on here, when, in order to find an Egyptian precedent for the Masonic initiation ritual whereby the novice is ritually 'slain' and raised from death, they posit an altogether unattested Egyptian coronation rite in which the new Pharaoh was united with the divine Horus by a ritual shamanistic death and flight through the netherworld and the stars to become divine. It is not as if Knight and Lomas have actually discovered a handy Egyptian rite that mirrors Freemasonry. No, they simply *surmise* that such a precedent would make sense – especially for their theory – and so it is henceforth a fact.

According to a Masonic ritual, a delver in Solomon's temple during Zerubbabel's restoration spelunks his way into a cavernous pillared chamber where he discovers a lost scroll of the Law of Moses, the Ten Commandments. This seems most likely to be simply a garbled (or artfully rewritten) version of the 'discovery' of the *Book of the Covenant* by the priest Hilkiah during renovations of the temple mentioned in 2 Kings 22:8-10. But in order to get their theory home, Knight and Lomas make the story refer instead to a hypothetical Templar discovery of early Christian (Nasorean) scrolls beneath the ruins of Herod's temple. And they feel sure this document trove must include the Q Document, even though they do not know what that is. They think Q underlies all fours gospels in the manner of the old Nazarene Gospel theory of Robert Graves and Joshua Podro (*The Nazarene Gospel Restored*, 1954).

There is indeed some evidence that the Templars may have done some digging beneath the Dome of the Rock, perhaps to get to the rumored treasures of Solomon's ruined temple. It is sheer surmise, though certainly not absurd, to suppose that they found such wealth. But it is wild speculation to dogmatize that they discovered a library of early Christian scrolls there, too. What is the basis for Knight and Lomas's certainty that there were Jesus scrolls waiting to be found? There is a reference in the *Testament of Moses*, a pseudepigraphical work from the first century CE where Moses commands his fellows to bury some scrolls beneath Mt. Moriah, the future site of Solomon's temple. Again, that is one major leap! What counts as authentic evidence is apparently whatever advances the case of the authors.

With modern critical scholarship, they dismiss most of the gospel 'history' as fiction and legend (and they are right to do so), but when it comes in handy for their theory, they will pick up and dust off the most blatantly legendary biblical material. For instance, Abraham was an historical figure who, like many other *Habiru*/Hebrews, migrated from Ur to Canaan and into Egypt. Moses is equally real, down to the bloodiest details of genocidal warfare against the poor Canaanites, because the authors enjoy using him as a whipping boy to illustrate the contempt they plainly feel for Judaism and Christianity. They need him, too, as a link between Egypt and later Israel, as the channel through which their hypothetical secret ritual of kingly resurrection passed on closer and closer to the Templars.

Their treatment of the supposedly historical Jesus is heavily influenced, it seems, by the work of Barbara Thiering, who reads the gospels as entirely symbolic of the career of Jesus as a member of the Qumran brotherhood of the Dead Sea Scrolls. When he raises someone from the dead, he is merely lifting the ban of excommunication. When he feeds the five thousand, he is giving the laymen access to the sacramental bread reserved for the priests. Oddly, they do not give Dr. Thiering a hint of credit. Of course whenever they do footnote any scholarly source, there are no page references.

Knight and Lomas also endorse (no doubt to his acute chagrin) the fascinating work of Robert Eisenman, who argues very powerfully that the Qumran sect was the same as the Jewish-Christian 'Nasorean' church of James the Just. Paul, as per Eisenman, was the rebellious heretic whom the Scrolls cryptically refer to as "the Spouter of Lies."

Knight and Lomas combine elements of Thiering and Eisenman by making John the Baptist, Jesus, and James the Just, Jesus' brother, all Essenes, and thus into Freemasons, then positing a breach between Jesus and his brother James (as Thiering sees one between Jesus and John the Baptist) and a subsequent break between Jesus and Paul.

Knight and Lomas believe John and Jesus played the roles of priestly and royal messiahs while John lived. Once the Baptist died, James the Just took John's place, but not without opposition from Jesus, who thought he deserved to occupy both posts. The Romans arrested them both, making the point moot. James? Arrested by Pilate? Yes, because he was also known as *Jesus* (a title denoting 'savior') *Barabbas* (son of God, or literally 'of the Father'). So there were two Jesus Christs, and Pilate let one go. James went on, without opposition, to become the Teacher of Righteousness of the Dead Sea Scrolls.

It is not that there is not something very intriguing about the occurrence of 'Jesus son of Abba' alongside of 'Jesus called Christ' in some manuscripts of Matthew 27:17, and whatever it may turn out to be will doubtless be something pretty strange. But must it be a pairing of Jesus and his brother as convict messiahs? Knight and Lomas have never heard of the cardinal principle of historical criticism: anything is *possible*, but what is *probable*?

Too Many Cooks

Paul they blame for creating a whole new religion, corrupting the Jewish nationalism and Essene Freemasonry. It was Paul who imported the ancient mythemes of the virgin birth and the dying and rising god (though it seems odd our authors would reject these, given the importance to their speculations of a ritual in which a king would die and rise and become the god Horus). They even credit Paul with the invention of the Trinity.

There is a similar Gordian Knot of gross anachronism when it comes to the Emperor Constantine, whom Knight and Lomas pretty much reduce to the level of a clever Mafia thug. According to them, Constantine never sincerely embraced the Christian faith, being instead an adherent of Sol the Invincible Sun. In fact it seems more likely that, not only was Constantine a believing Christian, but that he had been born and raised as such (see T. G. Elliott, *The Christianity of Constantine the Great*). He inherited the pontificate of the Sol cult as part and parcel of his duties as head of state. He did delay baptism till his deathbed, but that was only to avoid forfeiting salvation through post-baptismal slip-ups, a fear that haunted all Christians of the day. Theologically, the eager Christian emperor was like a bull in the china shop, intervening to settle the dispute over whether Jesus Christ was fully divine (as Athanasius taught) or semi-divine (as per Arius). But Knight and Lomas make him a cynical advertising executive like Knight himself. For them, it is Constantine and the Greek Christians who paganized Christianity — or was it Paul?

Our authors seem to be confused here. Part of the paganization, according to Knight and Lomas, was the addition to the Bible of the Deuterocanonical books including Tobit, Judith, Sirach, Esdras, Maccabees, *etc.*, as if their presence in the canon makes much difference. Yet later on in the book, when the history of Judah Maccabee seems to come in handy as a way of connecting the dots between ancient Israel and the Templars, Knight and Lomas suddenly damn the editors of the King James Version for omitting 1 and 2 Maccabees from the canon. But in fact the King James translators included the Apocrypha. It was Martin Luther who had previously caused these books to be bumped to a secondary status, though never suppressed, and the KJV was regularly printed with the Apocrypha until 1823.

Before their adventure is over, Knight and Lomas – tirelessly exploring from library book to library book – undaunted by context, and as far as automobile day-trips would take them into the British countryside, have established to their own satisfaction that Templar Knights discovered America before Columbus, and that they got the name America from Mandaean scripture. They have 'discovered' that the Turin Shroud (which the authors of *The Templar Revelation* 'reveal' as a hoax self-portrait by Leonardo Da Vinci) is actually the bloody image of Templar chief Jacques de Molay! On a second visit to the Roselyn Chapel (a Templar and/or Masonic?) edifice, Knight and Lomas suddenly intuitively realize that the whole structure is a miniature model of Herod's temple (which may indeed be so) and that the lost Scrolls of Jesus are hidden within! That's how the Templars, then the Masons, knew about Hiram Abif and all the other important secrets of Masonic lore. How else, they dare us, to explain the similarities between Masonic rituals and certain elements of ancient religion? But in fact, "there must be fifty ways…"

The endeavor of Knight and Lomas is but a step away from the sort of psychic history writing at which the Austrian esotericist and founder of Anthroposophy Rudolf Steiner [1861–1925] was so adept: just reading the past from one's own subjective impressions. They do not know the difference between a hunch and a discovery, between coincidence and confirmation. They do not seem to take seriously the difference between the diachronic analysis of evidence and the synchronic analysis. This means that they in effect ignore the great historical depth of centuries and centuries separating the various bits of evidence from one another and treat them as if they were all contemporary with one another, like dots on a common flat map surface, to be connected according to whatever pattern seems to appear, like a child's puzzle. But it appears like a pattern from a Rorschach inkblot test. It is completely subjective.

What Are They Now?

A different spin on the whole matter of ancient Templar discoveries and the mystery of Rennes-le-Chateau comes from yet another pair of authors, Richard Andrews and Paul Schellenberger (*The Tomb of God*, 1996). Like most others in this genre, *The Tomb of God* concerns itself with the mystery of a nineteenth-century village priest named Bergier Sauniere who is said to have discovered four (or five) parchments within an old pillar while his church was being renovated. He eventually took these documents to Paris and had their cryptic Latin translated. Hitherto poor as a church mouse, the Abbé Sauniere returned home a very wealthy man. The speculations offered in most of these books is that the priest had found a treasure map and decoded it, unearthing a fabulous trove of golden treasure brought back from Jerusalem by the Knights Templar — or else he discovered documentation of some shocking truth he was able to use to blackmail the Roman Catholic Church. One of the first things he did with his newfound funds was to spruce up his church in hideous bad taste, including some possibly heretical, Rosicrucian-tilting decorations. Our various authors see in this detail a sure sign of the priest's occult sympathies.

Another purchase was of copies of three paintings, traced down by Andrews and Schellenberger, which, as their painstaking analysis demonstrates, embody complex Platonic-Pythagorean geometric forms. Andrews and Schellenberger next turn their attention to the parchments discovered by Sauniere. There is no pretense or claim that these Latin texts represent ancient scriptures or the like. No, they are of admittedly recent vintage and convey, to the knowing eye, a set of geometric and verbal puzzles referring back to the three paintings. Someone had cracked a code, and it turned out that all these enigmatic charts and hints were pieces of a map of the Languedoc area of southern France.

Scrutiny of a fourteenth-century Templar map of Jerusalem disclosed the use of the same underlying geometric cipher, leading our researchers to the conclusion that the three eighteenth-century painters, some of whom are known to have had Hermetic or occultist connections anyway (such things were then quite chic), were in touch with an ancient geometric code, one of many bits of classical learning possibly rediscovered among the Arabs by the Templar Knights on their tour of duty in Jerusalem and its environs.

The question for us, however, is what any of this has to do with the contention of the remainder of the book that the treasure to which these enigmatic clues lead is the tomb containing the earthly remains of Jesus. Andrews and Schellenberger guess ('hypothesize' is too restrained a word) that either Jesus survived crucifixion and fled Palestine for less hostile territory, where he carried on his ministry; or, equally as likely as far as they are concerned, the Templars, in the course of their excavations, discovered the burial place of Jesus and decided to bring the holy relics back home to France.

The authors fairly leap from one phase of their argument into the other, hoping their momentum will carry them the whole way. They mention folk legends of Southern France that place the tomb of Jesus there, but they give no documentation for this assertion. There certainly are 'tombs of Jesus' available in Japan, in Kashmir, and perhaps other places, but where is the evidence for such a belief in the wine country? There is a statue of Jesus in the vicinity of the site (Cardou) to which the clues point. That need not mean much, though.

Perhaps the most fascinating hint they produce concerns the decipherment of a motto appearing in one of the relevant paintings, Poussin's *Les Bergers d'Arcadie* ('Shepherds of Arcadia'), where we see, chiseled into the lintel of a tomb, the words ET IN ARCADIA EGO. The phrase, which figures significantly in Dan Brown's novel, is usually rendered something like, 'I am present in Arcadia, too.' In this case, the sentiment is Kierkegaardian, a chill whiff reminding us that even in Paradise death intrudes. Actually, even this reading would comport with Andrews's and Schellenberger's theory, if one were to take the phrase as the words of Jesus, meaning, 'Though risen in heaven, I am also buried in Arcadia.' But they are still more imaginative. If one reads the line as an anagram, it comes out: ARCAM DEI TANGO: 'I touch the tomb of God' This would leave four letters left over: E, I, S, U, — reshuffled to form *Iesu*, or Jesus.

One must take care never to dismiss a radical thesis simply because it is radical and would require a realignment of belief and assumption if accepted. And let it be said just as quickly that one of the possibilities raised in Andrews and Schellenberger's theory, that Jesus *might* have descended the cross alive and lived to tell the tale, is by no means fanciful. The contemporary historian Josephus tells us that it was possible for the loved ones of crucified criminals to bribe or otherwise arrange to have the crucified taken down before they expired. And the gospels certainly bear traces of an underlying version of events in which some such possibility is entertained, else why note Pilate's surprise that Jesus was dead so soon (Mark 15:44), implying perhaps that he was not? Why remark on Joseph of Arimathea's wealth (Matthew 27:57), unless this detail is meant to supply motivation for grave robbers who will find a reviving Jesus in an opulent tomb and free him? Why does John emphatically reject the notion, that some must have held, that Jesus "went among the Greeks to teach the Greeks" (John 7:35)? No, none of that is impossible.

Likewise, if the Templars had somehow identified the corpse of Jesus in Jerusalem, there would have been every reason for them to spirit it away to France — the same reason that early bishops had for exhuming the relics of popular martyrs from countryside shrines and bringing them into city churches. This enabled the bishops to co-opt the charismatic clout hitherto possessed by the shrines and their owners. It was the same instinct that led the Jerusalem temple priests in King Josiah's day to close down the local hilltop shrines ("high places") and to restrict sacrifice to the temple, under their jurisdiction and to their profit. The Templars would have had every reason to bring the remains of Jesus with them especially if they feared the temple mount might fall once again, as it did, under the purview of the Muslims.

But then, if one's goal in such a game of capture the flag is to take the high ground relic-wise, one trumpets the fact! The last thing to do is to keep it a secret. Then again, no Christian would have announced such a find, nor rejoiced in it initially. So then we are back, logically, to the blackmail trump card version of the theory.

Sitting on the Secret

The arbitrary speculativeness of the second portion of *The Tomb of God* is troublesome enough, but what really kills it is the ill-founded assumption that the Templars, or the Masons, or whoever, could have sat on this secret, holding it in store as a trump card to disprove the resurrection of Jesus Christ. It is easy for a modern writer to imagine such a thing, for it rings true as a piece of a good mystery novel. But if one actually thinks out the implications of any attempt to cash in on this, to spill the beans and topple the Catholic Church, it immediately becomes apparent that the whole endeavor would be wasted effort. Who would believe such an announcement? Whoever made it would be considered insane. And what hope could the keepers of the body have had of corroborating their claim?

It is striking how the logic of this book mirrors that of fundamentalist apologists who argue that the tomb of Jesus must have been irrefutably empty; otherwise the Sanhedrin would have "produced the body," as apologists always like to say with a kind of Joe Friday self-assurance. Andrews and Schellenberger imagine that all the Templars would have to do in order to discredit Christian dogma is to "produce the body," even today, two millennia later, and it would smash Christian claims. In both cases, no one is taking seriously the absurd futility of trying to prove the identity of a moldering corpse after a very few days.

Andrews and Schellenberger try to lay a groundwork of religious history and theological warfare that would make sense of some Templar grave-robbing scheme. They seem to know they must make it sound reasonable that Christians, even heretical ones, would have thought it a good idea to announce the discovery of the corpse of Jesus. In their view, possession of the dead body of Jesus would be the vindicating token of a suppressed kind of Christianity for which Jesus Christ was a simple human being, albeit a great one, whose teachings have been lost behind the stained-glass curtain of his divinity, a later and artificial corruption of the historical truth by the Roman Church.

This is just one more version of an old reading of church history. The Anabaptists (the Radical Reformation sect from whom the Mennonites, Amish, Brethren, Hutterites, and others sprang) of Martin Luther's time centered their faith on the Synoptic Gospels (Matthew, Mark, and Luke) and their radical teachings to love one's enemy, turn the other cheek, give away possessions, *etc.* They were the pioneers of the separation of church and state and believed that Christianity experienced a "Fall into sin" when it succumbed to Caesar's invitation to become the state religion. The institutional privilege thus given came with the price tag of ethical compromise and state control of the church and its beliefs.

Adolf von Harnack (*What Is Christianity?,* 1901) in the early twentieth century renewed that theory, claiming that the historical Jesus taught a simple yet sublime gospel of the higher righteousness, the infinite value of the individual soul, and the loving Fatherhood of God and brotherhood of man. This, he said, was the religion *of* Jesus. But soon the institutional Church had replaced it with a sacrament-dispensing, superstitious religion *about* Jesus. Harnack and others implicated Paul as the "second founder of Christianity." So they placed the derailment of the faith even earlier than the Anabaptists had.

Andrews and Schellenberger are closer to Harnack's version, only they take into account some (not enough) more recent New Testament scholarship, which yields a more complicated schematic of early Christian history. Our authors appeal to Barbara Thiering to understand Jesus as an Essene, and his faith therefore as a type of sectarian Judaism. Essenism certainly embodied elite and restricted knowledge (lists of angelic names, for example, or battle plans for Armageddon), but Andrews and Schellenberger are too quick to identify Essenism with Gnosticism, which for them is pretty much equivalent to Rosicrucianism, a term they also (admittedly) use imprecisely as denoting 'esotericism.'

From Jesus' ostensible sectarian Judaism they derive the tenet of his mere humanity as one who gained whatever divine favor he had by his own spiritual self-cultivation. Notions like Jesus' inherent divinity, his incarnation, virgin birth, and resurrection they dismiss as inventions by Paul intended to lift Jesus and his achievements beyond the capacity of mere human beings. The point was to reduce people to passive servitude to the institutional Church, which could declare them original sinners and forgive them on certain conditions of fealty and quiescence. If we were to excavate the site where Jesus' bones lie buried and expose his lack of resurrection, our authors claim with hushed tones, maybe it would not be too late to restore the sort of freethinking self-help faith that the real Jesus preached.

But this is all hopeless confusion. It has been clear to critical New Testament scholars ever since Ferdinand Christian Baur [1792–1860] in the nineteenth century that the Pauline Epistles are among the most important roots of Gnosticism and that the Catholic Church represents a corruption of the Pauline faith with the Torah-piety of Judaism. Catholicism is seen by many as a declension from Paulinism, the emphases of which continued on primarily in the forms of Gnosticism and Marcionism. And while Gnosticism did encourage spiritual self-liberation and innovation, it certainly was not friendly to the simple humanity or mortality of Jesus. For them the human Jesus, if he even existed and was not some sort of a holographic phantom, was merely the unimportant channeler for the Christ-spirit who spoke through him.

What Andrews and Schellenberger are really interested in, it sounds like, is the victory of Liberal Protestantism or Unitarianism, a vaguely religious philosophy that will happily quote the maxims of a human Jesus and will rejoice equally to be rid of dogmas that make of him an oppressive theological abstraction. The irony is: what a subtle and tortuous path one must trace, over geometrical chasms and around historical mountains, to obtain the key to this supposedly commonsensical piety! Whose is the simple faith here?

Blizzard of Bunk

As we have already noted earlier, in the oldest and best manuscripts the Gospel of Mark ends quite abruptly — or so it has seemed to many readers both ancient and modern. The women visiting the tomb of Jesus find it empty of Jesus but nonetheless occupied by a young man posted, like a student in an empty classroom, left to tell any latecomers that class is canceled for the day, or that it has been moved. This attendant, perhaps an angel, tells them they have just missed Jesus but that they and the others can catch him in Galilee somewhere. The women are terrified, run away, and zip their lips. The end. Various scribes decided they would augment Mark and supply a 'better' ending. One of these, the so-called Longer Ending (Mark 16:9–20), familiar from the King James Version, reads like a slapdash combination of elements cribbed from the fuller Easter accounts of the other gospels. Well, when we read Peter Blake and Paul S. Blezard, *The Arcadian Cipher: The Quest to Crack the Code of Christianity's Greatest Secret* (2000), we may receive a similar impression. In many respects it appears to be a derivative digest of several of the books we have already discussed.

In the Introduction, our authors confess the similarity between their work and that published four years earlier, by Andrews and Schellenberger (*The Tomb of God,* 1996), in that both depend very heavily upon the notion of a hidden geometric coding contained in several Renaissance paintings — in fact, most of the same ones. But they maintain their research had run parallel in ignorance of the other book. If that were true, the fact certainly would tend to reinforce the plausibility of the analysis of the art and the use of the Platonic geometry, for what it is worth. In fact, where Andrews and Schellenberger try the reader's patience with (admittedly necessary) explanations of their calculations, Blake and Blezard spend the time providing a much fuller background for the relevant painters and their sponsors. The result is that the whole idea of the coded maps and diagrams seems a good deal more plausible than in the earlier book. In this one, we are shown how the individuals involved would have been interested in such esoteric matters. We are not left to infer, without much of a context, that they simply *must* have been. And with this we have reached the only strength of the book. Though Blake and Blezard are headed for pretty much the same destination as Andrews and Schellenberger, they are not destined to make it there by any more secure path, as we shall soon see.

Even before we make it out of the art museum we find we are in trouble. Blake and Blezard leave off the geometry lesson and begin interpreting the imagery of the paintings. Here one may escape total subjectivity only if one is able to draw upon established conventions of symbolism, and the authors try to do that, but unsuccessfully. For instance, in decoding the *Shepherds of Arcadia*, a painting that figures largely in all these books, we are told that the bold colors of this and that figure should tip us off to each character's identity with this or that Egyptian god to whom the color was sacred. A shepherd sporting a laurel wreath, a red robe, and white sandals — well, he might be the god Shu, "the representation of power of the godhead incarnate here on Earth in the form of man." The color red "has also been found to illustrate the presence of the Lord of Truth or the eye of Ra — in Christian terms a simulacrum of the Christ figure" (p. 34). Wait just a darn minute! Just because the guy's wearing red? This is word association, not interpretation of the author's intent. Likewise, a shoeless, bearded figure must be John the Baptist! "Could it be that Poussin is trying to indicate a continuing relationship between Jesus the preacher and John, whose sacrifice made that ministry possible?" (p. 35).

This book is heavily dependent, from this point on, upon the dreadful *Templar Revelation*, and from it Blake and Blezard have learned too many bad lessons. One of the worst is to plant bogus evidence for the conclusion one aims at reaching. Eventually, Blake and Blezard will be telling us that, as of the Transfiguration, Jesus became the vehicle for the spirit of the martyred Baptist. To pave the way for this notion, the authors need to make it appear that there was more of a connection between John and Jesus than appears on the surface of the gospels even when read at face value. So they smuggle already into the interpretation of the painting what they hope the reader will take as a signal from Poussin that, yes, there was such a connection.

But it is all a circle: it is only their belief in the spiritual possession of Jesus by John that even supplies the category they propose to use to interpret Poussin. Likewise, from Poussin's painting *The Deluge*, they arbitrarily peg one character, dragged ashore, as Jesus Christ, and another as Jesus' son! Why on earth should we imagine that Poussin could even have thought of such a creature? Simply because it would come in handy as a subtext, a kind of fictive sounding board built into the text. The reader is to recall it, perhaps dimly, so that when, later on, he or she gets to the 'revelation' of a Jesus Junior, it will ring some sort of a bell: "Yes, that seems to fit!"

Our authors turn next to a pseudo-historical survey of the evolution of religion, ritual, and mythology, from Pharaonic Egypt, on through the Mandaeans, the Kabbalah, *etc*. Most of this has been cribbed from *The Templar Revelation* and has the same problems. But the upshot is a Gnostic Jesus who learned both his religion and his magical techniques in Egypt. Celsus, the second-century Platonist critic of Christianity, it seems, is to be taken at his word, while the New Testament gospels are dismissed as disinformation except in the supposedly numerous places in which they make Jesus sound Gnostic. And as to this, no passages are specified.

At this point the whole thing goes to hell. Blake and Blezard think Joseph of Arimathea and Flavius Josephus the historian were the same person (p. 115). They have Herod Antipas thinking that he owed his defeat by Aretas IV (misspelled here) to his execution of John the Baptist (p. 110), though in fact it is Josephus who makes this connection in his *Jewish War*. They have Herodias formerly married to Herod Philip, when it was actually his brother Herod (not Philip as Mark thinks). They assert that the Essenes wrote the Nag Hammadi texts (p. 37) and that the Koran depicts Jesus as crucified but surviving it, then going on to teach in the Far East (p. 141-142). The Koran is innocent of such notions, which the authors have instead read in the apologetics of the Ahmaddiya sect (pp. 143-144) and misattributed to scripture. From the apocryphal *Acts of Pilate* Blake and Blezard derive the 'fact' that, as Jesus was marched into Pilate's presence, the Roman standards dipped in reverence to him. They treat medieval Grail romances describing Joseph of Arimathea's travels to Glastonbury as historical fact. Yes, it seems as if everything but the gospels is to be believed!

According to Blake and Blezard, Jesus' legs remained unbroken on the cross despite the approach of the Sabbath because the Sanhedrin had forbidden that he receive this act of mercy (p. 122), which would have put him out of his misery. This is not put forth as some new revelation or reconstruction; they have just forgotten what the text of John 19:31–33 said and did not bother checking. The authors imagine that all three Synoptic gospels mention the ascension, though of course only Luke does. They imagine that Tatian's combination of all four gospels, the *Diatessaron*, was called the *Detesteron*. They attribute spurious quotations to Jesus: "John the Baptist was ... the man who, in Jesus' own words, 'paved the way for my coming' " (p. 124).

When there are no facts to be skewed and misrepresented, Blake and Blezard just make them up. Speaking of Herod Antipas' ultimate exile to Gaul, the authors affirm, "although Herod had been banished from his homeland and stripped of all his Roman offices of state, his position as the titular King of the Jews was still respected enough for him to be allowed to take with him into exile the treasures of the Temple. These included... the remains of the head of John the Baptist" (p. 129).

Not only is this speculation impossibly far-fetched, it passes over the fact that Herod Antipas conspicuously *lacked* the title 'King of the Jews' (he was a mere tetrarch). Consider moreover the absurdity of Herod keeping the head of the Baptist as a souvenir (pp. 129-130) and yet imagining that sightings of Jesus performing miracles were actually resurrection appearances of John the Baptist (Mark 6:14): did he picture the miracle-worker lurching around as a headless, resuscitated corpse, as in the movie *Re-Animator*? Blake and Blezard think Jesus *was* John the Baptist raised from death, but only in the sense that the latter's spirit indwelt the former. But they themselves note the fact that Jesus told the disciples who accompanied him during the Transfiguration to tell no one about it (p. 124), so Herod Antipas cannot have been privy to such an incorporeal understanding of resurrection.

Blake and Blezard follow most of the other books in their genre by positing the final voyage of Mary Magdalene, as Jesus' pregnant wife, to Marseilles. Yes, yes, it's all based on a bunch of fanciful medieval legends the like of which no one would think of crediting unless they were looking pretty hard for evidence, but maybe in this case it's true. Why? "The validity of the legends and the claims for each in the wide range of localities in which they are based is both highly questionable and unverifiable. However, there are some places where the sheer number of claims and connections, coupled with the passion with which they are still held, leads one to think that there may be more to these stories than pure fabrication or desire to outdo neighboring parishes or areas" (p. 133).

All this means is that our two researchers have 'gone native,' becoming swept up in the local superstitions. It is like arguing that Martians actually invaded the earth because so many people heard the Orson Welles "War of the Words" broadcast and believed it was true.

The new wrinkle in this book is the suggestion that Jesus accompanied Mary Magdalene to Gaul. ("They look just like two gurus in drag.") Why are there not even any legends that suggest this? Well, Jesus' need to travel *incognito* was more pressing than Mary's (Crucified twice, shame on me!), so he managed a successful legends blackout. What perfect circularity! We posit a fact for which there is no evidence, and then we explain why there is no evidence, but then we must explain why we are thus left standing in midair. But, alas, even if there *was* a rabbit there, if it has covered up its tracks so perfectly, the rabbit would seem to have won! We no longer have any reason to suppose it was there in the first place.

Finally, when Blake applied to maps of the Languedoc region the three pentagrams abstracted from paintings, plus a star chart of Orion's Belt (seeing that Orion was depicted on one of the canvases), he decided to head, not for Cardou, where Andrews and Schellenberger ended up, but rather some distance away at the hill of Estagnol ('Lamb of the East.' Coincidence?). There, on the hillside, behind screens of obscuring moss, he found what appeared to be two abandoned and empty tombs, natural caves with artificially stone-tiled floors. Blake could not help linking this find with the story of Dagobert I's looting of a local tomb, leaving the bodies, which pious monks then retrieved and took to Rome.

For Blake, the connection was clear: Dagobert had stumbled upon the very resting place of Jesus and Mary Magdalene. The monks, no doubt heirs to local traditions signaling the true importance of the site, must have decided to place the sacred relics past further molestation by sending them to that great repository of all fanciful secrets, the Vatican. Given the earlier hints of a son of Jesus, it is surprising Blake and Blezard do not spin out their theory in the Baigent-Lincoln-Leigh direction pursued by Dan Brown, the dynasty of Jesus and the Merovingians.

Back to the God Head

Richard Laidler's *The Head of God: The Lost Treasure of the Templars* is a variation on the same collection of themes shared by all these books. The Templars discovered some Jesus-related shocker in their Jerusalem excavations that brought to light an ancient Egyptian connection, and which was later reflected symbolically as the Holy Grail. What did they come up with? What was the Grail? And what is Laidler's particular market niche? It was the embalmed, severed head of Jesus.

Like most of these writers, Laidler just has no idea what constitutes historical evidence. Anything anybody ever said sounds good to him. It doesn't matter who said it, how far from the supposed events his 'authorities' lived or wrote, what axe they may have been grinding — if it's in narrative form, it's apparently good enough for him. In Laidler's pages we find implicit trust in all manner of weird claims that the Druids were Jews, that Moses was the same man as Akhenaten the monotheist Pharaoh, that the Irish were Hebrews, that the Benjaminites were Isis cultists, *etc.* He relies upon speculative writers (like Baigent, Lincoln and Leigh, the spurious *Priory Documents*, or Ahmed Osman who thinks the Old Testament Joshua and New Testament Jesus were the same person suffering from a chronological glitch in scripture).

Focusing on the fascinating and macabre claim of their persecutors that the disgraced Templar Knights cultivated the worship of a living, oracular severed head called *Baphomet*, Laidler digs up as many literary references to severed heads as he can find, and then he strives mightily to connect the dots. Well, let's see now... some ancient peoples north of Lebanon appear to have collected, hence worshipped, human skulls, so it might be possible that Joseph and his family brought this custom into Egypt. Visions of disembodied noggins figure in the lore of modern Rosicrucians (the religion Woody Allen disdained for advertising in *Popular Mechanics*, and for good reason), and since today's Rosicrucians claim (vacuously, one might add) that Akhenaten was one of their founders, then this makes it likely that Akhenaten inherited and practiced this head-cult. And since he was Moses, we can trace it through the history of Israel. Well, we can't *really* trace it, because it was always part of secret lore not shared with most people, which is why the evidence is so scarce and so equivocal — hints, really. You get the picture.

One of the most hilarious blunders in this terrible book is Laidler's bizarre reading of Mark 6:14–29. He misreads the black and white as if verses 17–29, plainly an explanatory flashback (hence the perfect tense: "Herod had sent and seized John..."), follow verses 14–16 in temporal order. The result is that Salome dances for Herod Antipas long after the martyrdom of John. When she asks for the head of the Baptizer, it was already a severed relic from which Herod had sought oracles! Salome just asks her stepfather to give it to her. Maybe thereafter she used it for a hat rack. Who knows? But in any case, Laidler has ignored verse 27b: "He went and beheaded him in the prison."

But back to Jesus' noggin. Whether it would stand scrutiny or not must be left to an Arthurian specialist, but one observation of Laidler's on the Grail sagas is quite clever. He notes that in the Welsh *Peredur*, the Grail Knight beholds a platter with a bloody head, as if prepared for dinner, while in Chrétien de Troyes' version what the Grail contains, in the analogous scene, is a communion wafer. Laidler not unreasonably posits that the *Peredur* retains the earlier tradition, of the head, but that Chrétien's redactional change of the head into a communion wafer, signifying the body of Christ, implies whose the head originally must have been! On one hand, Laidler is possessed of a sharp eye; on the other hand, the *Peredur* itself identifies the head as having belonged to the hero's cousin, whose death he must avenge. Laidler could suggest that this identification itself was an attempt to cover up the truth of the hypothetical underlying tradition. But that's just the trouble. It's *all* hypothetical. An interpretation like his only becomes credible once one's theory already has a pretty solid body of argument and/or documentation under its belt. But here it just amounts to a meatball on top of a pile of speculative spaghetti.

What Laidler is doing in this book is best understood as a parallel to Margaret Murray's books *The Witch Cult in Western Europe* (1921) and *The God of the Witches* (1931). Miss Murray examined the forced confessions of the medieval witches, extorted from them by Inquisitors, and she found she could not simply dismiss them as false. That is, she saw a consistent pattern that suggested to her that, though the accusations were incorrect, this was because of Christian misinterpretation (or reinterpretation) of what the witches actually had believed. She saw a key whereby one might unlock the distinctive beliefs of the witches, separate them from the slanderous distortions. Where the witches had been forced to confess having had sexual intercourse with Satan, perhaps the truth was that these women had belonged to a pre-Christian paganism which venerated both a god and goddess of nature. Perhaps this god sported horns, like the Greek Pan, whose depiction had been borrowed to clothe the Christian Satan. Murray found it plausible that the witches had worshipped a horned pagan divinity, which, to Christians, *ipso facto* amounted to Satan.

And the sex? It would not be surprising if there was ritual sex intended as imitative magic, just like the sacred prostitutes of ancient Canaan, aimed at fertilizing the farmlands. Murray just could not believe the Inquisitors had dreamed the whole thing up. She figured there had to be *something* there for them to distort. Murray's reconstruction of this pre-Christian religion of the Goddess and the Horned God did not convince many anthropologists or historians in her day or ours. But her work has been rediscovered by the Wicca movement, which takes it as gospel truth and finds in it an ancient charter and a (counterfeit) continuity for their own neo-pagan beliefs.

Laidler, along with Picknett and Prince (*The Templar Revelation*), and several others are doing the same thing, their ultimate goal being to provide (fabricate) an ancient pedigree for the Masonic Lodge by linking it to the Templars, the Gnostics, and what-all. And, like Murray, Laidler does this by taking a second look at the confessions wrung from the persecuted Templars by their Inquisitors. Whence the strange business of worshipping heads if there were not something to it? Wouldn't it have been easier just to accuse the Templars of being sodomites (which they also did) and Satanists? And Laidler has a point. The problem is that we are simply no longer in any position to know what was going on, and his attempt to fill in the gap can be regarded as nothing more than a wild guess.

Conclusion

A review of these books which posit connections between the half-mythical Knights Templar and the half-mythical Jesus shows that their authors tend to combine them in such a fashion as to produce something that partakes of both myth-halves but sadly little fact. The writers take advantage of the fact that, the deeper into the New Testament and Christian Origins scholarship probes, the less we can know for certain. But for the once-comfortable certainties of pre-critical faith our authors have substituted elaborate tissues of vain speculation. Like the eighteenth-century Rationalists, they tend to eliminate supernaturalism only to replace it with the most tenuous card-houses of fantastic hunches and guesswork. The results seem compelling to their authors only because of a kind of parental pride. Those sad individuals flummoxed by these books' vain pretense of scholarly acumen are in effect enjoying these pieces of fiction as the novels that they really are.

The Talmud of Jmmanuel

Delving with the Devil

This awful book fully merits the epithets used by Edgar J. Goodspeed (in his great book *Famous Biblical Hoaxes*) for another modern apocryphon, *The Archko Volume*, namely "disgusting and ridiculous." Indeed, it takes the prize. There is the usual pack of lies about an underlying Aramaic document being discovered in 1963, imbedded, somehow, in resin since the first century when Jesus' loyal disciple, a guy named Judas Iscariot, wrote it down. Seems that an improbably named Greek Orthodox priest bearing the moniker *Isa* (= Jesus!) *Rashid* discovered Jesus' burial cave, and Eduard Albert 'Billy' Meier spelunked further, finding the present gospel. What we are reading represents, we are told with forked tongue in cheek, only the first quarter of the very long text, the rest being destroyed, or so Father Rashid figured, by Israeli troops who were violently pursuing him. (You will recognize the implicit element of uncertainty as a rat-hole through which Billy Meier may eventually squeeze the rest of the text if this portion sells well enough. At least if he can come up with that much baloney.)

Meier anticipates that the orthodox and the obscurantists will alike denounce his discovery as a hoax (p. *xv*). Well, let me tell you, you don't have to be particularly orthodox to denounce this thing as what we theologians like to call *Bullgeschichte*.

What does the title mean? *Talmud* is just a Hebrew word referring to a deposit of learning. We are more familiar with its use referring to the massive collection of Rabbinical law, lore, and commentary, the *Talmud of Jerusalem* and the *Talmud of Babylon*. So here it just denotes 'the teaching of Jmmanuel.' Of *whom*? Have you ever noticed something strange in Matthew's nativity story in which Matthew says Isaiah 7:14 was fulfilled by the advent of baby Jesus, and that though Isaiah says the child will be called *Emmanuel*, in Matthew's story Jesus is called, well, *Jesus*? That is pretty odd. I've never heard a good explanation. But Meier tries to harmonize the two names, producing the weird hybrid *Jmmanuel*. (Why do I keep thinking of pancakes?)

Meier says 'Jmmanuel' means 'man of godly wisdom,' but any Bible reader knows it does not. It means 'God with us.' At least *Emmanuel* does, but then I guess if you're making up a name, you can say it means whatever the hell you want. (For the record, Epiphanius of Salamis did the same thing back in the fourth century, pretending that one spells *Essenes* with a *J*, too: 'Jessenes,' so he could connect Jesus with them.)

Another improbability about the frame story: how, pray tell, did the mythical Father Rashid "discover" the cave-tomb of Jesus, since the book tells us Jesus was buried in the now-notorious tomb in Srinagar, Kashmir? This old structure has been promoted since the nineteenth century as Jesus' tomb by the Ahmadiyya sect of Islam. Orthodox Muslims believe Jesus was raptured to heaven before the crucifixion, with someone else put to death in Jesus' place. But the Ahmadiyya believe he was crucified and survived, then left the Holy Land to preach for decades longer, eventually winding up in Kashmir, where he died at a ripe, old age (110 or 120, Jmmanuel says). This site, though fraudulent, is well known. What was there for Rashid to discover?

And did I really say the book is supposed to be the work of Judas Iscariot? The disciple who betrayed Jesus? No, dear reader, as we soon find out, it was not Judas *Iscariot* who turned Jesus over to the G-men, but rather the similarly named *Juda Ihariot*! You see, it's pretty easy to mix up a couple of guys with names that close. This is just unintentionally hilarious!

Jesus as Ventriloquist Dummy

The Talmud of Jmmanuel is structurally just the same as other long-winded gospels like *The Aquarian Gospel*. It builds on a harmony of the four canonical gospels, picking and choosing favorite episodes and elements from them, then adding new bits of its own. The result is a glaring unevenness in quality. Grant me a seeming digression.

Scholars have noted a pattern in ancient apocalypses, in which some ancient worthy is depicted as predicting the history of his people from ancient times down to the end of the age. The 'predictions' match up with known historical events very well indeed till right near the end, at which point the train leaps from the tracks and careens wildly into the ditch. What happened? Well, of course, the actual author of the document lived at a historical position very close to the end-time his book anticipates. The preceding 'prophecy' matches up because the author knows it as history. He is only pretending to be the ancient character whose name he borrows (Daniel, Enoch, Baruch, whomever). So he has perfect 20-20 hindsight, but when he starts venturing real predictions, it is clear blue sky, and he plummets like Icarus.

Well, it's the same with these gospels: as long as they stay close to their source material, they sound pretty authentic, even if their authors do a bit of embellishing. But as soon as they kick away the training wheels, as soon as they stop using the tracing paper, the result is awful. And it is in the new material, obviously, that we have to look to find the main reason for writing the new gospel. What is the new teaching that this gospel wants to ascribe to its Jesus?

First, I think it is pathetic that people resort to such a gimmick. It plainly means the writer knows his ideas would carry no particular conviction if set forth under his own, utterly insignificant name, so maybe hanging them on Jesus will lend the ideas a degree of gravity they would otherwise lack. But he fails to see that the only reason we take seriously the words attributed to Jesus in the traditional Gospels is that they carry their own weight. By far the most of it has the ring of truth to it, whoever said it. In fact, that's how some of it came to be in the gospel in the first place! Someone heard some good saying and said, "Wow! That's good stuff! Worthy of Jesus!" as when we say, "It ain't in the Bible but it ought to be!" Believe me, no one is going to find himself saying that of the soporific gibberish (and worse) in this book, which 'Billy' dares to equate with the *real, true, original* teaching of Jesus before the fiendish churchmen, beginning with the nefarious fisherman himself, distorted the living daylights out of it.

The teaching here is warmed-over Theosophy, but very poorly expressed. We learn that there is a "god" who rules the earth but is essentially a long-lived mortal much like ourselves (16:55–56; 28:59). Above him is the 'supreme' entity, called "Creation"(16:52) which sounds something like unchanging Brahman (18:44). But then we are told that it, too, is incomplete and changing (18:43; 21:28) and defers to a still superior being (25:56). It is one without division (21:27), and yet it possesses parts (34:39). But while Billy/Jmmanuel is calling it infinite, he says we are part of it, so that what is true of it is *ipso facto* true of us, too. And if we tap into that fact by enlightened knowledge, we can do pretty much anything (16:44).

That is a prime case of the Division Fallacy in logic: what is true of an entity as a whole is not necessary true in the same way of its parts. I may understand the Theory of General Relativity, but it does not follow from this that my little finger understands Relativity.

Anyway, when Peter succeeded momentarily in walking on water it was because he had a fleeting grasp of this 'knowledge' and was able to suspend/defy gravity. But what sort of knowledge is it that refuses to reckon with elementary physics? It is substituting fantasy and wishful thinking for knowledge. This is all the more ironic since Jmmanuel is always talking about the "laws" of the Creation, which, I guess, do not happen to include gravity!

So what are we supposed to be doing about it? Well, it is our mission to realize our potential by efforts at self-perfection over the course of many lifetimes. Even Creation (a Him? Her? It?) experiences a kind of reincarnation, a series of eons-long periods of dormancy alternating with equal periods of life and activity (34:27–34), all the coin of Theosophy, borrowed from Hinduism. As Pogo once said about nuclear energy, "It ain't so new, and it ain't so clear."

The Ridiculous

I've borrowed Goodspeed's put-down of another modern gospel, calling this one "disgusting and ridiculous." Let's look first at the ridiculous part, because we may be quite out of patience or of any residual sympathy if we look at the disgusting aspect first. What's most ridiculous about *The Talmud of Jmmanuel* is its espousal of Flying Saucer religion. To get things straight here: I consider it plausible that extra-terrestrials have visited the earth. But the possibility, even the plausibility, of it does not entitle us forthwith to believe it is true. There does not yet appear to be compelling evidence for contact with Flying Saucers. But there sure is plenty of evidence that people who claim to be in regular contact with space men are a bunch of delusional nuts. Nor is it their belief in extra-terrestrial visitors what makes them nuts. No, no, there's way more than that. Some of these people make wild and extravagant claims that can only proceed from their imagination, at least because they sound like very bad science fiction. And all of this stuff does, from the Black Muslim 'Mother Plane' orbiting the earth with Elijah Muhammad in the captain's chair (so help me, I wish I were making this up), to the Raelian belief that aliens mutated apes to produce the first humans, to Heaven's Gate lemmings believing a spaceship hidden in a comet's tail was telling them to castrate themselves, to the Aetherius Society, to Unaria, *etc.*

Well, Billy Meier belongs in the same ranks. That's for damn sure. Nursing classic delusions of grandeur, including the persecution complex, Billy predicts his own eventual assassination: "the editor is even more endangered because he is the contact man for extraterrestrial intelligences and very highly developed spiritual entities on exalted planes who transmit to him true spiritual teachings that he disseminates without modification, thereby exposing the lies of the cult religions, which will lead to their slow but certain eradication" (p. *xix*). The "cult religions" are the major faiths. If this isn't classic Freudian projection, I don't know what is. Personally, I don't think the Islamo-fascist mullahs are going to be wasting a *fatwah* on this guy any time soon, much less the Catholic Church.

Not surprisingly, *The Talmud of Jmmanuel* embodies UFO theology. Its Jesus (Jmmanuel) is the result of Mary's impregnation by the angel Gabriel who is an alien arriving in a space ship for their date. Jesus is eventually taken aboard the same craft, much like Brian of Nazareth in the Monty Python movie. When he 'ascends' he is stepping aboard the spacecraft, though only for a couple of stops down the line, getting off in Damascus. Why bother with Spielbergianism? Simply because Billy wants to combine the usual props of UFO-Jesus-ism (beam-up ascension) with the Asian travels/Srinagar tomb scenario. He likes 'em both.

All science fiction reinterpretation of Christianity, the stock in trade of Flying Saucer religions, entails a dusting off of old eighteenth-century Rationalism: what looked like miracles to the ancients must have been advanced technology, at least as we, their far-superior pseudo-intellectual descendents, imagine it. Such science fiction, too, becomes dated and laughable after a while. Thus, UFO theology starts looking even more ridiculous than the supernaturalism it hopes to replace. In this case, the resurrection of Jesus is treated with a technique borrowed from old-time Rationalism rather than its twentieth-century sci-fi counterpart, though. Jesus does not die on the cross, but is taken down in a coma, then placed in Joseph of Arimathea's tomb, where he is given medical care and recovers. Usually the eighteenth-century Rationalists had Joseph call upon the Essenes to nurse Jesus back to health, but for some reason they are not good enough this time around. The 'risen' Jesus actually meets some Essenes later in the story, and they invite him to join their group, but he refuses. (Why does Billy not allow them a more positive role? You'll see in the next section: the trouble is that they're *Jews*.)

Joseph even somehow contacts Jesus' colleagues in India and summons them to come and treat him! Would there really have been time for this? I guess Gabriel could have picked them up in his space ship and rushed them into the OR, but then we'd have to wonder why the aliens didn't just revivify Jmmanuel like Gort did Klaatu in *The Day the Earth Stood Still*. Well, anyway, Joseph gets away with the scheme, despite Jewish and Roman guards at the tomb because he had taken the precaution of designing his tomb with a hidden back entrance! Why? How could he have known this day would come? It's all just so stupid.

Plus, *The Talmud of Jmmanuel* has its own theory to offer for the Shroud of Turin. It is a shroud on which Joseph of Arimathea had a likeness of Jesus' bloody body painted! But this nonsense clashes with the Carbon 14 dating test of the Shroud just as much as the Catholic belief in its genuineness: it goes back no earlier than the fourteenth century.

By the way, the book includes a pen sketch of Jmmanuel that is supposed to be based on an ancient portrait rendered by "Semjase, the pilot of a beamship, whose home planet, Erra in the Pleiades, is about 500 light years from our solar system" (p. *viii*). Actually, it appears to be based on an ancient Chinese Manichean painting of Jesus, an artist's conception. *Semjase* is the name of the leader of the fallen angels in the apocryphal *Book of Jubilees*.

The Disgusting

The Talmud of Jmmanuel is blood-curdlingly anti-Semitic. Its appropriation of the familiar Jewish title *Talmud* is offensive, but that is the least of it. Here are a few choice passages:

> Do not go into the streets of Israel, and do not go to the scribes and Pharisees, but go to the cities of the Samaritans and to the ignorant in all parts of the world. Go to the unenlightened, the idol worshippers and the ignorant after I have left you, because they do not belong to the house of Israel, which will bring death and bloodshed into the world. (10:5–6)

> Truly, I say to you: the nation of Israel was never one distinct people and has at all times lived with murder, robbery and fire. They have acquired this land through ruse and murder in abominable, predatory wars, slaughtering their best friends like wild animals. May the nation of Israel be cursed until the end of the world and never find its peace. (10:26--27)

> Therefore, beware of Israel, because it is like an abscess. (10:38)

> For the people of Israel are unfaithful to the laws of Creation and are accursed and will never find peace. Their blood will be shed, because they constantly commit outrages against the laws of Creation. They presume themselves above all the human races as a chosen nation and thus as a separate race. What an evil error and what evil presumption, for inasmuch

as Israel never was a nation or a race, so it was never a chosen race. Unfaithful to the laws of Creation, Israel is a mass of people with an inglorious past, characterized by murder and arson. (15:22–26)

You will be outcast among the human races, and then you will alternately lose your occupied land, regain it and lose it again until the distant future. Truly, I say to you: your existence will be continual struggle and war, and so the human races will strike you with their hostile thinking and enmity. You will find neither rest nor peace in the country stolen by your ancestors by means of falsehood and deceit, because you will be haunted by your inherited burden of murder with which your forefathers killed the ancient inhabitants of this continent and deprived them of life and property. (24:45–47)

...just like the Israelites who plundered this land and have dominated and oppressed the legitimate owners of the land. (27:12b)

I am the true prophet of all human races on earth: but in all truth I am not the prophet of those confused Israelites who call themselves sons and daughters of Zion. (30:8b)

And the time will come in five times 100 years when you will have to atone for this, when the legitimate owners of the land enslaved by you will begin to rise against you into the distant future. A new man will rise up in this land as a prophet and will rightfully condemn and persecute you and you will have to pay with your blood. [...] Even though, according to your claim, he will be a false prophet and you will revile him, he will nevertheless be a true prophet, and he will have great power, and he will have your race persecuted throughout all time in the future. His name will be Mohammed, and his name will bring horror, misery and death to your kind, which you deserve. Truly, truly, I say to you: His name will be written for you with blood, and his hatred against your kind will be endless. (30:10–11, 13–15)

What is this? Propaganda for Hamas? Okay, it's not as bad as the abhorred *Theozoologie* of the mad monk Jörg Lanz von Liebenfels [1874–1954], but it's still pretty revolting if you ask me. It appears to be Jew-hating, pro-Palestinian propaganda. What we have here is like the Gentile Jesus of the Third Reich theologians.

Random Observations

It seems anticlimactic to scrutinize this miserable travesty further. But it may be worth it after all, in case anything else is needful to discourage any adolescents who may still be interested in it. There are historical errors that would just not be possible in a writing from someone who lived in the period. Jesus is said to be born in the reign of Herod *Antipas* (2:1). Actually it was Herod the Great. *Talmud Jmmanuel* 16:9 repeats Mark's mistake (Mark 6:17), confusing Herod Antipas' brothers Philip and Herod. (That was an easy mistake to make, even for a contemporary, as Herod Antipas actually had brothers named Herod Philip and just plain Philip). Obviously *Jmmanuel* is dependent on the canon, hence by no means an ancient document.

Humble fellow that he is, Billy the Evangelist has Jesus predict him: "Not until two thousand years will an insignificant man come who will recognize my teaching as truth and spread it with great courage" (14:18). See also 15:75–81. But Jesus seems to underestimate just how insignificant the man will prove to be.

Jesus' audience in the Nazareth synagogue asks, "Is he not the son of the carpenter, Joseph, whose wife became pregnant by the son of a guardian angel?" "From where does he get all this wisdom and the power for his mighty works?" (15:18, 72). Oh, I don't know... could it have anything to do with his being the son of an angel?!

"A prophet is never esteemed less than in his own country and in his own house, which will prove true for all the future, as long as humanity has little knowledge and is enslaved by the false teachings of the scribes and the distorters of true scripture" (15:74). This nonsensical inflation of Mark 6:4 sounds like the rambling, bogus Ezekiel quote Samuel L. Jackson repeats again and again in *Pulp Fiction*!

We get a bit of invented soap opera in chapter 16, where it develops that Salome, dancing daughter of Herodias, was in love with the imprisoned John the Baptist and wistfully smooched his severed head.

Corrections of Canonical Gospel Teachings

The New Testament gospels set the ethical bar pretty high. From any standpoint, that's a good thing: set them lower and you are too easy on yourself. If your reach not only does not exceed your grasp, but does not even extend that far, you are just a lazy slob. But *The Talmud of Jmmanuel* doesn't mind taking Christian morality down a peg.

"Give to them who ask of you, if they make their requests in honesty, and turn away from them who want to borrow from you in a deceitful way" (5:42). In accord with the Rabbis, Jesus seems uncritical in his counsel to give to any beggar. The Rabbis were fully aware that there were cheats. In one of their tales, a man passes a hovel of beggars and overhears them deliberating on whether to feast that night on gold or silver dishes! But the sages said that didn't matter: you could never be sure if someone's professed need were real. It was up to you to be generous, period. Any other strategy would freeze out the genuine poor for the sake of stopping the cheats. But Jmmanuel seems to think you can tell the sincere sheep from the grifter goats. Good luck.

Everybody recognizes that, if it comes right down to it, it is noble to give your life for your country and what it stands for. Religious martyrdom is the same, as long as one does not seek it out as some kind of fanatic. In the last analysis, you have to preserve your integrity at whatever price. But not according to this gospel: "Flee from the unbelieving, because you should not lose your life for the sake of truth and knowledge. No law requires that of you, nor is there one that admits to such recklessness" (10:21).

"No Sabbath is holy and no law dictates that on the Sabbath no work may be done" (13:10) — or at least no law that an anti-Semite would take seriously, I guess.

"You are Peter, and I cannot build my teachings on your rock... I cannot give you the key of the spiritual kingdom, otherwise you would open false locks [=?] and wrong portals with it" (18:23–24). Take *that*, Papists!

Jmmanuel saith: "Do not suppose that prayer is necessary, because you will also receive without prayer if your spirit is trained through wisdom" (21:15). And yet Jmmanuel prescribes a prayer:

> My spirit, you are omnipotent.
> Your name be holy.
> Let your kingdom incarnate itself in me.
> Let your power unfold itself within me, on Earth and in the heavens.
> Give me today my daily bread, so that I may recognize my guilt and the truth.
> And lead me not into temptation and confusion, but deliver me from error.
> For yours is the kingdom within me and the power and the knowledge forever. Amen (6:12–18)

But what's the difference, I guess, since you'd be praying to your own self?

At first, one might be tempted to think this *Talmud of Jmmanuel* is a progressive, with-it kind of gospel for the New Age: "Do away with the enforcement of the old law that woman should be subject to man, since she is a person like a man, with equal rights and obligations" (12:25). But, Liberals, you may want to shield your eyes from this one. It looks like grief for Gays, though leniency for Lesbians: "And if two men bed down with each other, they should also be punished, because the fallible are unworthy of life and its laws and behave heretically; thus they should be castrated, expelled and banished before the people. If, however, two women bed down with one another, they should not be punished, because they do not violate life and its laws, since they are not inseminating, but are bearing" (12:6–7). How's that again?

*****

The Talmud of Jmmanuel, alas, seems to have plenty of fans. It deserves none. But then, on the other hand, maybe people get the gospel they deserve. Maybe there are some devout UFO skinheads who are ecumenical haters of Jews, Christians, and Muslims. This gospel is just right for them. But even so, a visit to a psychiatrist might be better.

Jonathan Z. Smith's
Drudgery Divine
On The Comparison Of
Early Christianities
And the Religions of Late Antiquity
(University of Chicago Press, 1990)

The Hands are the Hands of Jacob

George Tyrrell [1861–1909] said that the nineteenth-century questers after the historical Jesus were seeing their own visages reflected at the bottom of a deep well and mistaking it for the face of Jesus. Of course, they are still doing it, and Jesus hops aboard every conceivable politico-theological bandwagon. He is always a first-century 'precursor' of something, really a twentieth-century proof-text for something. Jesus the first-century Whitehead, the first-century E. F. Schumacher, the first-century feminist, the first-century Girardian — if only one reads the texts with the proper gematria. And what is good for Jesus is good for the early church as well. In these 1988 Louis H. Jordan Lectures, Jonathan Z. Smith demonstrates the surprising extent to which much that has passed for scientific study of early Christianity is more plausibly to be interpreted as theological apologetics.

It is, in brief, Smith's contention that the history of the work done by scholars in one particular corner of the vineyard, the relation of emergent Christianity to the Hellenistic Mystery Religions, has often functioned as a proxy-war between denomi-national super-powers reluctant to step into open combat. He argues that the earliest attention paid to the similarities between Christian myth and ritual and those of the Mysteries was that paid by Protestants who wanted to paint Roman Catholicism as an admixture of authentic proto-Protestant Pauline Christianity with the magic sacramentalism of heathenism. Likewise, Rationalists and Unitarians pressed the syncretistic process further back, making Paul the corrupter of the earlier, simpler, Jeffersonian faith of the Messiah Jesus. Adolf von Harnack [1851–1930] reflected this tradition when he made Nicene-Chalcedonian Christianity a bloodless Hellenization of a simple Galilean gospel.

Just as E. P. Sanders and others have recently suggested with some force that our reading of the Pauline writings has been distorted by the lens of Reformation-era polemics, Smith sees the study of Christianity and the Hellenistic religions as thinly veiled apologetics. Even if we no longer share this covert agenda, we are still fighting the same battle as long as we allow the game to be played by the same rules set down by the earlier polemicists. Or by the later ones, for, as some of us have long suspected and Smith demonstrates, the more recent apologetic *Tendenz* is still trying mightily to distance apostolic Christianity from any touch of the unclean Mystery Cults (or Gnosticism).

For this purpose Judaism is used as both buffer and whipping boy. This double, or as Smith says, duplicitous, use of Judaism as a foil has two moments. First one seizes upon any possible Jewish parallel with this or that feature of New Testament thought or myth that Rudolf Bultmann [1884–1976] or Richard Reitzenstein [1861–1931] had tagged a Hellenistic borrowing. Such a Jewish precedent is judged *ipso facto* preferable to any Hellenistic one. Albert Schweitzer [1875–1965] adopted this course already in *Paul and His Interpreters*, patching together from the Pseudepigrapha a vague but thoroughly Jewish apocalyptic "mysticism of the Apostle Paul" just so he wouldn't have to yield the Pauline corpus up to the radical surgery of Pierson, Naber, and W. C. van Manen [professor at Leiden 1885–1903]. These "Dutch Radicals" saw a Mystery Religion soteriology – *i.e.*, a scheme for the salvation of humanity – in the epistles that could ill be squared with the ostensible Jewishness of the apostle. The Hellenistic passages had, they judged, to be excised as secondary interpolations.

W. D. Davies' *Paul and Rabbinic Judaism*, hailed as a monument of scholarship, might better be described as a mountain that labored and brought forth a mouse (a mouse easily trapped by Hyam Maccoby in his recent *Paul and Hellenism*). Precious little in the Pauline letters emerges looking very rabbinic. The negligible results of the book demonstrate that the Judaizing path is a scholarly dead end, though its author and many readers did not think so. One may speculate that the acclaim given this work as well as that by Davies' disciple David Daube (a plastered cistern that lost not a drop), in his *The New Testament and Rabbinic Judaism,* stems from the imagined utility of both books for buttressing the bulwark against the incursions of parallels from the Mystery Religions.

The Dead Sea Scrolls were and still are proof-texted gleefully by scholars as a grand excuse to dismiss all the striking parallels drawn by Bultmann between the Gospel of John and various Gnostic and Mandaean sources, though it is hard to see how the minimal terminological agreements between John and the Scrolls can out-weigh the sheer number of striking parallels with the Mandaica — the sacred writings and traditions of the Mandaean followers of John the Baptist.

In all of this the reasoning seems to be that even a vague Jewish parallel is automatically to be preferred over even a close Gnostic or Mystery Religion parallel as the source of a New Testament doctrine or mytheme. And the reason for this bias can only be the traditional theological desire to have the New Testament grow out of the Old as by a process of progressive revelation. Let us widen the scope of Jewish origin to include Rabbinism, Qumran, and the Pseudepigrapha if we must, but God forbid we should have to admit that Christianity had non-Jewish roots as well as Jewish!

Semitic Scapegoat

The second moment in the use of Judaism that Smith describes is the deprecation of Judaism as a sow's ear from which the silk purse of Christianity was cut. Everywhere we meet with invidious comparisons leaving Judaism like Moses lonely on Mount Pisgah looking wistfully at the fertile plains of a Promised Land it was destined not to enter, a religion blindly studying the scriptures in which it thinks to have eternal life, but too near-sighted to behold the true Christian gospel.

I see here a covert use of what I call "dissimilarity apologetics," borrowing the term from Norman Perrin's famous *criterion of dissimilarity*. The idea is that Christianity will seem more truly to be a divine revelation the more we can isolate it from either Judaism or the Hellenistic world. First we employ Judaism to exorcise suggestions of Hellenistic influence, then we turn on Judaism and insist on its inferiority and utter inability to have produced the imagined distinctiveness of the revealed gospel. Judaism serves to minimize Christian similarities with the Mystery Religions, and once it has thus served its purpose, the apologist minimizes the similarities between Judaism and Christianity.

Yet for all his acuity in perceiving this agenda, Smith himself almost seems to be doing his best to seal off Christian origins from the possibility of syncretism. It is apparent that he so wishes to avoid the error of superimposing stereotypes of Catholicism onto the evidence of the Mystery Religions that he is unwilling to see any significant similarities between them and Christianity. And thus I fear he may be selling short some genuine and instructive parallels between them.

It is wise to seek to explain any religion, whether ancient Christianity or Mithraism or the Attis religion, on its own terms and not simply as a function of another religion it may have borrowed from; but in the case of significant similarities it is not unreasonable to suggest borrowing. Is it problematic to suggest, for instance, that Mithraism borrowed the representation of Mithras wearing the Phrygian cap, or accompanied by a divine consort, from the Attis cult; or that the Attis cult borrowed the Taurobolium (the ritual baptism in bull's blood) from Mithraism? Certainly not. Why then should one avoid the possible conclusion that Christianity borrowed from its competitors as well? One fears that Smith, having rejected the polemics of an earlier generation, fears too much being found guilty of being 'ecumenically incorrect.'

I Come Too Soon!

Here and elsewhere Smith declares the famous 'dying and rising god' mytheme a modern myth — one concocted by scholars, not an ancient one. If there were no such myth it would obviously be vain to claim that Christians had borrowed it for their own mythos. He seems to admit that Attis was eventually regarded as a resurrected deity, though he will not grant that Attis was thus pictured in the first century. It is certainly true that Attis was not always and everywhere regarded as a risen savior. Many variants have him die and remain dead, or simply survive his wounds. And much of the clear evidence of a cult of a resurrected Attis comes from the fourth century (*e.g.*, from Firmicus Maternus).

But it seems to me that here, as well as in the case of Osiris and Tammuz/Dumuzi, Smith is trying too hard to prevent these gods from rising. He dismisses Maarten J. Vermaseren's citation of BCE iconographic representations of a dancing Attis (his characteristic resurrection posture in later iconography) as "unpersuasive" (why?), but in doing so gives little idea of the breadth of Vermaseren's refutation of the work of P. Lambrechts (Vermaseren: *Cybele and Attis, the Myth and the Cult*, Thames & Hudson, 1977, pp. 119-124) on whose theories Smith seems dependant. (Not to mention that Lambrechts himself is a Roman Catholic apologist. Has Smith really transcended the old proxy warfare? Or has he just switched sides?) Hyam Maccoby's criticisms of Smith at this point deserve attention, too (*Paul and Hellenism*. SCM Press and Trinity Press, 1991, pp. 69–72).

Smith seems to be taking up the apologetical arguments of Bruce Metzger (recently deceased emeritus professor at Princeton Theological Seminary) and Edwin Yamauchi (retired professor of history at Miami University of Ohio) to the effect that the Mysteries borrowed the death and resurrection motif from Christians, surely an improbable notion — as Reitzenstein pointed out long ago. Which direction of borrowing is more likely when one religion is newer, and converts from the older faith are streaming into it bringing cherished elements of their familiar creeds with them?

Smith notes that it is *Christian writers* who make the death and resurrection parallels between their own faith and the Mysteries clearest, and thus he theorizes that Christians may have been projecting the categories of their own faith onto their rivals.' But this is just the opposite of what we might expect of embarrassed Christian apologists who already had to deflect the charge that Christian mythemes were copies of pagan ones (*e.g.*, that the supposed virgin birth of Jesus was nothing but a poor copy of that of Theseus). Why invite such criticism by suggesting just such parallels where pagans themselves had not previously seen them?

It is obvious that Christian writers would have special reasons for accentuating the aspects of rival religions that most closely paralleled their own. Here was where they had some explaining to do. If we had extant copies of Mystery Religionists' polemical writings against Christianity (a Mithras- or Isis-worshipping Celsus, so to speak) we might have more pagan testimony about the parallels; but, given the tastes of early Christian censors, that is just the kind of thing we do *not* have. We only have as much of Celsus (the second-century Greek philosopher) and Porphyry (the third-century Neoplatonist philosopher) as we do because these were preserved as quotations in the books of Christian apologists.

Smith seems to me to have contracted a certain contagious squeamishness now making the rounds among scholars. Apparently embarrassed by the bold synthetic visions of Reitzenstein, Bultmann, and others, contemporary scholars are beginning to practice a kind of theoretic asceticism, daring to move nary an inch beyond the strictest interpretation of the evidence. Such modesty leads to a mute minimalism. For instance we may compare the marks of the Mystery Religions listed in S. Angus' *The Mystery-Religions* (1928) with the spare and generic taxonomy of Helmut Koester in his *History, Culture, and Religion of the Hellenistic Age* (1995). For Angus the Mystery Religions offered redemption and purification from sin through sacramental identification of the initiate with the savior deity, elite gnosis of the gods, cosmological/astrological lore, the promise of rebirth and immortality, and participation in a syncretistic, Hellenistic pantheism or henotheism. Little of this survives in Koester, for whom Mystery Religions were marked by congregational polity, ritual initiation, regular participation in the sacraments, moral or ascetical requirements, mutual aid among members, obedience to the leader, and certain secret traditions. Is that all? What would exclude the Southern Baptists or the Knights of Columbus?

One senses here a certain fastidious *Angst*, a hesitancy to make any but the most innocuous generalizations about the Mystery Religions lest one be accused of painting with too broad a stroke, as some accuse Reitzenstein of doing. Was there really so little of substance that these exotic faiths shared in common? Koester has fashioned a lowest common denominator that obscures rather than reveals the distinctiveness of the Mystery Religions because he will not dare to venture an ideal type (as Angus and Reitzenstein did). As Bryan Wilson has pointed out, an ideal type is not some box into which the phenomenon must be neatly dropped. If it were, then one might be justified in either whittling away the rough edges of each religion or of making the box big and shapeless enough for all to fit. But an ideal type is a yardstick abstracted from admittedly diverse phenomena which represents a general family resemblance without demanding or implying any absolute or comprehensive conformity. Indeed the very lack of conformity to the type by a particular Mystery Religion would serve as a promising point of departure for understanding its special uniqueness.

Idol Types

In the same way, Smith seems unwilling to admit the viability of an ideal type of the dying-and-rising god mytheme. If the various myths of Osiris, Attis, Adonis, *et al.* do not all conform to type exactly, then they are not sufficiently alike to fit into the same box, so let's throw out the box. Without *everything* in common, he sees *nothing* in common.

Here he seems to me to approach the apologetical strategy of, *e.g.*, Raymond E. Brown in *The Virginal Conception and Bodily Resurrection of Jesus* (1972), where Brown dismisses the truckload of historical-anthropological, *religionsgeschichtliche* parallels to the miraculous birth of Jesus. This one is not strictly speaking a virgin birth, since a god fathered the divine child on a married woman. That one involved physical intercourse with the deity, not the overshadowing of the Holy Spirit. But, we have to ask, how close does a parallel have to be to count as a parallel? Does the divine mother have to be named Mary? Does the divine child have to be called Jesus? Here is the old 'difference without a distinction' fallacy. And it is strange to see Smith committing it. He becomes an improbable but real ally of the apologists he criticizes.

In his influential *Encyclopedia of Religion* article, "Dying and Rising Gods," Smith aims at prying apart the dying-and-rising god mytheme into disparate *skhandas*: disappearing and reappearing deities on the one hand and dying gods who stay dead on the other. Adonis, he says, is never said to die, but only to undertake a bicoastal lifestyle, splitting the year cohabiting with two romantic rivals, Aphrodite and Persephone. To winter with the latter, Adonis must head south, to Hades. And then, with the flowers, he pops up again in spring, headed for Aphrodite's place.

But what does it mean to say someone has descended to the Netherworld of the dead? Enkidu did not deem it quite so casual a commute 'to hell and back' as Smith apparently does: "he led me away to the palace of Irkalla, the Queen of Darkness, to the house from which none who enters ever returns, down the road from which there is no coming back." One goes there in the embrace of the Grim Reaper. Similarly, the second-century Greek traveler and geographer Pausanias tells of a myth of Theseus: "About the death of Theseus there are many inconsistent legends, for example that he was tied up in the netherworld until Herakles should bring him back to life" (*Guide to Greece*, I:17:4). Thus to abide in the netherworld was to be dead — even if not for good.

Aliyan Baal's supposed death and resurrection does not pass muster for Smith because the saga's text has big holes in it "at the crucial points." Mischievous scholars may like to fill them in with the model of the resurrected god, but Smith calls it an argument from silence. But is it? Even on Smith's own reading the text actually does say that "Baal is reported to have died" after descending to the Netherworld. There he is indeed said to be "as dead." Anat recovers his corpse and buries it. Later El sees in a dream that Baal yet lives. After another gap Baal is depicted in battle.

What's missing here? Smith seems to infer that in the missing lines it would have been discovered that Baal was the victim of a premature burial, that the reports of his demise, like Mark Twain's, were premature. But does he have any particular reason to be sure of this? And even if his guess were to prove correct, it seems evident that a premature burial and a rescue via disinterment is simply a variant version of the death and resurrection, not an alternative to it.

Baal's variant self, Hadad, is even less prone to dying according to Smith, since he is merely said to sink into a bog for seven years. He is only sick, but when he reemerges, languishing nature renews itself. For Smith, "There is no suggestion of death and resurrection." Nor any hint of ritual reenactment of the myth. What about Zechariah 12:11, where we read of inconsolable ritual mourning for Hadad-Rimmon? What are they mourning? Is this evidence too late for Smith? Probably not post-Christian, I'd say. And even if one were to deny that seven years' submersion in a bog is as good as a death, the difference would be, again, only a slight variation in a natural range for a wide-spread mytheme.

We see the same variation among the Nag Hammadi and other Gnostic texts as to whether the Redeemer took on flesh. Some deny he did. Others say he did, but it was a condescension, and the Savior stripped off the flesh-shroud as soon as he got the chance. Some have a fleshly body but an apparent death. Others a real death, but only of the human Jesus, once the Spirit Christ has fled. These are all equivalent versions, simply reflecting different choices from the menu of options. The differences are within a definite range along the paradigmatic axis, but the story is the same along the syntagmic axis.

Osiris, Smith admits, is said, even in very ancient records, to have been dismembered, reassembled by Isis, and rejuvenated (physically: he fathered Horus on Isis). But Smith seizes upon the fact that Osiris reigned henceforth in the realm of the dead. This is not a return to earthly life, hence no resurrection. But then we might as well deny that Jesus is depicted as dying and rising since he reigns henceforth at the right hand of God in Paradise as judge of the dead, like Osiris. The long constancy of the mytheme ought to make us wary of Smith's constant suspicion that later, Christian-era mentions of the resurrections of Adonis, Attis, and the rest may be late innovations. In the one case (that of Osiris) that we can in fact trace, it is no innovation. Why, in effect, assume as Smith does that it was originally absent in the other cases?

Smith describes how scholars early speculated from the fragmentary Tammuz texts that he had been depicted as dying and rising, though the evidence was touch and go. Then more texts turned up, vindicating their theories. Again, we must wonder why Smith is so quick to assume that speculations that make a god dead and risen are automatically suspect. But Smith quibbles even here. Though new material unambiguously makes Ishtar herself to die and rise, Smith passes by this quickly, only to pick the nit that Tammuz is "baaled out" of death only for half a year while someone else takes his place. Death, Smith remarks, is inexorable: you can only get a furlough for half a year. That makes it not a resurrection?

Anxiety of Influence

The general structure of Smith's arguments sounds as if, instead of trying to explode a baseless theory as he claims, he were trying to defend an established one against challenges. The tendency of his argument seems to be "there is not enough circumstantial evidence to sustain a conviction." And then you realize that is in fact just what he is doing: defending an old theory. But which one? Obviously not the one derived from Sir James Frazer's twelve-volume anthropological *magnum opus, The Golden Bough: A Study in Magic and Religion* of 1906–15. Rather, he seems to be defending the old apologetic line that there was no pagan prototype for the Christian resurrection myth (with the implication that it wasn't a myth). And he seems to be doing this, not so much for the sake of traditional Catholicism, but rather to rule out once and for all the old opportunistic use of the Mystery Religions as a polemical tool against Christianity. He wants to make that game impossible, so henceforth the Mystery Religions may be discussed on their own terms, free of theological or anti-theological polemics. But in doing so he bends over backwards so far that he winds up playing the game himself, taking the field as a pinch hitter for the Christian apologists.

There is no reason to give the benefit of the doubt to a reconstruction whose only merit would seem to be its function of overthrowing Frazer's hypothesis and allowing Christian apologists to breathe a little easier. In other words, it is special pleading. And why? Is it necessary to maintain that there were no Christian-pagan parallels or Christian borrowings? That the old polemicists fabricated or hallucinated everything? What is it Smith is trying to prove? I suspect it is part of his scorched-earth campaign against Frazer in *Drudgery Divine* and elsewhere.

Ultimately, in *Drudgery Divine*, Smith does come down, it seems to me, as an advocate of the principle of analogy. He champions the creative work of Burton Mack who, in *A Myth of Innocence,* suggests that the *Sitzen-im-Leben* of the various gospel pericopes may be as disparate as the pericopes themselves. That is, they may have emanated from quite different types of Christ cults or Jesus movements for whom very different aspects of the teaching or stories of Jesus were important. Smith asks if this implied diversity does not parallel the diversity of the Attis myth and cult. There were traditions of an Attis who did not rise as well as those in which he did. Different groups cherished them. Can we be sure that, *e.g.*, the Q community believed in a resurrected Jesus? Perhaps some did and some didn't. It hardly seems that the historical Jesus was important for the communities of the Pauline epistles. Smith suggests that we might be able to learn something about emergent Christianities as well as about the Mystery Religions if we can figure out what social or psychological factors led a group to adopt or to dispense with a resurrected savior. The same factors may prove to have been at work in analogous fashion in the cases of the Attis cult and of the Christian cult, with or without direct borrowing.

All of Smith's books are gems, and we as biblical students should be grateful for the attention given our subject by this wide-ranging anthropologist and historian of religion.

Gregory J. Riley's
Resurrection Reconsidered:
Thomas and John in Controversy
(Fortress, 1995)

John *versus* Thomas

I think those biblical scholars serve us best who cause us, like an unpredictable old Zen master, to view familiar things in a different way. Gregory J. Riley does the trick pretty well in *Resurrection Reconsidered: Thomas and John in Controversy*. He tries to demonstrate the dialogical relationship of the gospels of John and Thomas, reflecting the disputations of the communities supposed to have produced the two documents. The book is a wonderful example of the great utility of those gospels and revelations banned by fourth-century inquisitors and hidden away by desert monks to await rediscovery in 1945 in Chenoboskion, Egypt. The *Gospel of Thomas* is one of the Nag Hammadi texts, the surface of which has scarcely been scratched for all the attention paid them. Riley shows how illuminating the texts anciently excluded from the canon of official scripture can be for the ones included. One begins to see how the very fact of a canonical selection not only conceals the teaching of the one group of texts but distorts our understanding of the other.

Thomas, as Riley reads it, makes John sound suddenly quite different. It is as if we had finally gotten hold of the transcript of the other side of a phone conversation we had heard and long puzzled over. It is a shame that Riley's sharp-eyed book did not attain the public acclaim of Elaine Pagels's 2004 volume *Beyond Belief: The Secret Gospel of Thomas* the central chapter of which seems wholly derivative from Riley's and without acknowledging it.

Riley reminds us of the Fourth Gospel's co-optative use of John the Baptist, to make a rival sect's figurehead seem to espouse the Christian view instead. Shouldn't it be just as obvious that John's pointed use of Thomas as a doubter of correct belief, lately converted to the same, is of a piece with the polemical rewriting of the Baptist? Just as John the Baptist symbolizes the Baptist sect, Doubting Thomas stands for Thomasine Christianity. And the chief points of Thomasine 'heresy' are targeted in the scenes in which John features Thomas.

Chief among the points over which they differed was the fleshly reality of the resurrection of Jesus. Riley provides an interesting survey of ancient Israelite, Jewish, Hellenistic, and Christian belief about the fate of the dead. From these data emerge the assessment that the notion of fleshly resurrection emerged late and piecemeal within some strands of Judaism, was unheard of everywhere else, and dominant in no form of Judaism or Christianity we know of until formative Catholic Orthodoxy mainstreamed the belief in the second century and later. Riley shows that those polemicists who did accept the doctrine had fellow Christians, not just outsiders, to argue with.

Many converts to the Christian faith naturally interpreted their belief according to their inherited assumptions and thus believed Jesus had risen in spiritual form. (1 Corinthians 15 and 1 Peter 3:18 certainly seem to presuppose the spiritual body version of resurrection.) Riley shows how such traditional belief in soul survival was easily compatible with belief in *post-mortem* apparitions in which the dead might be identified by the death wounds they still visibly bore — even though they lacked physical substance. One recurring theme (not without occasional qualification) was that the dead, however lifelike they might appear, could not be touched or embraced. When the mourners tried to touch their loved one, they found themselves clasping empty air.

Riley argues plausibly that Thomas Christians believed Jesus was spiritually resurrected (sayings 28–29, 71). This, we are told, John rejected, as he did the Thomasine preference for saving *gnosis* that made the *illuminatus* the equal/twin of the Living Jesus, and their consequent lack of any demand for saving faith. Whereas Jesus tells the Thomas of the 'Fifth Gospel' he must no longer call him Master, having attained unto the same plateau of spiritual enlightenment (saying 13), in the Fourth Gospel Thomas is patted on the head for worshipping Jesus as "My Lord and my God." (20:28).

Hidden Agenda

All this makes good sense to me. But let me now propose a few 'friendly amendments' to Riley's reconstruction. I wonder if the issue separating the Johannine and Thomasine traditions was really that of the fleshly resurrection of Jesus. My hesitations begin with the resurrection appearance scene in John 20. Riley reads the passage as affirming the fleshly resurrection of Jesus, over against the supposedly Thomasine notion of a spiritual resurrection. Why does he see it so? Because of the business about Thomas vowing he will not believe unless allowed to probe the open wounds of Jesus for himself. This element of tangibility seems to Riley to push the issue beyond what might otherwise look like a *post-mortem* apparition. But is this issue really broached in the passage? I think not.

What is it that Thomas swears he will not accept till he can touch the wounds? Thomas is skeptical of the claim of his fellow disciples to "have seen the Lord." No one is said to be debating the Pauline question, "But how are the dead raised? With what sort of body do they come?" We do not read that the other disciples told Thomas, "The Lord is physically raised! It wasn't some ghost, you can count on that!" Neither do we hear that Thomas replied, "Okay, a ghost I could accept! See 'em all the time. No big deal there. But fleshly resurrection? You're going to have to do better than that!" The story doesn't get into that sort of detail. I suspect Riley is reading in, from Luke 24:37, the disciples' initial fear that they were seeing a ghost. But nothing of the kind figures in John 20. The issue there is simply whether it was really Jesus the disciples saw. "We have seen the Lord!" "I will not believe." He will not believe that they really saw Jesus. What the telltale wounds will convince Thomas of is that the dead Jesus has manifested himself, period.

Does John really mean to picture the manifested Jesus as appearing in the flesh? As Riley admits, even many in the early church did not read the passage so. After all, John makes a point of saying the doors were closed and locked (20:19–26), surely pointless unless to highlight the ghostly passage of Jesus through them, like Jacob Marley in Dickens' *A Christmas Carol*. What about the tangibility factor? Note that the point of Thomas' exasperated vow is that he must see for himself.

Actual touching proves unnecessary once Jesus appears and simply shows him the identifying marks. Thomas recoils abashed like Job: "I have uttered what I did not understand, things too wonderful for me, which I did not know. I had heard of thee by the hearing of the ear, but now my eyes see thee; therefore I despise myself and repent in dust and ashes" (Job 42:3b, 5–6). Literal touching must not have been the issue.

Riley too quickly couples John 20 and Luke 24. Both have reworked a common reappearance tradition, but the point in Luke 24 seems to me quite different. There, Jesus does specifically call attention to his fleshly corporeality. "No spirit has flesh and bones as you see me having." (As Riley points out, Ignatius had independent access to the same tradition: "Take hold of me and see, I am no bodiless demon.") But there is a form-critical point to be remembered here. Such scenes as Luke depicts (and Ignatius alludes to) appear elsewhere in the neighborhood. They are typically reunion scenes between friends or lovers, or master and disciples. In all such cases the point is that the unexpected return of the one feared lost does not mark a return from the dead, *i.e.*, the apparition of a ghost, but rather denotes unexpected survival, escape from death.

The parallel between Luke 24: and Philostratus' *Life of Apollonius of Tyana* is especially close. Apollonius' disciples, having fled the scene of his trial before Domitian, are gathered mourning their master who can scarcely have escaped the tyrant's ire. But lo and behold, Apollonius himself suddenly appears in their midst. He is no ghost as they first suspect, but has simply teleported miraculously from Rome, just as Philip does from Gaza to Ashdod in Acts 8:39–40. He invites them to handle him and prove to themselves it is really he, and no ghost. In other words, they should thus satisfy themselves that he is not back from the dead but has instead cheated death.

Luke 24 and Ignatius seem to rely upon a version of the Passion in which the suffering righteous one, Jesus, was delivered out of the hand of his enemies by premature removal from the cross, another standard feature of Hellenistic romances, whose heroes rather frequently get themselves sentenced to the cross or actually crucified, and then escape. Note how often Lukan redactional material has Jesus "suffering" or being "delivered into the hands of men," instead of actually and explicitly dying. Jane Schaberg (*The Illegitimacy of Jesus*) raises the possibility that the virginal conception of Jesus is not a New Testament doctrine/myth at all, but has been read into the texts of Matthew and Luke through the conventions of second-century patristic theology. In the same way, I wonder if it is really John and Luke, as Riley thinks, who argued for a fleshly resurrection of Jesus, or rather perhaps Riley is still too willing to take the second-century Christians' word for what Luke and John meant.

At any rate, it seems clear that John has reworked the Luke/Ignatius tradition. The original form of the story stressed tangibility so as to prove Jesus had not actually died. John clearly supposes Jesus had died. The Johannine Jesus does not stress fleshly corporeality but rather identifying marks. Luke's closed doors provided the occasion for the flabbergasted disciples to erroneously suspect him a ghost. John's closed doors denote that the *post-mortem* Jesus is a ghost, back from a genuine death. The point is quite different.

The Living Jesus

Riley does an admirable bit of detective work matching up clues from the Gospel of John on the one hand with those from the Thomas canon (*Gospel of Thomas, Book of Thomas the Contender, Acts of Thomas*) to indicate points where the two theologies collided, but I wonder if perhaps we cannot find a few more and, in the process, hypothetically reconstruct some theological evolution within Thomas Christianity. I suggest John is trying to correct Thomas Christians at two stages.

First, let us suppose that the Thomas Christians believed in a 'Living Jesus' who had neither died on the cross (despite being crucified) nor ascended to heaven shortly thereafter. We are acquainted with similar beliefs among Gnostic Christians who believed Jesus remained among his disciples for 18 months to 11 years after his resurrection. Similarly, Matthew's 'Great Commission' (Matt 28:19–20) says nothing of any ascension but rather pictures Jesus accompanying his disciples on their missionary journeys (of course, harmonizing, we never read it that way).

The Ahmadiyya sect and various others (including, recently, Barbara Thiering) pictured Jesus surviving or escaping the cross and leaving the Holy Land to continue his teaching elsewhere. Apart from whether such a thing happened, we may ask whether there is any textual evidence that any New Testament era Christians *thought* it happened. And there is some. As it happens, John, who habitually places what he considers current misunderstandings on the lips of Jesus' opponents, has someone *mis*-understand Jesus as predicting, not that he will ascend to heaven, but that he will "go to the Diaspora among the Greeks and teach the Greeks" (7:35). I submit that this means John knew some believed this is just what Jesus did. I'm hazarding the guess that the Thomas Christians believed this.

The second stage of John's anti-Thomas polemic would include the attempted refutation of the idea of a post-crucifixion Jesus continuing to travel and preach.

Let us take a look at the same three Johannine references to Thomas that Riley examines. He sees much. Taking his hint, we may be able to see more. First there is the Lazarus story in chapter 11. Riley notes that here Thomas is made implicitly to doubt the resurrection of Lazarus, just as in chapter 20 he will be made explicitly to doubt the resurrection of Jesus. How is that? Because, as Riley strikingly points out, Thomas' fatalistic sigh, "Let us go, too, so we may die with him" refers to dying not with Jesus (since Jesus has just assured Thomas that he is not yet in any danger), but to Lazarus. Jesus has announced his intention to raise Lazarus up (11:11), but all Thomas expects is Lazarus' death (and their own, in an ambush). On the one hand, we may ask Riley why it is that Thomas should take Jesus' word that Jesus is in no danger and yet expect that he and his fellow disciples will die in Bethany. On the other, we may ask if Riley's argument proves too much. If it is the fleshly nature of the future resurrection of believers (of whom Lazarus is an advance specimen) which is at stake here, does John mean that the dead will be merely resuscitated like Lazarus, whom we must imagine to have died again some time later, perhaps at the hands of the Sanhedrin (12:10)?

I suspect that the point of chapter 11 is to furnish a dress rehearsal for the death and resurrection of Jesus himself, and that the goal is to demonstrate the reality of the death of Lazarus explicitly and of Jesus implicitly. This is why John tells the tale of Lazarus rather than those of the daughter of Jairus or the son of the widow of Nain. Those did not pass muster precisely because it was not completely clear that the patient was really dead. Of Jairus' daughter Jesus actually says "The child is not dead but sleeping" (Mark 5:39), and in a number of contemporary stories (featuring Asclepiades the physician, Apollonius of Tyana, and several others) the point is that someone not yet dead is rescued at the last possible moment from being buried prematurely by people who lacked the keen diagnostic eye of the master physician. Form-critically, then, we ought to expect that any such story in which someone very recently dead is said merely to sleep is not a resurrection miracle but rather a rescue from premature burial. So the Jairus and Nain stories would very likely have been read by the ancients as *Scheintod*, apparent death, stories.

This was not good enough for John, who did not like the fact that some, including Thomas Christians, understood the crucifixion of Jesus the same way, as only an apparent death. So he supplies the Lazarus story as a prelude to the Passion of Jesus and as a guide for interpreting it. His point is to rule out the possibility that the death was only apparent. He seems first to set up the possibility (" 'Our friend Lazarus has fallen asleep, but I go to awake him out of sleep' " 11:11), only to knock it down ("Now Jesus had spoken of his death, but they thought that he meant taking rest in sleep. Then Jesus told them plainly, 'Lazarus is dead' " 11:13). This is obviously why John has Jesus stay put so that when he finally does arrive, Lazarus has been moldering in the tomb long enough that he must by now be a rotting corpse (11:39).

The point is not just that Jesus has rescued Lazarus from the tomb (which would still be the case even if Lazarus had been prematurely buried as in the other stories), but that Lazarus died and came back. (Even after all this, it must be pointed out, John has not completely succeeded, since we only hear that Martha *expected* there to be a stench. She *assumed* her brother was decomposing, but if he lay in a cataleptic state, he wouldn't have.) Are we to infer, then, that John also envisioned a grossly physical resuscitation of Jesus, since Lazarus returns physically? Apparently not, since, again, no one in the early church wanted Jesus raised in that way — a resurrection unto mere mortality. So John probably doesn't want Lazarus' resurrection to anticipate Jesus' in every respect. But he must have the reality of the death itself in mind, since this is where he goes out of his way to make that point.

In the Farewell Discourse of John 14:5, John assigns Thomas these lines: "Lord, we do not know where we are going; how can we know the way?" Of course Jesus replies that he himself is the way, but this scarcely contains all of John's answer to the question, an answer he certainly feels (as Riley says) the Thomas Christians do not know. And that, I suggest, is the way of the cross. "... if it dies, it bears much fruit... If anyone serves me, he must follow me; and where I am, there shall my servant be also; if anyone serves me, the Father will honor him... I, when I am lifted up from the earth, will draw all men to myself" (12:24, 26, 32). It is perhaps Thomas Christians who are in view at 19:34–35, where the narrator swears up and down that he saw Jesus fatally wounded and wants you to believe. Believe what? Simply that, as in *The Wizard of Oz*, Jesus was "morally, ethically, spiritually, physically, positively, absolutely, undeniably, and reliably dead."

As we have seen, finally, when the risen Jesus appears to Thomas, the point of showing the wounds (which conspicuously do not get touched!) is probably to show at once that Jesus did die but *is* now back, not in the first instance, *how* he is back.

Traveling Man

Perhaps the Thomas Christians pictured Jesus, like Elijah or al-Khadr ('the evergreen one'), as "with you always, even unto the consummation of the age" (Matt 28:20). No ascension rounded off their myth of Jesus such as wrapped up Luke's. John's emphasis on Jesus' ascension as an item likely to offend (John 6:61–62) might have been aimed at the Thomas Christians.

So my guess is that the Thomas Christians first believed that Jesus had survived the cross and set out to the East to resume his preaching, going as far as Syria or, as some would later say, Kashmir and India. Against this belief John aims (or preserves) the polemic that Jesus was "not only really dead, but most sincerely dead." The Thomas Christians then accepted this belief from the majority of Christians. But then what of their belief in the missionary travels of the post-cross Jesus? At this point they would have believed in the (saving?) death of Jesus, but not in his resurrection. So the bearer of their faith to the far reaches of Syria, Edessa, and India must not have been Jesus (martyred and seated in heaven at the right hand of the Father) but rather someone who might have been mistaken for Jesus, say, a twin brother of Jesus who carried on in his name. This stage of the Thomas tradition remains visible in the *Acts of Thomas* in the several places where Jesus is said to appear in the form of his brother Thomas as well as those in which Thomas is said explicitly to resemble his brother Jesus. (Keep in mind, the name *Thomas* means 'twin.')

This was not good enough for the Johannine community, who sought to correct the belief by means of the Doubting Thomas pericope. As an exegete of an earlier day (alas, I cannot recall whom) suggested, the reason the risen Jesus must appear to Thomas in particular is to counteract the belief of some that the resurrection was a case of mistaken identity, that people saw Jesus' twin brother Thomas and took him for Jesus himself returned from the dead. By showing the risen Jesus and Didymus Thomas ('Twin-Twin'!) side by side, as in a Superman cartoon wherein the Man of Steel contrives to be seen side by side with Clark Kent (probably a robot double), John means to show that the two cannot be the same. The subsequent orthodox overlay on the *Acts of Thomas* (which Riley discusses) implies that eventually the Thomas Christians were drawn into the Johannine orbit, and the theological gaps closed. Part of this redaction was the scene in which the reader again is shown Jesus side by side with Thomas, as the former orders the latter to missionize India, making it clear that even though it was Thomas who had missionized India, he was not replacing a dead Jesus but acting on behalf of a risen one.

Thomas the renegade left his mark in the New Testament. Riley notes how only Judas Thomas and Judas Iscariot are characterized in the New Testament as "one of the Twelve," and needless to say, both are shown in a dubious light. I suggest this is because they were originally one and the same character. From the 'Orthodox' side, Thomas' heresy became narratively transformed/concretized into Judas' betrayal of Jesus, while the subsequent cooptation of Thomas Christianity created the repentant Thomas of John 20.

Gary R. Habermas's
"The Resurrection Appearances Of Jesus,"

In: R. Douglas Geivett and Gary R. Habermas, eds., *In Defense of Miracles: A Comprehensive Case for God's Action in History* (Downers Grove: InterVarsity Press, 1997)

Gary Habermas is the closest thing to a New Testament critic one will ever find teaching in the hallowed, but far from hollow, halls of Jerry Falwell's Liberty University. Exceedingly well read, Professor Habermas is the epitome of what James Barr called the "maximal conservative" approach to New Testament scholarship. The maximal conservative proposes to examine an issue in a neutral scholarly way but *always* comes out defending the traditional view, often explicitly appealing to the (inappropriate) rationale: "innocent until proven guilty," as if the orthodox view of any matter must claim the benefit of the doubt. That is to say, he poses as an objective researcher into open questions regarding the early Christian literature and history, but his conclusions are determined in advance by a dogmatic agenda. As a member of the Liberty University faculty, Dr. Habermas is honor-bound to believe in the absolute inerrancy of the Bible, the dogma that the Bible is free from all historical errors, and even that its authors never expressed differences of opinion on religious matters.

The inerrantist believes either that the text of the Bible was verbally dictated by the Almighty (whether or not the human penman knew it at the time) or that at least the result was the same as if God had dictated it, even if 'all' he did was to oversee the writing process providentially. Someone with a view like this adopts the posture of the biblical critic not because he or she believes it will shed new light on ancient texts but rather in order to defend traditional, orthodox readings of the text from 'heretical' new research that threatens by its very nature to render such readings obsolete, depriving orthodox dogma of its seeming proof texts.

The unstated goal is to beat the genuine critic at his own game so as to defend the party line. That is the business Gary Habermas is in. That is the approach of the many books he has written. They are all exercises in apologetics, the scholastic defense of the faith. The position is an ironic one, since such attempts to clamp the lid on the open Bible would have prevented just the sort of bold, open-ended investigation that led to the Protestant Reformation and the Biblical Theology Movement.

Three major difficulties beset this erudite and clearly written essay. The first is the character of the whole as essentially an exercise in the fallacious argument of appeal to the majority. Habermas does not want to commit this logical sin, so he admits in the beginning that the mere fact of the (supposed) consensus of scholarly opinion to which he repeatedly appeals does not settle anything, and as if to head off the charge I have just made, he says he supplies sufficient clues in his endnotes to enable the interested reader to follow up the original scholars' arguments, which, he admits, must bear the brunt of the analysis. I'm sorry, but that is simple misdirection like that practiced by a sleight-of-hand artist. You can say you reject the appeal to consensus fallacy, but that makes no difference if all you do afterward is to cite 'big names' on the subject. And that is what happens here.

The second besetting sin is Habermas' omission of much recent scholarship that has put well into the shade much of the reasoning of Joachim Jeremias, C. H. Dodd, and even Rudolf Bultmann, to which he appeals. I am not trying to play posturing here, as if to score points against Professor Habermas. For all I know, he is quite conversant with these works and is just not impressed by them. Who knows? All I am saying is that I *am* impressed by them. And if you are, too, you will know that contemporary studies of Acts are increasingly inclined to treat the narrative as a tissue of second-century fictions and legends no different in principle and little different in degree from the Apocryphal Acts, though it is better written than these others (see Richard I. Pervo, *Profit With Delight: The Literary Genre of the Acts of the Apostles*, 1987).

You will know that J. C. O'Neill (*The Theology of Acts in its Historical Setting*, 1961) and others regard the supposed bits of early tradition found in the speeches in Acts to be signs of a late date, of the Christology and theology of the Apostolic Fathers, not of the primitive church.

You will know that many regard the so-called Semitic flavor of Acts not as a sign of an underlying early Aramaic tradition, but as an attempt to pastiche the Septuagint and so lend the book a biblical flavor.

You will be familiar with the fact that a number of scholars (not just I!) have spotlighted the appearance list in 1 Corinthians 15:3–11 as a later interpolation into the text, an alternate explanation for all the non-Pauline linguistic features Habermas invokes as evidence that Paul is quoting early tradition. (Arthur Drews, Winsome Munro, R. Joseph Hoffmann, William O. Walker, J. C. O'Neill, and G. A. Wells have all argued or asserted this.)

Since not everyone has memorized this list, it may be useful to quote it here for reference.

> For I delivered to you as of first importance what I also received, that Christ died for our sins in accordance with the scriptures, that he was buried, that he was raised on the third day in accordance with the scriptures, and that he appeared to Cephas, then to the twelve. Then he appeared to more than five hundred brethren at one time, most of whom are still alive, though some have fallen asleep. Then he appeared to James, then to all the apostles. Last of all, as to one untimely born, he appeared also to me. For I am the least of the apostles, unfit to be called an apostle, because I persecuted the church of God. But by the grace of God I am what I am, and his grace toward me was not in vain. On the contrary, I worked harder than any of them, though it was not I, but the grace of God which is with me. Whether then it was I or they, so we preach and so you believed.

Perhaps most importantly, however, you would realize that, as Burton L. Mack, Jonathan Z. Smith and their school argue, the very idea of Christianity beginning with a Big Bang of startling visions of Jesus on Easter morning is highly dubious — very likely the fruit, not the root, of Christian theological evolution, alongside other versions of early Jesus movements and Christ cults that had no need for or belief in a resurrection. You would know that there may be quite a gap between whomever and whatever the earliest Christians may have been (if you can even draw a firm line where proto-Christianity split off from 'Essenism' or the Mystery Religions) and what we mean by the term today. Like Habermas, I must be content to recommend these writings, but I am not trying to win an argument here, merely to challenge Habermas' contention that there is a safe consensus among today's scholars on these issues. There is no substitute for studying the issues oneself.

The third big problem with the essay is the lamentable leap in logic whereby, like a 'Scientific Creationist,' Habermas seems to assume that the (supposed) absence of viable naturalistic explanations of the first resurrection-sightings proves the objective reality of the resurrection. This is to pull the reins of scientific investigation much too quickly! And in fact one may never yank them in the name of miracle, for that is a total abdication of the scientific method itself, which never proceeds except on the assumption that a next, traceable, *i.e.*, naturalistic, step may be found. And if it never is, then science must confess itself forever stymied. To do otherwise, as Habermas does, is to join the ranks of the credulous who leap from the seeming improbabilities of ancient Egyptians engineering the Pyramids to concluding that space aliens built them with tractor beams! But let us go back and examine some of Habermas' claims in detail.

Habermas' *Ennead*

Our apologist lays out a hand of trump cards he thinks will justify him gathering up all the stakes. But does he win the game? We need to take a closer look at his cards.

First, "There is little doubt, even in critical circles, that the apostle Paul is the author of the book of 1 Corinthians. Rarely is this conclusion questioned" (p. 264). But there *is* reason to question it, and this is where the appeal to the majority is so misleading. Bruno Bauer and a whole subsequent school of New Testament critics including Samuel Adrian Naber, A. D. Loman, Allard Pierson, W. C. van Manen, G. A. van den Bergh van Eysinga, Thomas Whittaker, and L. Gordon Rylands all rejected the authenticity of 1 Corinthians as a Pauline epistle.

And they did so with astonishing arguments that remain unanswered to this day, the major strategy of those few 'consensus' scholars who even deigned to mention them being to laugh them off as *a priori* outrageous. These arguments have been revived and carried further today by Hermann Detering, Darrell J. Doughty, and myself. Again, appealing to authoritative names in the manner of an exorcism is vain in scholarly matters. I mean only to indicate that there are real and open issues here, and that one must not over-simplify the debate by taking important things for granted.

Second, "Virtually all scholars agree that in this text [1 Corinthians 15:3*ff*] Paul recorded an ancient tradition(s) about the origins of the Christian gospel. Numerous evidences indicate that this report is much earlier than the date of the book in which it appears" (*ibid.*). This is not really a separate argument from the next two following, but let us briefly note the oddity of the whole notion of Paul, if he is indeed the author, passing down a *Christian* 'tradition,' much less an 'ancient' one (though perhaps Habermas means ancient in relation to us, but then that's true of the whole epistle, isn't it?). Habermas has set foot on one of the land mines in Van Manen's territory: the anachronism of the picture of Paul, a founder of Christianity, already being able to appeal to hoary traditions, much less creedal formulae! All this demands a date long after Paul.

Not only that, but as Harnack showed long ago, the 1 Corinthians 15 list is clearly a composite of pieces of two competing lists, one making Cephas the prince of apostles, the other according that dignity to James the Just. The conflation of the lists (to say nothing of the addition of gross apocryphal elements like the appearance to the half-thousand!) presupposes much historical water under the bridge, way too much for Paul.

Third, "The vast majority of critical scholars concur on an extremely early origin for this report. Most frequently, it is declared that Paul received the formula between two and eight years after the crucifixion, around A.D. 32–38" (*ibid.*) because..."

Fourth, "Researchers usually conclude that Paul received this material shortly after his conversion during his stay in Jerusalem with Peter and James (Gal 1:18–19), who are both included in Paul's list of individuals to whom Jesus appeared (1 Cor 15:5, 7)" (*ibid.*).

One may ask concerning all this what it is that Paul was supposed to have been preaching *prior* to this visit, since 1 Corinthians 15:1 makes the list the very content of his initial preaching to the Corinthian church! The text as we read it gives no hint that Paul is supposed to be citing some older material (though I agree the material is alien to the context, not being the writer's own words. I just make it a later interpolation, not a Pauline citation of prior material. It's just that the text does not mean to let on to this). But if he does regard the list as a piece of earlier material, he leaves no interval between the beginning of his apostolic preaching and the learning of this so-crucial list. Ouch!

Nor should we forget how Galatians tells us in no uncertain terms that the gospel message of Paul was in no way mediated through any human agency, which would just not be true if he was simply handing on tradition "like a plastered cistern that loses not a drop."

Besides this, it is sheer surmise that Paul would have memorized this text at the behest of Peter and James when he was in their company in Jerusalem on the occasion mentioned in Galatians. In fact, to bring the list and the visit together in the same breath is already a piece of harmonization after the manner of hybridizing Mark's empty-tomb story with Luke's by saying one of Luke's angels was out buying a lottery ticket when Mark got there, pen in hand. It is like pegging the visionary ascent to the third heaven (2 Corinthians 12:1–10) as the same as the Damascus Road encounter of Acts. Purely gratuitous.

To make things worse, there is the serious question of whether the fortnight's visit of Paul to Jerusalem in Galatians 1:18–24 is original to the text either. It bristles with odd vocabulary, even in so short a text!, and neither Tertullian's text nor Marcion's seems to have contained it. It looks like a Catholicizing interpolation trying to shorten the span between Paul's conversion and his first encounter with the Jerusalem apostles, fourteen years after (Galatians 2:1).

I realize that evangelical readers will be snickering by this time. They have been led to scoff at this way of scrutinizing the text for interpolations too early for the extant manuscript sources to attest them. I recommend William O. Walker's *Interpolations in the Pauline Letters* as a good introduction to this methodology and its inherent plausibility. Conservatives have elevated to a dogma the premature and groundless judgment that we can take for granted that no important interpolations crept into the text during that early period for which there is absolutely no manuscript evidence either way.

Fifth, Habermas takes it as independent corroboration of Paul's (= the list's) claim that various people saw the Risen Jesus that Paul got the creed from James and Peter: "if critical scholars are correct that Paul received the creedal material in 1 Corinthians 15:3*ff* from Peter and James in Jerusalem in the early 30s A.D., then we have strong evidence that the reported appearances of the risen Jesus came from the original apostles." (p. 267). If they gave him the list, they must have drawn up the list to begin with, or at least informed those who did. I don't see how this follows. And the whole scenario reminds me too much of the old legend that the Apostles Creed was written, an article at a time, as each apostle added on his favorite tenet.

Habermas points to Galatians 1:18–20, the mention of Paul heading for Jerusalem to seek Peter's expertise, presumably on the main features of his gospel or about the life of Jesus: if they had told him something very different concerning the resurrection than we read in Paul, wouldn't he have said so? But again, this is part of that harmonizing interpolation, inserted just to make things easier for apologists like Habermas himself.

In general, we must recognize that references to what the apostles may or may not have said, occurring not in writings by them but rather in writings by a different author, have no independent historical value. We might as well invoke John the Baptist's endorsement of Jesus from the gospels as independent evidence for the historical Jesus!

Sixth, Paul (= the list) *includes an appearance to Paul himself.* I think the interpolated list mentioned Paul in the third person, and that the redactor (inevitably) made it first person, an adaptation the interpolator of 2 Corinthians 12:1–10 could not competently carry through. In any case, if it is an interpolation, it is post-Pauline and pseudepigraphical, so this one depends on a prior decision as to authorship.

Habermas notes that the three accounts in Acts of Paul's encounter with the Risen One on the road to Damascus tend to corroborate the statement of the 1 Corinthians 15 list about a Pauline appearance. This is ironic, since Luke seems instead to want to ring down the curtain on the resurrection appearances with the ascension, allowing Paul and Stephen to have mere visions afterward. This he does to rebut claims for their non-twelve apostleship. And, as Detering notes, the element of Paul being blinded (borrowed ultimately from the conversion of Heliodorus in 2 Maccabees 3) surely means to deny that Paul saw the Risen Jesus in any manner analogous to the twelve, who, after all, had tea with the Risen Savior on more than one occasion.

Seventh, Habermas cites Paul's Jerusalem visit in Galatians 2:1–10, which issued in an A-plus report card, as further evidence that Paul and the Jerusalem apostles had no serious disagreement. Suffice it to say that the text is very clear on the point at issue in these discussions: not resurrection but rather circumcision of the Gentiles. We simply do not know if the question of the resurrection came up on that occasion. There is no point in pretending we do, or we are making it up as we go along. Habermas warns: "rather than highlight what many contemporary scholars think cannot be known about the New Testament testimony, I want to concentrate on the evidence that we do have" (p. 262). But this isn't part of it.

Eighth, "After recounting the creed and listing key witnesses to the appearances of Jesus, Paul declared that all the other apostles were currently preaching the same message concerning Jesus' appearances (1 Cor 15:11–15). In other words, we have it on Paul's authority that these resurrection appearances were also being proclaimed by the original apostles" (p. 267). But we cannot say we know they were preaching the same list or the same listed appearances until we read some other document by one of them that has the list in common with 1 Corinthians 15. And we have no such text. You can't blithely quote Paul as evidence for what others were saying. The 1 Corinthians text does not take us out of the range of what Paul is saying — unless we recognize that the material is interpolated! And then the point is that it is a Catholicizing gloss, rewriting history to make it look like Paul agreed with the Jerusalem apostles when in fact he hadn't.

Ninth, "Another indicator of the appearances to the original apostles is the Gospel accounts... Even from a critical viewpoint, it can be shown that several of the appearance narratives report early tradition [an apologetical euphemism for 'early rumor'] as Dodd argues after a careful analytical study. He contends that the appearance narratives in Matthew 28:8–10, 16–20 and John 20:19–21, and, to a lesser extent, Luke 24:36–49, are based on early material [again: apologetical euphemism — "material"!]. The remaining Gospel accounts of Jesus' resurrection appearances are lacking in typical mythical tendencies and likewise merit careful consideration" (p. 268). Now isn't that special?

It is hard to stop cringing and to know where to begin after this fusillade of fustian. Matthew 28:8–10 — based on early tradition?

> So they [*Mary Magdalene and 'the other Mary'*] departed quickly from the tomb with fear and great joy, and ran to tell his disciples. And behold, Jesus met them and said, "Hail!" And they came up and took hold of his feet and worshiped him. Then Jesus said to them, "Do not be afraid; go and tell my brethren to go to Galilee, and there they will see me."

This is simply part of Matthew's fictive add-on to Mark's empty tomb narrative which itself does not manage to make Dodd's list! Not only that, it represents editorial rewriting and contradiction of the Markan original! Likewise, 16–20 are a mere pastiche-summary of a resurrection-commission narrative, as if the evangelist knew more or less what this kind of story sounded like but couldn't quite pull it off, much like the inept paraphrase of earlier materials in the Longer Ending of Mark. The disciples meet Jesus on the mountain he had specified — where? And when did he tell them? This is a reference back to something he forgot to include in his story, like somebody getting ahead of himself and spoiling the ending of a joke. Verse 17 means to have the epiphany of Christ quell all doubt, but instead the narrator rushes through it with the incoherent "they worshipped him though they doubted" (masked by translations because it wouldn't sound good in Easter sermons). Some of the language is Matthean ("unto the consummation of the age;" "to disciple"); the rest is derived from both the Septuagint and Theodotion's translation of Daniel 7, as Randel Helms (*Gospel Fictions*, 1988) has shown. And then what is left?

Habermas says Dodd valued John 20:19–21 above the parallel Luke 24:36–49, though I think the evidence points to John's version being a redaction of Luke's (and not just of the 'underlying tradition' as apologists would prefer, trying to maintain some semblance of the old notion of the gospels being independent reports). John has omitted Luke's redactional material in Luke 24:44–49, retaining only a paraphrase of the Great Commission ("As the Father has sent me, so I send you."). And let's get it straight: *vv*. 44–49 are *not* "independent L tradition," which is to appropriate source criticism as apologetics. No, Luke just made it up, as one can see from the material's similarity to the speech in 24:25–27 as well as to many of the speeches in Acts — also Lukan compositions (see Earl Richard, *Acts 6:1–8:4. The Author's Method of Composition*, 1978; Marion L. Soards, *The Speeches in Acts: Their Content, Context, and Concerns*, 1994).

But beyond this, John has edited Luke so that Jesus no longer offers just his (*corporeal*) hands and feet, but now his *wounded* (only in John) hands and *side*. This fits with John's having added the piercing of Jesus' side and anticipates Doubting Thomas with the mention of nail holes and a chasm in the side. All this uniquely Johannine redaction rewrites the story in order to suppress a current reading of Luke's story in which Jesus is understood to have survived crucifixion, evaded death, and means to show the disciples that, like Mark Twain's, the reports of his death are premature.

In fact, this way of reading Luke's story makes it remarkably similar to the episode in Philostratus' *Life of Apollonius of Tyana* (also supposedly based on local oral tradition as well as eyewitness memoirs!) in which the sage vanished from the court of Domitian, where he was up on capital charges, to reappear across the Mediterranean among his astonished disciples, who naturally take him for the ghost of their presumably late master. He stretches forth his hands and invites them to examine his corporeal flesh! Subsequently he ascends into heaven alive, as also in Luke. Or so some read Luke in John's day, and that is why the latter sought to reinforce the real death of Jesus with spear-thrusts and nail wounds.

See for yourself!

Let's take stock: John's version, far from being straight-forward reporting, is a redacted version of Luke's — which is already redacted and embodies a common Hellenistic epiphany theme attested also in Philostratus. You can hold your breath and keep quoting the fantasy novelist C. S. Lewis about how none of this smacks of mythology, or you can stop citing authorities and examine the matter for yourself.

Are the remaining gospel resurrection accounts free of mythological traits, as Habermas suggests Dodd contended? Hardly! In the Emmaus Road story, we have another epiphany mytheme, closely matched in an Asclepius story predating Luke by centuries. In that one, frustrated seekers of a miracle in Asclepius' temple return home and are met on the way by a concerned stranger who hears their sad tale, performs the desired healing, reveals himself, and vanishes.

The empty tomb tale itself is clearly cut from the same cloth as the numerous apotheosis stories discussed by Charles H. Talbert (*What Is a Gospel? The Genre of the Canonical Gospels*, 1977), in which a famous sage or hero mysteriously vanishes, companions search for the body, can find no trace, and are assured by an angel or heavenly voice that he has been raptured by the gods, henceforth to be worshipped.

The Doubting Thomas story closely parallels one from Philostratus in which a stubborn young disciple is the sole hold-out against belief in immortality. His brethren are startled to witness the fellow having a vision in which Apollonius manifests himself from heaven for the sake of the doubter who henceforth doubts no more.

The farewell to Mary Magdalene in John 20 is highly reminiscent of the last words of the departing angel Raphael to Tobias and Sarah in Tobit chapter 12, as Helms has noted.

The miraculous catch of fish in the Johannine Appendix, like its pre-resurrection cousin in Luke 5, stems directly from a Pythagoras story in which the vegetarian sage wins the forfeit lives of a shoal of fish by preternaturally 'guessing' the number of them caught in the nets.

The idea that these stories do not smack of mythology is just palpably absurd. Rather than functioning as an argument on behalf of faith, the claim has by now itself become an article of faith, so drastically does it contradict all manner of evidence.

Is there a worse example of the fallacy of special pleading, the double standard, than to dismiss all these mythical stories from other ancient religions and to claim that in the sole case of the gospels they are all suddenly true? Laughable in the one case, convincing in the other?

Truth or Method

Let us not miss Habermas' gambit here. First he recommends Dodd's judgment that at least 2.0 or maybe 2.5 of the gospel resurrection stories are, if not factually true, at least based on early story-telling. That is what one might call damning with faint praise on Dodd's part. But it is good enough for Habermas. And then Habermas says those stories not taken seriously by Dodd are to be taken seriously anyhow. His agenda is clear. Because he is a spin-doctor on behalf of inerrantism (the real presupposition underlying all this blather), he has never met a resurrection story he doesn't like. And if you (or Dodd) don't like this one, maybe you'll buy that one. Habermas himself obviously cares nothing for the judgment of the critical scholars he cites except that he may use them cosmetically in a warmed-over piece of fundamentalist apologetics.

Habermas will take what he can get from mainstream scholars, at least those of yesteryear who are nearer orthodoxy anyway. This is clearest in his nose-count of scholars lining up in favor of the 'heavenly telegram' or 'objective vision' theory of the supposed Easter experiences. Taken on its own, this version of resurrection belief is abhorrent to Habermas because it amounts to an 'Easter docetism,' a non-fleshly resurrection. That isn't good enough for Habermas, and he finally takes refuge with the pious equivocation of John A. T. Robinson: "a body identical yet changed, transcending the limitations of the flesh yet capable of manifesting itself within the order of the flesh. We may describe this as a 'spiritual' (1 Cor. 15:44) or 'glorified' (*cf.* 1 Cor. 15:43; Phil. 3:21) body... so long as we do not import into these phrases any opposition to the physical as such" (cited on p. 273).

What specious clucking! We may say half-fish, half-fowl, or anything else we may fancy, as long as we stonewall and insist that the result is not a matter of docetism — the claim that Christ merely *appeared* to have a human body. As if Robinson has not just given a good working definition of docetism: the doctrine of only apparent fleshly reality, the polymorphousness of a divine being who can change forms precisely because he has no true physical form! It all comes down to saying the proper shibboleth when you get to the river bank. Coherent meaning is strictly secondary, if even that. How pathetic. The poor apologist is forever engaged in a bruising game of dodgeball, imagining he has vindicated the Bible just because he has contrived a way of never having to admit he was wrong.

Less Real than a Hallucination

Gary Habermas thinks to convince us that the earliest disciples did *see something*, something that walked like the Risen Jesus, talked like the Risen Jesus, and therefore must have been the Risen Jesus. He thinks those theologians who posit "objective hallucinations," *i.e.*, true but intrapsychic visions sent by God, are headed in the right direction, but he wants finally to quell all talk of hallucinations. Slippery ground, you know. So he rehearses the standard arguments against the resurrection appearances of the gospels being hallucinations. This formula argument, unvarying no matter which apologist dusts it off, is the kind of instrument apologists like Habermas think Paul was using and bequeathing in 1 Corinthians 15:3–11. They are making Paul over in their own image.

Hallucinations are not shared by groups. Then I guess Habermas accepts the historicity of the dancing of the sun in the sky at Fatima. Plenty of people saw that, too. *The disciples could not have been hallucinating, since such visions come at the behest of the longing of mourners, who thus have their dreams fulfilled. But the disciples are shown as skeptical of the reality of the Risen Jesus.* Come on: by now Habermas must have learned from those "critical scholars" whose opinions he professes to respect so much that the skepticism element is simply a common plot-prop in any miracle story. It in no way marks the story as eyewitness testimony. To even argue that way reveals that Habermas and his colleagues are mired in the eighteenth century when these arguments were first framed: they were arguments against Rationalistic Protestants who denied supernatural causation but believed in the accuracy of the gospels. Only against such convenient opponents does it make any sense to take for granted that the gospel scenes are historically accurate and so the implied causation must be miraculous.

Hallucinations are the stock in trade of weirdos, and there is no reason to think the disciples were all weirdos. Oh no? People who abandoned their jobs to follow an exorcist so they could get a piece of the action when the Millennium dawned? Fanatics eager to call down the lightning bolts of Jehovah upon inhospitable Samaritans? Not exactly your average Kiwanis Clubber or Methodist, I'd say. *People would not die as martyrs for mere hallucinations.* Well, sure, as long as they didn't realize that's what they were! *People are not changed from cringing cowards to men who turn the world upside down by mere hallucinations.* How do we know? And besides, the New Testament itself attributes the evangelistic zeal of the apostles not to the resurrection appearances but to the infilling of the Spirit at Pentecost, seven weeks later.

But the salient point is this: Habermas is still locking horns (in the mirror) with the eighteenth-century Protestant Rationalists when he simply assumes we know that the earliest Christians were the named people in the gospels and Acts who did the deeds and said the words depicted in those texts. But as Burton Mack says, these stories are themselves the final products of a myth-making tendency in some quarters, and not all, of early Christianity. They represent the end result *of one kind of Christian faith*, not the root and foundation of *all* Christian faith. There is not only no particular reason to think the gospel Easter narratives or the 1 Corinthians 15 list preserve accurate data on the Easter morning experiences. There is no particularly compelling evidence to suggest that the stories even go back to anyone's experiences. They are one and all mythic and literary in nature. Or they sure look like it, and there's nothing much on the other side of the scale.

N. T. Wright's
The Resurrection of the Son of God
(Minneapolis: Fortress Press, 2003)

If you have seen any of a number of ABC or PBS documentaries on the historical Jesus question, you have certainly seen N. T. Wright. He is one of the 'usual suspects' rounded up by Peter Jennings and his producers, along with John Dominic Crossan, Paula Fredricksen, Ben Witherington, and others, all of whose views are comfortably homogenized by the pleasant host (along with the pronouncements of Pentecostal choir directors and Middle Eastern tour guides) to reinforce the comfy prejudices of the audience. Wright always adopts the stance as of a career historian in the field of ancient history, as if approaching the gospel texts as an admiring outsider. In fact, he is a bishop of the Church of England celebrated there for his reactionary theological opinions. He has expressed these opinions in a number of books that seek to rehabilitate pre-critical views of the Bible by a sophistical appeal to recent scholarly research.

Wright's massive book on the resurrection is, even for the garrulous bishop, an exercise in prolixity. It is several times longer than it needs to be, as if designed to bludgeon us into belief. One might save a lot of time and money by finding a copy of George Eldon Ladd's *I Believe in the Resurrection of Jesus* (Eerdmans, 1975), which used most of the same arguments at a fraction of the length — and without skimping. The arguments have not gotten any better. They are the same old, stale, fundamentalist apologetics we got in Ladd — essentially the same old stuff we used to read in Josh McDowell and John Warwick Montgomery.

It is the same hash reslung — only now it is getting pretty smelly. Perhaps that is why Wright seeks to perfume it, reminiscent of Joseph and Nicodemus attempting to fumigate the decaying corpse of Jesus by encasing it in an extravagant hundred-pounds weight of spices (John 19:39). Wright backs up much too far to make a running start at the resurrection, regaling us with unoriginal, superfluous, and tedious exposition of Old Testament and Intertestamental Jewish ideas of afterlife and resurrection, resurrection belief in every known Christian writer up into the early third century, *etc., etc.*

The mountain thus laboring is doomed to bring forth a messianic mouse, alas. All this erudition is perhaps intended to intimidate the reader into accepting Wright's evangelistic pitch. But it is just a lot of fast talking. In the end, Wright, now Bishop of Durham, is just Josh McDowell in a better suit. His smirking smugness is everywhere evident, especially in his condescension toward the great critics and critical methods of the last two centuries, all of which he strives to counteract. He would lead the hapless seminary student (whom one fears will be assigned this doorstop) backwards into the pre-critical era with empty pretenses of post-modern sophistication, shrugging off the Enlightenment by patently insincere attempts to wrap himself in the flag of post-colonialism.

Genuine criticism of the gospels he dismisses as the less advanced, muddled thinking of a previous generation, as if 'cutting-edge' scholarship like his were not actually pathetic nostalgia for the sparkling Toyland of fundamentalist supernaturalism. It is a familiar bag of tricks, and that is all it is. The tragedy is that many today are falling for it. Witness Wright's own prominence in the Society of Biblical Literature, to say nothing of his ecclesiastical clout.

The weight of this book's argument for orthodox traditionalism is to be found, of all places, in the acknowledgements section, where Wright thanks the hosts of the prestigious venues where he first presented bits of this material: Yale Divinity School, South-Western Theological Seminary, Duke Divinity School, Pontifical Gregorian University, St. Michael's Seminary, *etc., etc.* Wright is the mouthpiece for institutional orthodoxy, a grinning spin-doctor for the Grand Inquisitor. What credibility his book appears to have is due to the imposing wealth, power, tradition, even architecture, of the social-ecclesiastical world that he serves as chaplain and apologist. It is sickening to read his phony affirmations of the allegedly political and radical import of a literal resurrection (if you can even tell what Wright means by this last).

Does Bishop Wright espouse some form of Liberation Theology? No — for just as he emptily says that Jesus redefined messiahship, Wright redefines politics. When he says the early Christians were anti-imperialistic, all he has in mind is the fact that Christians withstood Roman persecution, valiant enough in its way, but hardly the same thing. Like a pathetic Civil War reenactment geek, he is sparring at an enemy safely dead for centuries. In attempting to co-opt and parody the rhetoric of his ideological foes, Wright reminds me of Francis Schaeffer, a hidebound fundamentalist who began as a children's evangelist working for Carl MacIntyre. Schaeffer, posing as an intellectual and a philosopher, used to stamp the floor speaking at fundamentalist colleges, shouting "We are the true Bolsheviks!" Right.

Part of Wright's agenda of harmonizing and de-fusing the evidence is to smother individual New Testament texts beneath a mass of theological synthesis derived from the Old Testament and from the outlines of Pauline theology in general. He is a victim of what James Barr long ago called the "Kittel mentality," referring to the approach of Kittel's *Theological Dictionary of the New Testament* (TDNT), in which articles on individual New Testament terms and words are synthesized from all uses of the term, creating an artificial and systematic semantic structure that leads the reader to suppose that every individual usage of the word was an iceberg tip carrying with it implied reference to all other references.

In other words, each article in the TDNT composed a 'New Testament theology,' topic by topic. In just this manner, Wright first composes a streamlined Old Testament theology of historical and eschatological redemption. Then he synthesizes a Pauline Theology, then a New Testament theology, and then an early Christian theology. Finally, he insists that the synthetic resurrection concept he has distilled must control our reading of *all* individual gospel and Pauline texts dealing with the resurrection.

In short, it is an elaborate exercise in harmonizing disparate data. The implications of 1 Corinthians 15, for example, with its talk of spiritual resurrection, are silenced as the text is muzzled, forbidden to say anything outside the party line Wright has constructed as '*the* biblical' teaching on the subject. Another example is his insistence on translating the Greek *Christos* as 'the Messiah' in Pauline passages, lending them a falsely Jewish coloring belied by their content. Wright even admits that the Pauline writings are already pretty much using 'Christ' as simply another name for Jesus, yet he wants to tie Paul's theology in with the grand arc of Old Testament theology, 'redemptive history,' or whatever. Similarly, he sees everything in the context of second-temple Judaism.

Again, we detect here a phony ecumenism, as if he thought Jews were not all going to hell for rejecting Jesus as the Son of God. The same is true with his cosmetic use of politically correct inclusive language and ecumenical mistranslations of *Jews* as 'Judeans,' *etc*. It is all to butter up the reader, like a used-gospel salesman closing in for the sale. Wright is a better-educated Anglican Zig Zigler. In reality, the only value he sees in Judaism is the safe haven it gives him from taking into account the patent influence on early Christianity of Hellenistic Mystery religions, which are really all we need to account for the empty tomb legend and the resurrection myth. For Wright 'Judaism' really denotes Old Testament and rabbinic interpretation of it.

Here we spot the reason for – and the character of – the unholy alliance between mainstream Judaism and Evangelical Protestantism in the pages of the *Journal of Biblical Literature* and *Bible Review*. They are closing ranks against radical critics in both traditions: Old Testament minimalists and Jesus Seminar-type scholars alike. It is rather like the Moral Majority, uneasy allies with certain goals in common.

There are three fundamental, vitiating errors running like fault lines through the unstable continent of this book.

Fault-line I

The first is a complete unwillingness to engage a number of specific questions or bodies of evidence that threaten to shatter Wright's over-optimistically orthodox assessment of the evidence. The most striking of these blustering evasions has to do with the dying-and-rising redeemer cults that permeated the environment of early Christianity and had for many, many centuries. Ezekiel 8:14 bemoans the ancient Jerusalemite women's lamentation for Tammuz, derived from the Dumuzi cult of ancient Mesopotamia. Ugaritic texts make it plain that Baal's death and resurrection and subsequent enthronement at the side of his Father El went back centuries before Christianity and were widespread in Israel. Pyramid texts tell us that Osiris' devotees expected to share in his resurrection. Marduk, too, rose from the dead. And then there is the Phrygian Attis, the Syrian Adonis.

The harmonistic efforts of Bruce Metzger, Edwin Yamauchi, Ron Sider, Jonathan Z. Smith and others have been completely futile, either failing utterly to deconstruct the dying-and-rising god mytheme (as Smith vainly tries to do) or trying to claim that the Mysteries borrowed their resurrected savior myths and rituals from Christianity. If that were so, why on earth did early apologists admit that the pagan versions were earlier, invented as counterfeits *before the fact* by Satan? Such myths and rites were well known to Jews and Galileans, not to mention Ephesians, Corinthians, *etc.*, for many centuries. But all this Wright merely brushes off, as if it has long been discredited. He merely refers us to other books. It is all part of his bluff: "Oh, no one takes that seriously anymore! Really, it's so *passé!*"

Wright comes near to resting the whole weight of his case on the mistaken contention that the notion of a single individual rising from the dead in advance of the general resurrection at the end of the age was unheard of, and that therefore it must have arisen as the result of the stubborn fact of it having occurred one day — Easter Day. This is basically absurd for reasons we will attend to in a moment, but the premise is false. Even leaving out the resurrections of the savior gods, Wright mentions that the resurrection of Alcestis by Hercules is an exception to the rule, but he seems to think it unimportant. Worse, though, is his utter failure to take seriously the astonishing comment of Herod in Mark 6:14–16 to the effect that Jesus was thought to be John the Baptist *already* raised from the dead!

Can Wright really be oblivious of how this one text torpedoes the hull of his argument? His evasions are so pathetic as to suggest he is being disingenuous, hoping the reader will not notice. The disciples of Jesus, who was slain by a tyrant, may simply have borrowed the resurrection faith of the Baptist's disciples who posited such a vindication for their own master who had met the same fate. Wright should really be arguing for the resurrection of John the Baptist, if its being unprecedented means anything!

Equally outrageous is Wright's contrived and harmonistic treatment of the statements about a spiritual resurrection in 1 Corinthians 15, where we read that "flesh and blood cannot inherit the kingdom of God" (v. 50) and that the resurrected Jesus, the precedent for believers, accordingly possessed a "spiritual body" (v. 44). Wright labors mightily and futilely to persuade us that all Paul meant by "flesh and blood" was 'mortal and corruptible,' not 'made of flesh and blood.'

Who but a fellow apologist (like William Lane Craig who sells the same merchandise) will agree to this? What does Wright suppose led the writer to use a phrase like "flesh and blood" for 'mortal corruptibility' in the first place if it is not physical fleshiness that issues inevitably in mortal corruption? How can the Corinthians writer have used such a phrase if he meanwhile believed the risen Jesus still had flesh and blood?

It is no use to protest that none of the "second temple Jewish" writers we know of had such a notion of resurrection. This supposed fact (and Ladd knew better: he cited apocalypses that have the dead rise in angelic form, or in the flesh which is then transformed into angelic stuff) cannot prevent us from noticing that 1 Corinthians 15:45 has the risen Christ "become a life-giving spirit."

Likewise, when he gets to Luke, Wright laughs off the screaming contradiction between Luke 24:40 ("Touch me and see: no spirit has flesh and bone as you can see I have.") and 1 Corinthians 15:50 and 45 ("Flesh and blood cannot inherit the kingdom of God." "The last Adam became a life-giving spirit."). The contexts of both passages make it quite clear that the terms are being used in the same senses, only that one makes the risen Jesus fleshly, while the other says the opposite. Wright's laughable hair-splitting is a prime example of the lengths he will go to get out of a tight spot. Similarly, when he gets to 1 Peter 3:18 (Jesus was "put to death in the flesh but made alive in the spirit, in which he went and made proclamation to the spirits in prison," *etc.*), Wright rewrites the text to make it say what he wants: "he was put to death *by* the flesh, and brought to life *by* the Spirit." This is just ridiculous. It is the exegesis of that faith that calls things that are not as though they were.

Fault-line II

Wright's second mortal sin is his desire to have his Eucharistic wafer and eat it too. He takes refuge on either side of an ambiguity when it suits him, hopping back and forth from one foot to the other, and hoping the reader will not notice. For instance, Wright is desperate to break down the 'flesh/spirit' dichotomy in Paul and Luke (not to mention that *between* Paul and Luke!), but he builds the same wall higher outside the texts. That is, he wants to say *resurrection* always meant bodily, not merely spiritual, resurrection. The latter would mean just 'going to heaven,' and that will not do. But Wright confesses he has no clear idea of what sort of physical presence the risen Jesus might have had. He calls it "transphysical" and admits he cannot define it.

What then is he arguing? He just knows he wants a bodily resurrection, but it has to be a body capable of passing through locked doors and teleporting, appearing and disappearing at will. Yet he despises the notion that the risen Jesus was docetic — a spiritual entity that could take on the false semblance of physicality. Wright doesn't want any early Christians to have believed this. He doesn't want it even to have existed as an heretical option that the evangelists were trying to refute — because that would mean that a spiritual resurrection was one form of early Christian belief, which Wright is trying to rule out.

Most scholars rightly see the business about the risen Jesus requesting a fish sandwich (Luke 24:42–43) as demonstrating, against Gnostic Docetists, that Jesus had a fleshly body. But Wright will have none of this. He is right to point out, as A. J. M. Wedderburn does in *Beyond Resurrection* (1999), that anti-docetism is inconsistent with the same narratives' depicting Jesus walking through locked doors like Jacob Marley. But why cannot Wright see this simply attests the inconsistent piecemeal nature of the redactional attempts to 'anti-Docetize' the very same narratives? But Wright is stuck with both contradictory features as "eye-witness testimony" or "early tradition" which he seems to think mean the same thing. So his "transphysical" Jesus must be the equivalent to a comic book superhero like the Vision or the Martian Manhunter — possessing a physical body but able to vary physical density at will. But wait a minute — if *this* is not Docetism, *what does Docetism mean?*

Fault-line III

The third strike against Wright is by far the most important. He loathes Enlightenment modernity because it will not let him believe in miracles. So he must change the rules of the game. Like all apologist swindlers, Wright makes a fundamental confusion. He thinks it an arbitrary philosophical bias that historiography should be "methodologically atheistic." Why not admit that miracles might have occurred? It may be that a miracle turns out to be the most simple and economical explanation of the data. If we are unalterably opposed to that possibility, Wright says, we are bigots and arbitrary dogmatists. But if Wright should ever make a serious study of the 'miracles' of the pagan religions, would he not himself adopt a 'methodologically atheistic' approach, even as Benjamin B. Warfield did in his skeptical *Counterfeit Miracles* (1917)? Would he too then be a bigot and an arbitrary dogmatist?

Freud would readily peg Wright as a victim of 'reaction formation.' Long ago, the Ionian philosopher Thales understood that it explains nothing if we piously say that it rains because Zeus turned the faucet on. No, even if there is a god, it is to short-circuit the process of scientific explanation to invoke divine fiat. The same point is made in the cartoon where a lab-coated scientist is expounding his theory with a chalkboard full of figures. He points his pencil to a gap in the long equation and says, "Right here a miracle occurs." It is funny for a reason Wright apparently does not understand.

To say that the rise of Christian resurrection faith requires a divine intervention is tantamount to saying we just do not know how it arose. One resorts to such tactics of desperation when all else fails, as Wright thinks mundane explanations have failed. But in that moment one has not found an alternate explanation at all. It is like the fundamentalists who say their god must have ignited the Big Bang since scientists cannot yet account for what chain of causation led to it. How is a *god* an explanation, even if there is a god? 'God' is a mystery, unless one is an idolater. And to claim one has explained a problem by invoking a mystery is no advance at all. You are trying to invoke a bigger enigma to explain a smaller one. "I have the answer to *X*! The answer is *XX*!"

Erudite Bishop Wright reveals himself to be on the same level with evangelical cartoonist Jack Chick who 'explains' that the unknown Strong Nuclear Force is really *Jesus Christ* because scripture says "in him all things hold together" (Col. 1:17). What's the difference? The instant one invokes the wildcard of divine miracles, the game of science and scientific history comes to a sudden halt. But then that is just what Wright, unsuccessfully disguising himself as a humble historian, wants to do. The good bishop would reassure the faithful that superstition is really science, harmonization is criticism, fideism is evidence.

And why does Wright think a miracle is necessary? Only a real space-time resurrection, he insists, can account for the birth and spread of resurrection faith. Of course there are many viable explanations, not least Festinger's theory of cognitive dissonance reduction, whereby more than one disappointed sect has turned defeat into zeal by means of face-saving denial. Wright suicidally mentions this theory, only to dismiss it, as usual, with no serious attempt at refutation. So totally does his predisposition to orthodox faith blind him that he cannot see how lame a gesture he makes. No argument against his faith can penetrate his will to believe. Every argument against his evangelical orthodoxy seems *ipso facto* futile simply because he cannot bring himself to take it seriously.

But suppose a miracle *were* required. What sort of a miracle might it be? Wright maintains that the earliest evangelists must have been galvanized, electrified, by something mighty convincing! Set aside the fact that all manner of supposed eyewitness enthusiasts – not least UFO abductees – have equal and equally sincere zeal. This is not nearly enough. Wright needs to account for the spread of this improbable-seeming belief *among those who had not themselves seen the risen Christ,* if he thinks the spread of the faith requires a miracle.

Wright himself is at pains to show how resurrection seemed absurd and distasteful to nearly everyone. If that were so, and I am not convinced it was, what Wright needs to posit is something like the Calvinist notion of *the effectual call,* a supernatural mesmerism whereby God makes the gospel attractive to sinners. The miracle is needed at a later stage if it is necessary at all — not that I think it is.

Wright's wrongs

Wright (though by this time one is tempted to start calling him *Wrong*) uses sneer quotes, dismissing with no argument at all Crossan's claim (which I deem undoubtedly and even obviously correct) that the empty tomb traditions stem from women's lament traditions like those mentioned in Ezekiel 8 and attested for the Osiris cult and others. Having merely sneezed at rather than refuted this contention, Wright insists that the empty tomb narratives are eyewitness evidence, evidence that is all the stronger for the supposed fact that ancient Jews did not admit legal testimony from women.

How's that? Wright's evangelical early Anglican Christians in togas just felt they had no choice but to include this vital eyewitness testimony even though it would surely invite ridicule by Celsus and his ilk. They were stuck with it. But why? Wright himself imagines that the framers of the 1 Corinthians 15 list of resurrection appearances knew the empty tomb tale but omitted it so as not to invite ridicule. It was thinkable to do so. But the unwitting logic of Wright's whole argument presses ineluctably toward saying that the empty tomb story is not even *supposed* to be evidence and is not offered as such. It must be there for an entirely different reason. Crossan had it right. He made sense of it. Wright doesn't, because he does not want anything to link the Easter story to the Mystery Religions.

Wright's insistence on limiting himself to the canonical Judeo-Christian continuity blinds him to other crucial parallels to the Easter stories. The Emmaus story (Luke 24:13*ff*), where two apostles meet the Risen Jesus on the road to Emmaus but do not recognize him, is cut from the same cloth as numerous ancient 'angels unawares' myths, but it bears a striking resemblance to a demonstrably earlier Asclepius story where a couple returns home dejectedly after failing to receive the desired healing miracle at Epidaurus. They are intercepted by a curious and concerned stranger, the divine savior *incognito*, who ferrets out the reason for their sadness, reveals himself, performs the hoped-for healing after all, then vanishes.

The miraculous catch of fish in John 21 is patently based on an earlier Pythagoras story in which the no-longer relevant detail of the number of the fish made some sense. As Charles H. Talbert pointed out years ago (*What Is a Gospel?*, 1977), the abrupt ending of Mark (as it seems to readers familiar with the other gospels) fits quite naturally as a typical apotheosis story, where the absence of the body combined with a heavenly voice is sufficient to attest the hero's exaltation to heaven. Talbert showed how an empty tomb story made sense by itself, and how the gospel tomb scene may have originated as window-dressing for an apotheosis narrative. We are *not* stuck with the empty tomb as a stubborn historical fact as Wright would like us to think.

These Hellenistic parallels tell us that we hardly require eyewitness testimony of miracles to explain the origin of the gospel Easter stories. Occam's Razor makes that altogether unnecessary. But they also explain something else Wright thinks explicable only by miracles: the absence of scriptural allusions in these stories. Wright throws down the gauntlet to Crossan, who says that the gospel Passion Narratives are historicized prophecies from the Old Testament, rewritten as New Testament stories.

Why, then, is there so little scripture reflected in the burial and Easter stories? Well, there is a good bit. Matthew has supplemented Mark with Daniel, as Randel Helms shows in *Gospel Fictions* (1988) — and as Wright himself eventually admits! But Crossan has also shown how similar Mark's burial and resurrection stories are to the entombment alive and subsequent crucifixion of the enemy kings in Joshua 10:16–27. Helms also shows how John 20:17 is based on Tobit 12:16–21. But there is a good bit of the gospel story that is not derived from scripture — and that is because it comes from pagan mythology and novels where prematurely entombed heroines are inadvertently rescued by tomb robbers and heroes survive crucifixion (another body of highly relevant textual evidence that Wright haughtily laughs off).

Wright piously tells us that, faced with the resurrection narratives, we ought to bow in awe and wonder. That may or may not be so, but we must blink in astonishment at Wright's comments upon them! In another case of his both/and harmonizations (one found frequently with Evangelical scholars, *i.e.*, apologists), Wright both claims that the resurrection narratives lack artifice (hence must be authentic "raw footage") and that they have been thoroughly worked over by each evangelist so as to function as consistent extensions of themes and even narrative structures running through each gospel. This sort of analysis, demonstrating the thorough permeation of Mark's Passion story by themes ubiquitous throughout the previous chapters led the contributors to Werner H. Kelber's symposium *The Passion in Mark* (1976) to conclude that Mark had no preexistent passion tradition but composed the whole thing. Such an obvious conclusion never occurs to Wright. For him, each narrative is both early, unadorned tradition and thoroughly modified. It is either one as he needs it to be.

The bishop throws source criticism out the window when he needs to, claiming, astonishingly, that there is so little apparent interdependence between the tomb tales of Mark, Matthew, and Luke that we cannot be sure they are not independent tellings of the same story, learned by each evangelist via different channels. This is a way of discounting the great degree to which Luke and Mathew have rewritten Mark, maintaining they are all separate collectors of 'early traditions,' a slippery repristination of the old Sunday School notion that the four evangelists are independent witnesses, as if to the same auto accident. Again, there is no stale crust of apologetical sleight-of-hand that Wright will not claim as a critical advance upon Enlightenment scholarship.

For Wright, Matthew's accuracy is demonstrated by the fact that he seems to have added no new stories to the resurrection plot-line. What about the repeated earthquakes, the descent of the angel, the guards at the tomb, the embassy of the Sanhedrin to Pilate, the rising of the dead saints on Good Friday? Without a word as to the improbability of other evangelists omitting it if it had happened, Wright confesses himself ready to swallow the historical accuracy of the guards. Wright thinks it makes sound sense that the guards are to tell that the disciples stole the body while the guards were asleep? How did they know what happened while they were snoozing? Wright seems not to recognize comedy if there is no laugh track.

Wright insists that the gospel writers must have believed in a literal resurrection (whatever that would be: Jesus becoming the Martian Manhunter again?). But can we be so sure of that, given certain elements of their narratives? Luke's Emmaus scene is transparently symbolic of the invisible presence of Christ among his followers every Sunday at the breaking of the bread. (Wright finally admits this, but he insists that it also really happened, more of his both/and-ism.) Matthew ends not with an ascension to get Jesus off the stage of history (as in Acts), but with Jesus assuring the readers (at whom the Great Commission must be aimed) that he will continue with them until the end of the age. Does this not imply that the resurrection was after all the inauguration of the metaphorical/spiritual sense in which Matthew's readers, like modern Christians, sense Jesus intangibly with them?

John's story of Doubting Thomas concludes with Jesus making an overt aside to the reader: "Blessed are those who have not seen yet have believed." Can this writer have seriously intended his readers to think they were reading history? Such asides to the audience are a blatant and overt sign of the fictive character of the whole enterprise. As Barr pointed out long ago (*Fundamentalism*, 1977), the fact that Luke has the ascension occur on Easter evening in Luke 24 but forty days later in Acts chapter 1 (something Wright thinks utterly insignificant!) shows about as clearly as one could ask that Luke was not even trying to relate 'the facts' and didn't expect the reader to think so.

One could easily go on and on and on, even as Wright does — and *because* Wright does. What we have in this book is not a contribution to New Testament scholarship, any more than Creationist 'Intelligent Design' screeds are contributions to biological science. Both alike are pseudoscholarly attempts to pull the wool over the eyes of readers, most of whom will be happy enough for the sedation.

A. J. M. Wedderburn's
Beyond Resurrection
(Hendrikson Publishers, 1999)

Back of *Beyond*

A J. M. Wedderburn has nothing but credibility among mainstream biblical scholars. He serves on the Protestant Faculty of the University of Munich, and his well-received books including *Reasons for Romans* and *Theology of the Later Pauline Letters* were not particularly liable to ruffle anyone's feathers. The same, fortunately or unfortunately, cannot be said of his *Beyond Resurrection*. This one is sure to have pious heads shaking and praying for the author.

In a sense, though, the newly radical character of Wedderburn's take on the gospel narratives of the resurrection should not be surprising. The issues in the study of the gospels are rather different from those at stake in the epistles. It's a commonplace that evangelical scholars sometimes go into 'safe' fields of biblical study such as textual criticism ('Lower Criticism') because there they are liable to find little that will upset their own faith or that of their public. Truly scholarly, truly important, but not very controversial. The same is true of Pauline studies. There one may play the theologian more than the critic.

I always wondered how the brilliant evangelical theologian Clark H. Pinnock could say the things he said against New Testament critics and in favor of biblical infallibility since he himself had earned a PhD degree in New Testament. The answer, as I later discovered, was that he had studied the Pauline epistles under F. F. Bruce at Manchester University. Thus, for example, he never had occasion to read D. F. Strauss. If he had, I suspect he would have seen matters much differently, for Strauss had thoroughly refuted virtually every apologetics argument for the gospels and the resurrection still in use today, and he did it long before any of today's apologists were born.

Well, A. J. M. Wedderburn here emerges from the safety zone of Pauline literature into the battlefield of gospel studies.

Doubters will be as delighted as believers will be shocked to read Wedderburn's views on the gospel Easter materials, for they are anything but conservative. In this book we are witnessing a milepost along the way that has led so many of us, as thoughtful Bible readers, from uncritical fideism to a critical standpoint that becomes inevitable as soon as one begins engaging the text on a technical level.

This book has a title that might be taken two ways: does he mean to take the resurrection of Jesus as an established point of departure and then ascend to ever-higher realms? Or does he mean the resurrection somehow fails to pass muster and must be discarded in favor of something else? The latter, perhaps surprisingly, is closer to the truth, and as he anticipates, some colleagues will not much relish what they read here. Wedderburn writes as a scholar who has quietly taken seriously the professed zeal of his fellow New Testament historians and found himself passing beyond the rest, in the process charting the sandbars and rocks where each of his fellows has run aground. For instance, he writes knowingly and well of intellectual stratagems nearly ubiquitous in the world of 'maximal conservative' evangelical scholarship, including the idea that any viable reconstruction of Christian origins must be theologically adequate and must meet the needs of preaching.

This bizarre and arbitrary axiom is precisely why anyone refers to "evangelical scholarship" at all; what makes the scholarship "evangelical"? It is tweedy rationalization at the service of teary-eyed revivalism.

But Wedderburn will have none of it. Not that he is unsympathetic to the concerns of the pious pew-potatoes; he has simply come to the realization that the scholar's role cannot be that of the Grand Inquisitor, shielding people from the uncomfortable truths they fear. (And in the last few chapters he strives manfully to reconstruct some sort of theological stance that will fake neither the biblical evidence nor that of the senses. The result is inevitably pretty modest.)

In the same way, Wedderburn commendably repudiates the controlling axiom of all evangelical scholarship: if there remains any open space for doubting that the traditional view (of Petrine authorship, gospel accuracy, literal resurrection) has been refuted, then the believer need not yield to the critic.

Now if one were honest about it and admitted one's convictions were held by simple will power (C. S. Lewis' old friend "obstinacy in belief"), this might fly. But to shut one's eyes and chant "innocent until proven guilty," while pretending to be a historian is the very height of hypocritical posturing. And to his great credit, Wedderburn has had enough of it. One of the surprising cases he discusses of such will-to-believe masquerading as historical judgment is Wolfhart Pannenberg (*Jesus: God and Man*, 1968), Professor of Theology at the University of Munich until 1994. Pannenberg was a student of Karl Barth. Dismayed at the existentialist element in Barth, he sought to restore revelatory value to history and argued for a historical resurrection of Jesus. He once enumerated a list of criteria that would serve to debunk the resurrection as history:

> (a) if the Easter traditions were demonstrable as literarily secondary constructions in analogy to common comparative religious models not only in details, but also in their kernel, (b) the Easter appearances were to correspond completely to the model of self-produced hallucinations.... (c) the tradition of the empty tomb of Jesus were to be evaluated as a late (Hellenistic) legend (Wedderburn, p. 18).

Pannenberg seems to think he has erected a strong fortress around his faith, like Warfield's series of hurdles the denier of inerrancy must leap. But in fact he was crouching within a melting igloo and trying not to get wet. What was he waiting for? Have not all the criteria been long ago met? Pannenberg's inability to see the obvious can only be compared to the supernatural blindness of the Emmaus disciples.

Swatting the Plague of Flies

In a number of specific cases Wedderburn has seen how the Risen Lord is wearing no clothes. He is quick to point out the unfalsifiable game of "heads I win, tales you lose" as applied to the gospel resurrection accounts. Which is it? Are these stories more credible because their contradictions show there was no collusion between their authors? (Of course there was, in the sense that one may easily demonstrate how one has embellished and rewritten the other.) Or are the stories powerful evidence because they do not contradict one another? (The latter is a barely disguised instance of the absurd claim that an 'apparent contradiction' may be treated as no contradiction at all so long as one can devise some contrived harmonization. In fact, the need to harmonize must itself count, and would in any other field, as a disqualification of the texts as evidence.) One cannot have it both ways. (And I am saying one cannot have it *either* way!)

Wedderburn offers several other helpful refutations of the bombast of conservative apologists. *Contra* today's leading evangelical apologist William Lane Craig and others, he shows that the Acts 13:29 tradition of Jesus' burial by his enemies is more widely attested, occurring also in Justin Martyr, *Dialogue with Trypho* 97:1 and the *Gospel of Peter* 6:21.

Again, he explodes the claim of apologists that Paul knew of the empty tomb tradition because he says Jesus "was buried" in 1 Corinthians 15:4. Surely, Wedderburn points out, the "was buried" is intended to cap what precedes it, "Christ died," *i.e.*, 'dead and buried,' not what comes after — "he rose."

Indeed the situation is precisely parallel to the futile Protestant argument against the perpetual virginity of Mary (itself, of course, a legend). Protestants think that the fact that Joseph "knew her not until she had borne a son" (Matthew 1:25) implies they went at it afterward — when the point is not what *followed* Jesus' birth but what *preceded* it: nothing! So the baby cannot have been Joseph's. Does Luke 2:7 ("She gave birth to her first-born son") imply anything afterward, *i.e.,* more children? No, surely the point is to underline her previous virginity.

James D. G. Dunn (who once seemingly strove for critical scholarship, but has seemed sorrier and sorrier to have hewn himself from the fundamentalist rock), Craig, and a multitude of others maintain that the lack of any known veneration of a tomb for Jesus attests the resurrection. The point seems to be that if there had ever been a time when a Jesus movement had not believed in the resurrection of Jesus (*e.g.*, the Q community as envisioned by Burton Mack), we would hear of pilgrimages to where Jesus was buried.

But I wonder: once the resurrection creed became ascendant, any such site might have been expunged with the ferocity of a King Josiah closing down the high places. That is, if anyone had regarded tomb-veneration as incompatible with belief in the resurrection in the first place. Wedderburn astutely observes that no one would have seen any incompatibility. They never have since Constantine 'discovered' the tourist-trap tomb site in the fourth century. Surely the *best* commemoration of the resurrection would be to visit the empty tomb! And yet, as Dunn and Craig and their fellows contend, there is no early tomb-veneration! Might this lack be construed as evidence that there was no dominant early belief in an *empty* one?

Texts Not Facts

Wedderburn shows how the Easter tales of Matthew and Luke stem from their rewriting of Mark — and to show this is to show the purely literary character of at least Matthew and Luke. The problem with the contradictions between the gospel Easter stories is not that they are goofs casting doubt on the details of stories we might otherwise be inclined to take seriously. No, the point is that the contradictions are keys enabling us to trace *the purely literary history* of the narratives. And Wedderburn pursues the point.

It is not only glitches *between* gospels but also *within* them that betray a literary rather than historical origin. For example, it is simply by crude authorial fiat that Luke 24:16, John 20:14, and the longer ending of Mark (16:12) make the resurrected Jesus unrecognizable to the mourning disciples. Try to picture the scene (as Strauss, in his *The Life of Jesus Critically Examined*, 1835, bade us try to envision Jesus multiplying loaves of bread by stretching them out like sponges!) and you wind up with absurdities. Was Jesus heavily robed? Was he flogged and bruised into hamburger meat and thus unrecognizable? (Never mind that Jesus should have been recognized precisely by means of his wounds, as in John 20:25, 27.) In one sense the literary gimmick here is an excellent one: the element of uncertainty preserves the supernatural chill of the scene without resolving it into pat certainty, a technique

Tzvetan Todorov explains in his *The Fantastic (1975)*. But on the other hand, it is done artlessly: no narrative explanation is given for the uncertainty. The evangelists just baldly tell us the disciples did not recognize him, something as abrupt and arbitrary as their incredible failure to grasp what the passion prediction meant (Mark 9:32). There, Mark was just trying to account for why the passion and resurrection predictions did not prepare the disciples, as they are supposed to do for the reader, for the subsequent events. But all this, both the stories' skill and their lack of it, is a matter of literary composition, not of historical reporting.

Similarly, the question in John and Luke is whether the Risen One is solid flesh or can pass through locked doors like Jacob Marley. If what Jesus wanted to demonstrate was the physical reality of his body, that he was *not* a ghost, he certainly had a funny way of showing it! But the incoherence arises from the literary character of the story: the evangelists wanted to show two things: that Jesus was corporeal, and that, as a resurrected being, he could make a heck of a surprise entrance! The two contradict one another, but that does not occur to the storyteller as long as both individual goals are met. It is just like the Transfiguration story in Mark: did Elijah appear personally in the time of Jesus? Yes he did: you just saw him with Moses. And no, he didn't: he appeared only in a manner of speaking, as John the Baptist. Mark inherited both apologetical arguments and decided he might as well include both. Never mind that they are incompatible; he couldn't bring himself to choose between them. Nor here; hence a fleshly Jesus who can nonetheless walk through walls! The only explanation is that we are dealing with fiction, whether well told or badly — or both.

Blindness and Insight

It is perhaps surprising to see the limits of Wedderburn's critical vision, for he still seems trapped in the clinging Lazarus-bands of conservatism — more individual assumptions than modes of argument. For instance, he imagines that "It is an indubitable historical datum that sometime, somehow the disciples came to believe that they had seen the risen Jesus"

(p. 13). I should say not! Any more than we know about any 'changed lives' of these disciples from before to after the resurrection.

As Pannenberg feared and Wedderburn seems to realize, the gospel resurrection accounts are secondhand — or worse, completely fictive. And what other evidence do we have about what the first disciples may or may not have experienced? 1 Corinthians 15:5 and 7 are hardly firsthand evidence. It is after all, a pair of formulas, standardized, official credential lists that even seem to undercut one another, one presupposing James as the leader of the apostles, the other Peter (as Harnack knew and Wedderburn seems aware). We have this set of formulas from a third party, even if we regard the text in which it appears as genuinely Pauline.

As for Paul's own vision, Wedderburn recognizes the difficulties in knowing what Paul may have experienced and how similar or different it may have been to the experience (if any!) of the 'original disciples.' Burton Mack is right: the empty tomb and appearance stories can simply no longer be taken as either univocal or equivocal ("it might have been hallucinations") evidence of a Big Bang that started Christianity. No, these stories are themselves growths from one of the several kinds of early Christianity, whose origins are unknown. The stories of the apostles and the dawn of their faith are a product of one particular 'apostolic' Christianity and betray an agenda that makes sense best in the second century where well-defined sects (including 'catholic' 'orthodoxy') vied with one another and made parallel boasts of apostolic succession. In the gospel Easter stories we are seeing not the root of the plant but the tip of the iceberg.

Wedderburn still lingers in the pleasant shade of the historicizing bias when he arbitrarily retains individual elements of the resurrection narratives seriously as history. He thinks the women looked for the body, probably without much luck. Isn't it obvious by now that the whole scenario parallels and is derived from ubiquitous Mystery Religion myths where goddesses (Isis and Nephthys, Ishtar, Anath, Cybele) seek for the slain god (Osiris, Tammuz/Dumuzi, Baal, Attis) and anoint him to raise him from the dead? Let Occam's razor rip! Granted, women's testimony may not have been worth much in the ancient world, so the empty tomb stories wouldn't have begun as apologetics — Celsus showed the futility of using them for that. But surely they began instead not as factual reports but rather as mythic scripts for women's mourning rituals such as those long familiar in Israel for Tammuz (Ezekiel 8:14) and Haddad-Rimmon (Zechariah 12:11).

Wedderburn thinks there may be some reliable tradition underlying the Sea of Tiberias story in John 21, but the whole thing must be based on the famous tale of Pythagoras, a vegetarian, who came upon a group of fishermen unloading a huge catch, whereupon he made them an offer. If he could guess the right number of fish, would the fishermen free them? He was right, and back they went. The miracle wasn't the size of the haul, but rather the Rain Man-like acuity of the sage's calculations. The point has been shifted in the Johannine version, but that it stems from the Pythagorean legend is still apparent from the fact that the number of fish – one hundred fifty-three – not only presupposes someone counting them (pointless in the Johannine version we now read) but happens to be one of the holy Pythagorean 'triangular' numbers.

Wedderburn wrestles with the origin of the 'third-day' motif and wonders if something did not after all happen that day. Hosea 6:1–2 ("on the third day he will raise us up") seems insufficient to have fixed the day if there had not also been some event that day, even if that should prove to have been the failure of the women to find the body!

> [The] earliest Christians were convinced, thanks to their experiences at Easter and afterwards, that Jesus' fate was according to God's will. Because they also believed that God had revealed that will in the Old Testament scriptures, they... searched in those scriptures for the proof that the anointed one of Jewish expectations had indeed to suffer and die and be raised again, that his fate was therefore according to the scriptures (plural). As a result of this basic enquiry which convinced them that Jesus' fate did correspond to what the scriptures had foretold, they... sought for the confirmation of their basic search in as many details of the passion story and its sequel as they could... Even when only one passage could support, rather precariously, a detail like the third day, it confirmed the general character of the story as scriptural. But this analysis leads to the conclusion that the [Hosea]

passage did not originate the date, as some have claimed; on the contrary, the date led to the discovery of the text that showed its basis in scripture" (p. 52).

But this seems superfluous and unnatural. What would have been the point if the event of the resurrection, the experience of the risen Jesus, had first convinced them? Would these Easter morning believers and their immediate heirs have been dissuaded if they had not been able, like the Pharisees of John 7:52, to document every detail from scripture? No, the whole scenario bespeaks a scribal atmosphere like that of the rabbis or of Qumran, where new secrets are coaxed out of the sacred page by means of esoteric combinations and out-of-context exegetical atomism. Surely a more natural picture is the one hypothesized by Earl Doherty *(The Jesus Puzzle*, 1999) whereby early Christians sought to historicize their spiritual messiah by filling in details from scripture *peshers*. When they said Christ died for sins, was buried, rose, *etc.*, according to the scriptures, they probably, like Matthew with the 30 pieces of silver, the two donkeys, *etc.*, derived the supposed events from reading texts out of context for their secret predictive value. Thus most likely either Hosea 6 was the origin of the third-day motif, or it was invoked to supply a Jewish, biblical pedigree for a mytheme derived from a Mystery Religion (Attis, too, rose on the third day).

Has Wedderburn abandoned his one-time evangelical compatriots? Or, as I deem more likely, have they abandoned him? That is, someone here has taken seriously and consistently the exhortation all evangelicals hear to love the truth above all, but not everyone has seen that the truth cannot be identified with a given dogmatic-exegetical party line. I should say Wedderburn has chosen the better part.

William Lane Craig's "Contemporary Scholarship and the Historical Evidence For the Resurrection of Jesus Christ"

William Lane Craig is a meticulous researcher and a smooth platform speaker. Those attending one of his debates will readily come to see they have chanced upon an evangelistic rally in academic clothing. His goal is not so much to win debates as to win souls. But he makes a good showing at the lectern, or the pulpit, whichever it is. He is a kind of 'Mister Science' purporting to convey the increasingly conservative results of contemporary scholarship in order to convince sophomoric skeptics and doubting believers alike. The most remarkable thing is the degree of respectability Craig (like his twin N. T. Wright) has managed to obtain in the ranks of mainstream scholarship. There is no denying Craig's brilliance, and yet his arguments strike me as being pretty much gussied-up versions of hackneyed old platitudes. How is it, then, that they show up now and again in the pages of the super-elite *New Testament Studies* and similar venues?

I believe the welcoming of views like Craig's and Wright's attests a demographic shift that is easy to explain. The 1970s resurgence of emotion-driven, revivalistic religion has resulted in the mushrooming of evangelical seminaries and Bible colleges. These institutions are able to employ large numbers of graduate-schooled Bible professors — all trained, like Creationist biology teachers, in the trappings of mainstream scholarship, though most of them only endured courses in criticism with gritted teeth long enough to get the requisite sheepskins. Thus was created, too, a wider scholarly market for textbooks of a neo-conservative slant, eager to stultify the results of generations of the Higher Criticism of scripture. Then the Society of Biblical Literature flung wide its once closely guarded doors, admitting anyone who applied.

The result of all these trends was a demographic shift in the "plausibility structure" (as Peter Berger and Thomas Luckmann, *The Social Construction of Reality*, call it). In short, the reactionary backwater of one generation succeeded in becoming the mainstream of the next. Genuine critics have been forced back to the defensive ramparts we once occupied in the early days of critical scholarship, distracted from positive, pioneering work by the need to try to undo some small part of the damage. Hence the need for essays like this one, to try to indicate the vacuity of the regnant neo-fundamentalist scholarship.

My acquaintance with Dr. Craig goes back to 1985 when I was privileged to be invited to represent a critical viewpoint in a Christian-sponsored confab on apologetics in Texas. Dr. Craig was one of the organizers. Once we got there, we were all told that our presentations, already pared to the bone to fit 30-minute time slots, had to be reduced by half. One exception to this rule was Dr. Craig, who gave the keynote speech. I can only wish that he had been subject to the same strictures, and that he had allowed me to take the editing knife to his remarks. I was astonished at their wrong-headedness then, and I have only grown more astonished in the years since, years in which I have read his essays on the resurrection and debated him in person. Here I will restrict myself to a rejoinder to one particular exercise in apologetics, Dr. Craig's article "Contemporary Scholarship and the Historical Evidence for the Resurrection of Jesus Christ" (available at http://www.leaderu.com/truth/1truth22.html).

Philosophical Presuppositions

Dr. Craig begins by stacking the deck, driving home to the reader (almost certainly already a fellow believer looking for some salve for his chafing doubts) the dismal alternative to faith in an afterlife and a creator God. We are left bereft of hope, he says, if we are but the chance products of evolution, doomed to be set adrift in the vacuum of eternity, our atoms commingling randomly with those of the forgotten pterodactyl and the unremembered community college administrator. A sobering prospect, to be sure, but not for that reason a bad one. As Bertrand Russell ("A Free Man's Worship") showed so splendidly, such a nihilistic vision may instead yield a noble Stoicism of purpose and duty. As Nietzsche proclaimed, such a gospel of the Death of God may be received, as Epicurus' was, as decidedly good news! It implies that Man is born from the forehead of precisely nothing, a clay Adam awaiting his self-creation as he himself wields the tools of will and intelligence. He need not mutely await orders from some higher being, for whose puppet-show he has been carved as a marionette. It does no good to say that this is what Hitler thought (though he didn't — he was a Roman Catholic); any creed may be abused by the wicked, as the sorry history of knaves and demagogues who have manipulated Christianity for their own ends shows too well.

Craig reassures the reader that he need not look into the Nietzschean void, because there is the hope of eternal life with God, and that hope is founded upon the resurrection of Jesus. We will shortly see whether that hope is well founded. But for the present, let us ask ourselves: if this life has no discernible purpose, how would lengthening it unto eternity suddenly *make* it meaningful? Add an infinite number of zeroes to zero and what have you got?

Endless quantity does not create quality, as if one should watch millions of episodes of *Laverne and Shirley* or *Charles in Charge*. Would that make them good viewing? Craig believes life would be pointless without an eternal extension of it. I don't see why. We would first have to settle the question of what would make it meaningful here and now. And if we can answer it, then the question of how long it may last is a completely different issue. For example, if we decided that loving and serving a god gives meaning to life, that conclusion alone tells us nothing about possible life after death. Ancient Israel apparently believed in a loving god to whom one bade farewell on one's deathbed. It was just part of the humility of the human condition. Still not a bad way to look at it.

But in all this, Craig is rushing to embrace the very danger Kierkegaard warned awaited the interested partisan in any intellectual problem: if one has a vested interest in a certain conclusion being reached, one's hand rests too heavily upon the saw, and the needful fine consideration of factors becomes clumsy and violent. Craig should have heeded that warning. Failing that, he is a raging bull stampeding through the china shop of delicate evidence.

Resurrection of the Resurrection

Craig next laments the abandonment of the belief in the historical resurrection of Jesus by nineteenth-century liberal Protestant theologians, under the influence of Rationalistic Deism, which denied the possibility of miracles. Schleiermacher would be a case in point. Like the Deists, he disdained miracles as clumsy mid-course corrections by a god who surely was wise enough to get it right the first time, when he planned the universe and set in place its natural laws. As a result, Schleiermacher justified the resurrection appearance narratives as factual (something the Rationalists were eager to do!) by positing (as many of them did) that Jesus had not died but been taken down alive from the cross, then revived in the tomb, whence he emerged for a brief period, which Schleiermacher called "the second life of Jesus" before he finally succumbed.

We will see, however, that it is Craig and his fellow apologists who are mired in eighteenth-century Rationalism, for like them and their contemporary Orthodox opponents, Craig believes that the terms of the debate over the resurrection include a prior acknowledgment by both sides that the gospel narratives are historically accurate even down to the details. The debate must concern the lines employed to connect those details, like dots in a puzzle. Can we connect them without resort to miracles and the supernatural? The Rationalists said *Yes*; their Orthodox opponents said *No*. Craig and the apologists are still trying to play that game. There is no other team; there are only tackling dummies — for the other team has long since moved on, not only to a different stadium, but to a different game altogether.

Already in the eighteenth century, the Empiricist David Hume [1711–1776], the scourge of philosophical Rationalism, mounted an argument that apologists seem perversely to refuse to understand. In their writings, one continuously reads as if in a recurrent nightmare the erroneous refutation by C. S. Lewis in *Miracles: A Preliminary Study*, that Hume's argument is circular. It is not. Hume did not argue, as Rationalists had done, that we know natural laws are inflexible and do not allow for the barest possibility of miracles ever having occurred. For Hume, we know no such thing!

The most radical of Empiricists, Hume simply pointed out that, faced with a report of a miracle, the responsible person would have to reject it, not because he has a time machine in the garage and can go prove it didn't happen, but because he knows the propensity of people to exaggerate, to prevaricate, to misunderstand, to be tricked, *etc*. Balance against the possible truth of this report of a miracle all the evidence of contemporary experience against violations, suspensions, whatever, of the regular occurrence of events, and where will you come out? You do not know for a fact that the miracle report is mistaken, because you can never absolutely know the past. But you have to make your call whether the thing is plausible or not. Let's let Hume himself tell us what he thought about miracles:

> No testimony is sufficient to establish a miracle, unless the testimony be of such a kind that *its falsehood would be more miraculous than the fact which it endeavors to establish....* When anyone tells me that he saw a dead man restored to life, I immediately consider... whether it be more probable that this person should either deceive or be deceived, or that the fact which he relates should really have happened. I weigh the one miracle against the other... and always reject the greater miracle. If the falsehood of his testimony would be more miraculous than the event which he relates — then, and not until then, can he pretend to command my belief or opinion. [Hume, "Of Miracles"]

What Hume argued was essentially the same as what Ernst Troeltsch in the next century would dub the *principle of analogy*: claims of past events must be judged by today's standards of what does and does not happen. Otherwise there simply is *no* standard. We are stuck believing every fairytale and political promise. And if we say one must be equally open to things having gone differently in the past, we are begging the question, since what basis do we have to think they did? And besides, the apologists' own case, though it turns out to be futile, depends no less on the scarcity and astonishing nature of miracles in whatever age they may occur. In other words, they are imagined as always violating the analogy of the experience of every age, or no one would take notice of them and say, "Surely God is among you!" Hume would agree that by a leap of faith, *i.e.*, sheer will power, one may insist on believing the improbable, but then all talk of the supposed importance of 'evidence' must end — *has* ended except as window dressing.

Craig is equally disgusted with the successors to classical liberal theology: Neo-Orthodoxy and Bultmannian existentialism. They didn't have a taste for the historical resurrection either. But the clouds parted starting with Käsemann and the New Quest for the Historical Jesus — or did they? Käsemann certainly did not believe in the empty tomb of Jesus. He and neo-Bultmannians simply sought to find evidence, in what fragments of Jesus' authentic teaching they had left after critical scrutiny, of any continuity between Jesus' own 'authentic existence' and that made possible for Christians in the wake of the Christ-event.

Craig has found something more like an ally in Wolfhart Pannenberg [1928–], whose belief in a physical resurrection is based on one of the weakest of old-time apologetics: what changed the Disciples from craven cowards to lion-hearted preachers? The whole thing depends upon a naïve reading of the gospels, where the disciples' flight at Gethsemane is dramatically requisite so the hero may face, and triumph over, danger alone. And it entails a dubious reading of Acts, according to which *it is not the resurrection appearances at all which have emboldened the disciples*, but rather the advent of the Holy Spirit seven weeks later, until which time they are pictured as still huddling together in private.

At any rate, Craig is delighted to be able to point to a movement among scholars backwards towards belief in an empty tomb and a historical resurrection. There are various ways to explain such shifts in the scholarly plausibility structure, and each has its own strength in the eye of the beholder. To me and my colleagues, for example, the trend toward such beliefs is the product of a failure of nerve beginning already with Rudolf Bultmann [1884–1976], a fearful backing away from the radical insights of F. C. Baur [1792–1860]. Higher Criticism of the old school was gradually abandoned because of a move toward retrenchment in an age that sought the comfort of the familiar, that rejoiced to return, as Freud would say, to the oceanic bliss of the womb that bore them. Craig is wrong to disdain Neo-Orthodoxy. It, and Karl Barth [1886–1968], charted the course back to churchliness that pulled biblical studies exactly where Craig thinks it belongs, as the handmaid of Christian dogma.

Holy Hearsay

One can chart the tidal movements of currents of opinion, but that really counts for nothing. One must look instead at the evidence. Craig announces that the scholarly shift rightward is due to scholars considering "the resurrection appearances, the empty tomb, and the origin of the Christian faith." As to the first of these, Craig credits Joachim Jeremias [1900–1979] with restoring credibility to the list of appearances in 1 Corinthians 15 by inferring that it was a piece of tradition, practically a creed, memorized by Paul on a visit to Jerusalem where he met earlier apostles, who must have composed the list. This, Craig and many other apologists tell us, takes the list of appearances back to within five years of the events.

True, the witnesses cited there *might* have been hallucinating, but what reason is there to think so? To which one must respond, Oral Roberts might have been hallucinating or lying or what-not when he saw, as he said, a Jesus the size of Godzilla standing next to his hospital building, telling him to raise the money to pay for it. *Ditto* for the numerous claims of UFO abductees, witnesses of the Virgin Mary, *etc.* As Hume said, why should anyone take *any* of these claims seriously? What are the chances these people have not misunderstood, hallucinated, been deceived, *etc.*, given the dismal record of the human race in this regard?

But I do not grant the point of the tradition even being old. Craig and I have tangled on this, and I cannot take the time to repeat it all here. One may read my case ("Apocryphal Apparitions: 1 Corinthians 15:3–11 as a Post-Pauline Interpolation") together with Craig's reply and my reply to him at *infidels.org.* Suffice it to note that if this text, this list, were as old as apologists make it – if it even fell within the first century! – *we should certainly see the business about the appearance to more than five hundred brethren reflected in the gospels*, which instead give us nothing but disappointing scenes of Jesus appearing to small groups behind locked doors! The notion of the eyewitness apostles composing this list is no different from the identically bogus claim that the twelve of them got together and composed the Apostles Creed.

As an inerrantist, a conviction that controls his every move though he keeps it tactfully tacit during these machinations, Craig cannot leave it at 1 Corinthians 15. He cannot throw the gospel appearance stories to the wolves. So he takes the circuitous path to nowhere and starts with deductive arguments about how quickly legends can and cannot form, how long it takes for remembered public events to become distorted, and then says that the gospel Easter stories just don't have the time to be anything but newspaper-type reporting. He buttresses his case with the sweet assurances of A. N. Sherwin-White (*Roman Society and Roman Law in the New Testament*) who agrees that much more time would be needed for such distortions to creep into the record.

Craig is proud to appeal to Sherwin-White as an objective witness, not a biblical scholar but an impartial historian of secular matters! Yes, about as impartial as William Foxwell Albright, a Presbyterian apologist for biblical historicity who misled a whole generation of biblical archaeologists (who wanted desperately to be misled — part of that Neo-Orthodox retrenchment). Scarcely the disinterested drop-in from an alien field, Sherwin-White wrote as a Christian apologist, proof-texting Roman studies to vindicate the gospels. But whoever he was or whatever the reason he wrote, he is just wrong. Studies of actual cases of myth-mongering in far less than a generation (such as I give in my book *Beyond Born Again*) show these deductive pontifications about "what would have happened" are absolutely worthless, as arbitrary a presupposition as that naturalism which Craig delights in ascribing to biblical critics.

In the final analysis, all this hair-splitting is really quite superfluous and unnecessary. Craig asserts the 1 Corinthians 15 list of Jesus' alleged appearances takes us back to within five years of the events. Really? How on earth could he know that? How does he *know* when Jesus died? How does he *know* that Jesus ever lived at all, let along died in a particular year? How does he *know* when, where, and by whom the text of 1 Corinthians 15 was committed to writing? How long had the 'tradition' therein been circulating at the time of writing, and how could he prove it? What proof does he have that someone named Paul wrote it? How does he know the text is unitary and has never been altered by a later hand? How does he know that any particular appearance ever occurred? How can he know the whole thing is not a total fiction concocted for theopolitical purposes in a historical milieu unrecognizably different from the primitive Christianity of Orthodox tradition?

Confederacy of Dunces

Craig says "a significant new movement of biblical scholarship argues persuasively that some of the gospels were written by the AD 50's." I will not assume Craig is hallucinating here. Let's suppose he has actually read something to this effect: he can only be referring to other evangelical pietists grinding out fatuous apologetical arguments like the ones we are dealing with here. To dignify this nonsense with a term like "a new movement of biblical scholarship" is like calling Henry Morris and the Creationists "a new movement in paleontology." Oh — I forgot: Craig is a Creationist, too, isn't he? I refer the reader to my book *The Incredible Shrinking Son of Man*, chapter one, "The Sources," for a discussion of gospel dating. It is too much to reproduce here.

Similarly, Craig fantasizes that "All NT scholars agree that the gospels were written down and circulated within the first generation, during the lifetime of the eyewitnesses." With this, Craig has begun to do with contemporary history what he has been doing all along with ancient history: recasting it according to his fond desires. This is not even a good generalization! Does Craig now read nothing but fundamentalist apologists? Unless the reader has so restricted himself, he will know at once how wide of the mark Craig's assertion is.

"It is instructive to note that no apocryphal gospel appeared during the first century. These did not arise until the generation of eyewitnesses had died off." What does that have to do with it? First, we aren't close to knowing that any of the canonical gospels occur within the first century. Second, the distinction hints at Craig's theological bias: inside the canon is good; outside the canon is bad. Anything we have to say to make the canonical look good, we will say. If what he means is that the familiar four gospels are blessedly free of exaggeration such as we find in things like the Gospel of Nicodemus and the Gospel of Peter, he still fails. Comparing Matthew with Mark shows how Matthew added to Mark's crucifixion account the 'details' of the mass resurrection of dead saints and their eerie return to Jerusalem, as well as earthquakes that shattered stones. If these are not prime examples of 'apocryphal' embellishment, nothing is. True, Nicodemus' gospel goes even farther, but so what? Matthew must be measured as much against Mark as against Nicodemus. And if Craig snickers at the giant angels accompanying Christ out of the tomb in Peter's Gospel, I hope he gets a belly laugh out of the giant angel within the canon at Revelation 10:1–2, or those seen by Elchasai and Muhammad. Of course his face straightens right up if you flip over to Revelation 10, because the issue, as it always is with Craig, is theological apologetics, not the scholarly study of ancient documents.

Veritas versus Verisimilitude

"If the burial account is accurate, then the site of Jesus' grave was known to Jew and Christian alike. In that case, it is a very short inference to [the] historicity of the empty tomb." Right off the bat, one is tempted to say, "Yes, but then if the raft account is accurate, then the direction of Huck and Jim's flight would have been known to Tom and Aunt Polly alike. In that case it is a very short inference to the historicity of Huck Finn." But on to details.

Craig says the first disciples could never have sustained their own belief in Jesus' resurrection had they known Jesus was still in the grave, since there is no known form of Jewish resurrection belief compatible with a rotting body. He quotes fellow evangelical apologist E. Earl Ellis to this effect. (I am reminded of the laundrymen who stayed in business by taking in each other's wash.) But this is just not so. Even the scene in John in which Jesus is recognized by his wounds is reminiscent of Hellenistic (including Jewish) *post-mortem* appearance scenes by ghosts. The ectoplasmic body would have looked like the physical one, so pointing to a wound sustained while being put to death would not have to mean physical resurrection. One would have "returned from the dead" in any event.

Besides, as Burton L. Mack and many others (if one wants to name drop and nose-count as Craig likes to do) have shown, there is no way of knowing that the earliest Christians even believed in the resurrection of Jesus. Whoever compiled the Q document gave no hint of it, that's for sure. (Craig rejects Q, by the way, but he's going to be waiting a long time for New Testament scholarship to catch up to him on that point!). Others seem to have believed Jesus was initially assumed into heaven, where he served as an intercessor in the manner that Jews believed Jeremiah and Onias III did, from whence he would one day return via the resurrection, a belief with which an occupied tomb would not be at all incompatible. This is exactly what Lubavitcher Hasidim believe about the late Menachem Schneerson today.

Craig assets that "Even the most skeptical scholars admit that the earliest disciples at least believed that Jesus had been raised from the dead. Indeed, they pinned nearly everything on it." Such assurances are gratuitous. All we *do* know is that it served the interests of some segments of early Christianity to tell stories in which Jesus returned from the dead and appeared to his disciples. We have no way to know whether such stories came from the original disciples, especially since Craig knows good and well that the similar resurrection appearance scenes of the apocryphal gospels are by no means historical. But then how can we be sure the scenes in the canonical four are? It is begging the question, in precisely the same way the old Rationalists used to do, to take for granted all sides in the dispute must assume the substantial accuracy of the gospels and Acts going in!

"The Jewish authorities would have exposed the whole affair. The quickest and surest answer to the proclamation of the resurrection of Jesus would have been simply to point to his grave on the hillside." I love the buttoned-vest peremptory tone of these dismissals, carrying with them the English club atmosphere of the older generation of apologists (*e.g.*, J. N. D. Anderson) whom Craig and his pals are emulating. But this is surely the lamest of arguments. Remember, the only evidence we have one way or the other as to when anyone began preaching the resurrection is Acts 2, where it began *fully seven weeks after the death*. If the Sanhedrin had produced the body, it would have by then been a lump of liquescent putrefaction, unidentifiable as anyone in particular. Remember, the mourners held their noses when Jesus ordered Lazarus' grave stone to be taken away: "Lord, by this time he stinketh!" And that was only the fourth day!

Plenitude of Emptiness

Craig offers a Pentateuch of pleadings to get us to accept the historicity of the story of Jesus' burial.

Firstly, "the burial is mentioned in the third line of the old Christian formula quoted by Paul in 1 Cor. 15:4." But, again, it may not be an early list. Even if it is, so what? It may be history, or it may be verisimilitude if someone is building up to a resurrection fiction.

Secondly, "It is part of the ancient pre-Marcan passion story which Mark used as a source for his gospel." But are we so sure there ever *was* such a source? I for one do not think so. To posit one is itself, I think, another sleight-of-hand scheme to narrow the gap between Jesus and the earliest gospel. That is why Craig assumes without question the existence of a pre-gospel source here, but denies it in the case of Q, the implications of which he dislikes. As for me, I am only saying we can't rely on a merely hypothetical source if we are, like Craig, trying to narrow down the possibilities, not trying to open them up as I am seeking to do. And the more possibilities there are, the less the case seems to "demand a verdict."

Thirdly, "The story itself lacks any traces of legendary development." Oh does it, now? The fretting of the women – "Who shall roll aside the stone for us?" – is an obviously literary anticipation of the supernatural opening of the tomb. John's account, which only he has, and involving a character unique to his gospel, Nicodemus, smacks of legend, especially the extravagant hundred pounds' worth of spices! The burial in a garden recalls the relevant fertility-god mythemes (which also include the searching for the savior's body by the divine sisters, *e.g.*, Isis and Nephthys looking for Osiris, Cybele looking for Attis, Anath seeking Baal). The element of Jesus' burial in a rich man's tomb (implicit in all versions, explicit in Matthew) sounds like the typical lead-in of the Hellenistic novels to the discovery by grave robbers of the person prematurely interred, awakening from a coma. In fact, if we were not, in the gospels, reading a piece of fiction, there would be no burial story at all! In a historical account the burial would be implicit, not rising above the threshold of the noteworthy. Whereas a historian never bothers telling us how a character was dressed, a fiction writer will tell us how the character is dressed if it is going to prove relevant in what comes after. Even so, here we are told that Jesus was buried in a particular tomb simply to pave the way for the narration to return there and see what happens next.

Fourthly, "The story comports with archaeological evidence concerning the types and locations of tombs extant in Jesus' day." But even if that were true, that need be no more than verisimilitude in fiction. If the story were guilty of gross errors of geography (as the gospels do seem to be elsewhere, not least on the question of there having been synagogues in Galilean villages), this might militate against its historical accuracy, but the absence of them means nothing. One might as well argue that *War and Peace* is a record of real events since, where it does use historical coloring, it gets it right.

Fifthly, "no other competing burial traditions exist." Not so, *mon ami*. As Craig knows, Acts 13:29 has the executioners of Jesus see to his burial. Craig, as I recall, wishes to subsume this as mere summarizing of the fact that Joseph of Arimathea was a member of the Sanhedrin. But that is a very strange way of putting it! If you were generalizing from the gospels' Joseph story, would you subsume Jesus' benefactor amid the mob howling for his blood? It is a strange bit of synecdoche! Besides, Justin Martyr and the *Gospel of Peter*, not to mention the *Toledoth Jeschu*, give alternate burial stories. What they hold in common may be very old, and that's all we have to show in order to show Craig has not eliminated all the variables.

Paul-Bearers

Craig next tries to find the body of an assertion of the empty tomb inside the vacant cavity of 1 Corinthians 15:4. In that verse the author says "he was buried," then passes on to "he was raised." It is begging the question to assume that "no Jew" could have understood a resurrection to be compatible with a decaying body. And yet what does 1 Corinthians 15 itself go on to say? The discussion compares the dead body to the seed husk from which the newborn plant emerges (verses 37–38). It requires no great stretch to see how one who wrote in this manner could have easily envisioned the husk lying there to decay. The impact of this point is not lost even if, with me, one deems 1 Corinthians 15:3–8 an interpolation. My point is simply that here we have what Craig says cannot exist: an apparent understanding of the resurrection body compatible with the sloughing off of a mortal body of flesh.

The fact that 1 Corinthians 15:4 has Jesus raised "on the third day" seems to Craig (and others) to require some historical peg to hang from. If there had not been some historical event, even a hallucination, on that day, why choose "the third day" for the resurrection? But the passage itself gives us a broad hint when it says he rose on the third day "in accordance with the scriptures." I join many who read this as meaning that the early Christians derived "the third day" midrashically from Hosea 6:2, "On the third day he will raise us up." That is certainly the simplest alternative. How else did Matthew 'know' Judas had been paid thirty pieces of silver? He surmised it, and a great many other details of his story, from Zechariah.

Craig appeals to Rudolf Pesch for two arguments for the antiquity of the burial tradition. First, the account of the Last Supper in 1 Corinthians 11:23–25 seems to reflect Mark's and to be based on it. This implies that the pre-Markan passion narrative (if there was one) would have been older than Paul, already available to him. But this ignores the strong possibility that 1 Corinthians 11:23–25 is itself an interpolation, as has been argued by William O. Walker, Jr. But let us assume it is genuine. In that case, as Hyam Maccoby says, we have a passage in which Paul seems to claim knowledge of the proceedings of the Last Supper by means of direct revelation, not by historical tradition: he received it "from the Lord" and passed it down to the Corinthians. But I think it is an interpolation based on canonical Mark and thus very late.

Furthermore, Mark (or his source) never refers to the officiating high priest by name, which Pesch absurdly takes to mean that the narrator was writing for contemporaries who naturally knew the identity of the priest. But might it not just as easily mean that the narrator did not himself know who the priest was, because he was writing too much later? I don't see why not, or how we could decide between the two options. For how many fairy tales do you know the names of the kings and queens?

Shall We Join the Ladies?

In lock-step with the legions of yesterday's apologists Craig next asks why women are credited with discovering the empty tomb if the story was made up? Women's testimony was suspect in the eyes of many (though the degree to which that is true is newly debated these days). So if someone were making it all up, he should never have had the empty tomb discovered by women. So it must be true.

Really, now? There is another approach. *We might conclude that since it would have been altogether pointless to adduce the testimony of women, then testimony is not what we are reading.* What *would* make sense in an ancient context? The presence of the women at the tomb is exactly what we should expect if the whole story hails from the cognate resurrection myths of Osiris, Baal, Attis, and Dionysus, whose major devotees were inspired women who sought out the body of the slain savior, then raised it from the dead.

It is virtually an article of faith among apologists to disclaim and despise such myth-pattern cross-references, as if to suggest such parallels were tantamount to denying the Holocaust. Apologists like to scorn this observation, one suspects, because it is so deadly to their case. If there were well-known myths of dying and rising gods similar at many points to the Passion and Easter stories of the gospels, then anyone could see, *à la* Hume, that these gospel stories are much more likely to be whatever the others are: beautiful and profound myths.

Despite the repeated assurances of Bruce Metzger, Edwin Yamauchi, Ronald Sider, and Jonathan Z. Smith that no pre-Christian evidence for such pagan resurrections exists, the claim is absurd. Pyramidal evidence for the risen Osiris, textual evidence for the resurrections of Tammuz and Baal, iconographic evidence for the risen Attis all predate the New Testament. Besides, why on earth would early Christian apologists resort to the argument that Satan counterfeited the true resurrection *in advance* if they thought no such myths predated theirs? In short, then, the stories of the women at the tomb are not intended as evidence for anything. Rather, they are remnants of the rubrics for the Easter vigil of the holy women. That makes the most sense to me. If I'm wrong, I'd like to know why. It sure fits the pattern of ancient religion.

Craig defies the critic to explain where Christianity came from in the first place if there were no 'Big Bang' (if I may borrow Burton Mack's term) to give it the initial momentum. Well, if the resurrection of Jesus as a historical fact is the only answer, then I guess we're stuck believing in the historical victory of Mithras over the cosmic Bull, the historical resurrection of Attis, Osiris, Tammuz, *etc.* Craig has no difficulty believing these fine religions began amid the hoary mists of antique myth. Why should this one be any different? Of course, what makes it different in Craig's estimation is that this one started relatively recently, which is why he is so concerned to pin down everything to within a few years of the alleged events. But that is, again, begging the question, since precisely what is at issue is whether it makes more sense to trace Christianity to a local mutation of the resurrection myths that thickly foliated the region.

Craig is myopic when he says Christian faith in the resurrection could only have come from Jewish influences, since there weren't any "Christian influences" before Christianity began. But Mack is right: there may well have been non-resurrection Christianities that eventually created the belief in the resurrection at a certain stage of their evolution. Anyway, Craig discounts the possibility of Christianity emerging from Jewish resurrection belief since in all our evidence for such belief there is never any reference to the possibility of someone rising from the dead before the eschatological denouement when everyone rises together. Does Mark 6:14 mean nothing? "King Herod heard of it; for Jesus' name had become known. Some said, 'John the baptizer has been raised from the dead; that is why these powers are at work in him'."

It sure seems to mean that Jewish contemporaries (mis)understood public appearances of Jesus as resurrection appearances of John the Baptist. I'd say that's a pretty good possible source for the idea. Craig protests that this-worldly resurrections, *e.g.*, that of Lazarus, are no real parallel, because these people, like Jairus' daughter, must have died again one day. How does Craig know this? In view of the faith of early Christians that the world would end in their own generations, I would have to assume they were believed to "tarry till I come again."

But notice Craig does not even mention the possibility of Christian resurrection faith arising from contact with the cults of Baal, Osiris, Attis, Tammuz, *etc.*, all of which were still going strong. He wants to explain Christian origins as a case of creation *ex nihilo*, by a miracle of God, the historical resurrection.

Does the slander attributed to the Jewish elders in Matthew 27:62-66; 28:4, 11-15 at least imply Jews admitted the tomb of Jesus was empty? Would one resort to claiming Jesus' body had been stolen if one did not have to reckon with an empty tomb and come up with some other explanation for it?

No, not at all. Here we have an exact analogy to the Jewish slur that Jesus was a misbegotten bastard. It does not require that Jews had to admit that Joseph was not Jesus' father and had to resort to gossip to avoid admitting the virginal conception! No, the whole point is that they were just sneering at, spoofing Christian preaching. "Empty tomb? Sure! Have it your way! Now what could account for *that*, eh?"

When Craig quotes D. H. van Daalen, "It is extremely difficult to object to the empty tomb on historical grounds; those who deny it do so on the basis of theological or philosophical assumptions," this is sheer libel.

Empty Tombs and Shell Games

In classic style, Craig finishes up with the argument from the process of elimination: none of the alternative explanations serves to explain the Easter morning events, not the Wrong Tomb Theory, the Swoon Theory, the Hallucination Theory, the Theft Theory, *etc.* I have dealt with all these tired arguments, as full of holes as a pair of moth-eaten socks, in my book *Beyond Born Again*. Please look it up at *infidels.org*. Let me just point out that it is just here where Craig shows himself completely mired in the apologetics of the eighteenth century, to which he seeks to turn back the scholarly clock. What he has shown is that, *à la* the Rationalists and Orthodox, these theories cannot be wedged in around the edges of a literalist reading of the gospels that takes their stories all at face value.

These arguments only ever sounded good to Rationalist inerrantists who (freakishly, to our ears) denied the miraculous. They were in the bizarre position of upholding the entire accuracy of the texts as they stand, yet explaining them without miracles! You could disqualify this or that alternative theory by pointing out how it was inconsistent with this or that feature of the story, *e.g.*, the guards at the tomb. This is why apologists, who are after all writing to reassure worried insiders, love these arguments. They allow them to keep their big gun: an inerrant scripture. With this taken for granted, any opponent who falls for their strategy is trapped, having to suggest far-fetched ways of reading the texts against the grain, twisting texts written pretty much out of whole cloth to proclaim the resurrection, as if to make them look like they were saying something else, say, that it was all a case of mistaken identity. (That is pretty much what Hugh J. Schonfield does in *The Passover Plot*, another late growth of the old Rationalism.)

What critics see, ever since David Friedrich Strauss, is that we are not dealing with historical writing here, but with legend and scriptural pastiche. We can easily trace the growth of the Easter stories from gospel to gospel as one evangelist tried to improve or correct his predecessor. To suggest that the variations between the gospels are like street reports of a car accident seen from different angles is just laughable, given the patent interrelationships between the texts and their rootage in Old Testament sources and mystery religion mythemes.

If contemporary New Testament scholarship is going Craig's way, it is devolving back into Protestant scholasticism. It reminds me of the time that Reinhold Niebuhr decried Billy

Graham's evangelistic efforts, over-simple and crass as they seemed to him: "Billy Graham has set Christianity back a hundred years!" Graham's response: "That's too bad! I'd like to set it back two thousand years!"

James Patrick Holding's "How Not to Start an Ancient Religion"

Internet apologist James Patrick Holding (as he chooses to be known) has thus far seen fit to by-pass the pages of published books, though one can only imagine that numerous evangelical publishers would love to have him. He maintains a Web-site containing a whole raft of apologetical essays, most of them aiming to refute unbelievers and biblical critics — all of whom he considers to be enemies of the faith. He is amazingly prolific and erudite as well, though he seems to me sometimes perversely to misread his opponents' arguments and to reduce them to straw man status. In the essay to be addressed here, Holding sets forth a wide-ranging version of an old argument one hears more and more these days from fundamentalist apologists: that the initial success of Christianity defies sociological common sense and demands a miraculous explanation. The sheer scope of the argument, as well as its increasingly common use in debate, make a critical review of it advisable.

Holding here attempts "to put together a comprehensive list of issues that we assert that critics must deal with in explaining why Christianity succeeded where it should have clearly failed or died out" like many another messianic cult. For example, that of Sabbatai Sevi in the seventeenth century? Holding deems it unlikely, first of all, that Christianity could have begun with the hoodwinking of a sufficient number of gullible dupes. Imposture is no basis for a successful religion, a notion asserted as if self-evident by many apologists past and present. And yet it is easy to show how Mormonism started with a hoax, though, given the paradoxes of human psychology, we cannot for that reason dismiss Joseph Smith as not also being a sincere religious founder. But a hoax it was, and here today, look at it: it is a thriving world religion in its own right.

So such things *can* happen. On the other hand, I believe the parallels to Sabbatai Sevi are important and show how some of the greatest challenges facing early Christianity may have been overcome, especially the crushing defeat in the wake of its Messiah's death. It also illustrates the thinking that led to retrospective claims of 'passion predictions' and scriptural prophecies, as well as the framing of atonement theories as after-the-fact rationales of an embarrassing death — plus resurrection appearance (and miracle) rumors. Most devastating of all, as I show in *Beyond Born Again*, the rapid, contemporary formation of legends – and that against the attempts of an Apostle such as Nathan of Gaza to prevent miracle-mongering – utterly destroys the apologist's claim that such legendary embellishment could not have taken place in the case of the Jesus tradition.

Holding argues that "Christianity 'did the wrong thing' in order to be a successful religion" and that thus "the only way Christianity did succeed is because it was a truly revealed faith ... and because it had the irrefutable witness of the resurrection." Here he serves notice that we will be asked to 'admit' that miracles are the only way to account for the rise and success of Christianity. In any other field of inquiry this would be laughed off stage. I am thinking of a cartoon in which a lab-coated scientist is standing at the chalkboard, which is full of symbols, and he is pointing to a hollow circle in the midst of it all, saying, "Right here a miracle occurs." Appealing to miracles as a needful causal link is tantamount to confessing bafflement. But in fact, there will be no need for this.

Cross Examination

Citing 1 Corinthians 1:18 ("For the preaching of the cross is to them that perish foolishness; but unto us which are saved it is the power of God."), Holding asks rhetorically, "Who on earth would believe a religion centered on a crucified man?" He contends that crucifixion was so repulsive and degrading a punishment that no one could have taken a crucified man seriously as a religious founder. On top of that, no one could have envisioned the notion of a god stooping to undergo such treatment.

> This being the case, we may fairly ask... why Christianity succeeded at all. The ignominy of a crucified savior was as much a deterrent to Christian belief as it is today — indeed, it was far, far more so! Why, then, were there any Christians at all? At best this should have been a movement that had only a few strange followers, then died out within decades as a footnote, if it was mentioned at all. The historical reality of the crucifixion could not of course be denied. To survive, Christianity should have either turned Gnostic (as indeed happened in some offshoots), or else not bothered with Jesus at all, and merely made him into the movement's first martyr for a higher moral ideal within Judaism. It would have been absurd to suggest, to either Jew or Gentile, that a crucified being was worthy of worship or died for our sins. There can be only one good explanation: Christianity succeeded because from the cross came victory, and after death came resurrection! The shame of the cross turns out to be one of Christianity's most incontrovertible proofs!

This is completely futile and does not begin to take into account the religious appetite (in many people) for the grotesque and the sanguine. Just look at the eagerly morbid piety of Roman Catholics and fundamentalist advocates of "the Blood" who wallow in every gruesome detail of the crucifixion, real or imagined. Consider the box office receipts of Mel Gibson's pious gore-fest *The Passion of the Christ*. In ancient times, think of the Attis cult that centered upon the suicide of its savior who castrated himself and bled to death. Street corner celebrations of such rites invariably attracted bystanders, even initially hostile ones, swept up in the music and chanting, to castrate themselves and join the sect on the spot!

Even if one stops short of the Christ Myth theory, one must still reckon with the possibility, as advocated by Bultmann and others, that the crucifixion of Jesus would still have been readily embraceable as a means of salvation because of the familiarity of the dying and rising god mytheme. It was a familiar religious conception, and no less so because of Hellenistic Judaism's martyrdom doctrine as glimpsed in 2 and 4 Maccabees, where the hideous deaths (much more fulsomely dwelt upon than the crucifixion is in the gospels) are set forth as expiations for the sins of Israel. See Sam K. Williams, *The Death of Jesus as Saving Event*.

Finally, crucifixion was not a taboo subject — as witnessed by the frequent occurrence of crucifixion in dream interpretation manuals, where dreaming of being crucified was typically taken as a good omen of impending success.

Good Jews, Bad News?

Holding thinks that "Jesus' Jewishness... was also a major impediment to spreading the Gospel beyond the Jews themselves. Judaism was regarded by the Romans and Gentiles as a superstition. Roman writers like Tacitus willingly reported... all manner of calumnies against Jews as a whole, regarding them as a spiteful and hateful race. Bringing a Jewish savior to the door of the average Roman would have been only less successful [than] bringing one to the door of a Nazi."

This is ludicrous. There were Roman anti-Semites aplenty, though this seems to have prevailed mainly during periods of Jewish revolt against Rome. But in fact, Judaism was quite attractive to Gentiles in general, Romans in particular, as witnessed by the number of conversions and the unofficial adherence of Gentile 'God-fearers' (like Cornelius in Acts 10 and the Lukan Centurion who bankrolled the synagogue). It had the appeal of an 'Oriental religion' as well as the sterling teaching of Ethical Monotheism to recommend it.

> The Romans... believed that superstitions (such as Judaism and Christianity) undermined the social system established by their religion — and... anyone who followed or adopted one of their foreign superstitions would be looked on not only as a religious rebel, but as a social rebel as well.

No, Judaism was considered a legitimate religion and for that reason Jews were exempt from military service. The Roman attitude seems to have been that an ancient religion was okay, even if silly by the standards of Romans like Juvenal, who felt the same way about the religion of Isis and Osiris, Cybele and Attis, *etc*. But these, too, were legal and quite popular. It was only *new* religions, like Christianity or the Bacchanalia (new to Rome), that aroused suspicion. (Holding will acknowledge this fact later, when it seems to prove useful to him.)

This Accursed Multitude

Furthermore, says Holding, "Christianity had a serious handicap [in] the stigma of a savior who undeniably hailed from Galilee — for the Romans and Gentiles, not only a Jewish land, but a hotbed of political sedition; for the Jews, not as bad as Samaria of course, but a land of yokels and farmers without much respect for the Torah, and worst of all, a savior from a puny village of no account. Not even a birth in Bethlehem, or Matthew's suggestion that an origin in Galilee was prophetically ordained, would have [de]tached such a stigma: Indeed, Jews would not be convinced of this, even as today, unless something else first convinced them that Jesus was divine or the Messiah."

I cannot imagine anybody would have been this snobbish. Romans and other non-Palestinians could hardly have drawn much of a distinction between Galilee and Timbuktu. But even if they had been so choosy, does Holding seriously imagine that any such blue-nosed scoffer would have been convinced only by the miracle of the resurrection, as opposed to the assertion of the resurrection? *They would no longer have been in a position to be convinced by the real thing*, though they might have found the preaching of the resurrection emotionally or spiritually compelling, as many still do. It is foolish to argue in effect that "They were convinced by it, so it must have been convincing. So you, too, should be convinced."

Again, "Assigning Jesus the work of a carpenter was the wrong thing to do; Cicero noted that such occupations were 'vulgar' and compared the work to slavery." Must early Christian preaching have won over the worst sort of snobs? No one, not even the special-pleading Crossan, argues that Jesus was one of the Untouchables or Outcasts. Don't tell me there weren't plenty of people then as now who would not have relished the notion of a faith started by a rustic carpenter. But I think the identification of Jesus as a carpenter, *à la* Geza Vermes, was an early error, a Gentile misunderstanding of the Jewish acclamation that he was an erudite rabbi, skilled in scripture exposition. At any rate, it did not seem to hinder the fantastic success of Stoicism that one its most beloved sages, Epictetus, had been a slave, even less classy, one might suppose, than a carpenter.

> Placing Jesus' birth story in a suspicious context where a charge of illegitimacy would be all too obvious to make would compound the problems as well. If the Gospels were making up these things, how hard would it have been... to take an 'adoptionist' Christology and give Jesus an indisputably honorable birth (rather than claiming honor by the dubious, on the surface, claim that God was Jesus' Father)?

Tell that to all the myth-mongers who ascribed divine paternity to their saviors and heroes! Must these miraculous nativities be factual, too?

Let's Get Physical

Holding ventures that a fabricated religion such as he supposes critics imagine Christianity to have been, would never have chosen a version of exaltation for its hero that entailed a physical resurrection since many ancients are on record as finding the whole notion repugnant, preferring Platonic soul-survival. Indeed, many rejected the idea: Sadducees, some philosophers, even pagan Arabs in Muhammad's day. Does that mean no one else liked it? We never find denunciations of a belief that no one holds. I find fundamentalism grossly repugnant, but that doesn't mean everyone else does.

Holding knows that many Jews *did* share the Christian belief in a physical resurrection, but he says this would not have facilitated their belief in Jesus' resurrection, since Jews supposedly restricted resurrection to the end of the age (John 11:23–24, "Jesus said to her, 'Your brother will rise again.' Martha said to him, 'I know that he will rise again in the resurrection at the last day.'") Holding, like all evangelical apologists, claims that belief in a man rising from the grave before the time, in the midst of "this age," would have been unthinkable. Hence on the one hand, it cannot even have occurred to Christians as a possibility unless they knew Jesus had actually arisen. And on the other, it would have struck the ears of other Jews as the rankest heresy.

But think of John the Baptist, transformed into a miracle-working entity by virtue of resurrection, according to the belief of many (Mark 6:14). Of course Mark makes it a false opinion, but the point is that such a belief, closely paralleling the preaching of Jesus' own resurrection, was readily available in the immediate environment of early Christianity according to the gospels themselves.

As for the venue of the Gentile Mission, "what makes this especially telling is that a physical resurrection was completely unnecessary for merely starting a religion. It would have been enough to say that Jesus' body had been taken up to heaven like Moses' or like Elijah's. Indeed this would have fit... what was expected, and would have been much easier to 'sell' to the Greeks and Romans." But this only means the early Christians didn't concoct Christianity like a bunch of network execs fashioning a sitcom according to focus group surveys.

The question is: where did they get the belief in resurrection that they were shortly saddled with? It might have been because of a real resurrection, sure, but they might simply have inherited it from an environment more friendly to the idea.

Too New To Be True

Holding first argued that Judaism was repulsive to Romans, but now he has to switch hats. He says, correctly, that Romans paid grudging respect to Judaism because it had an ancient pedigree. "Old was good. Innovation was bad." Thus a new faith like Christianity should have failed. Should we then conclude that no new religions ever started or were accepted on their appearance in the West? You just can't take the opinions of the intellectual caste as definitive for what everyone would have thought. Especially since the very expression of such opinions presupposes a regrettable (to these snobs) prevalence of precisely such 'superstitions' as the snobs were condemning.

Such faiths famously could and did succeed — even to the extent of becoming the official religion of Rome: Mithraism and even Baalism, for example. Holding argues as if the success of Christianity couldn't happen and so it must have taken a miracle for it to have happened. The scientific approach, taken by Rodney Stark (*The Rise of Christianity*) and others, is to take as established that it did happen and then explain it — not piously refuse to explain it and claim, "It's a miracle!" With that utter abdication of the scientific method, we would still be in the Dark Ages.

Of course, no one denies there were persecutions of the Christian faith and, before that, the Isis and the Dionysus cults. They were occasioned by the fact that many, many people *did* like these religions and practiced them. That is why Juvenal has occasion in the first place to ridicule them, why Plutarch warns young matrons against them — because they were so prevalent, even among the aristocracy. Their husbands didn't like it, but they couldn't ultimately stop it.

Novelty was in large measure responsible for official distaste for the new faith. But as always, many people are looking for something new, however much the establishment hates and forbids it. And even they may eventually succumb: they yielded to Mithraism as the official state religion, and similarly later to Christianity. Hurdles are meant to be jumped, and hardy religions have jumped them. Christianity had much going for it, many noble features, just as Judaism did, and they won out.

Raising the Bar

Where, Holding wonders, would potential converts have derived the wherewithal to repent of their nice, cozy sins to swallow the bitter pill of early Christian abstinence, if the whole thing were simply a matter of joining one more man-made religion? Can he ignore the fact that *all* the (very popular) Mystery Religions called their recruits to an initial stage of repentance and purification, too?

Neither must we suppose that all Christians were heroic cross-bearers. The whole crisis of a second repentance seen in the *Shepherd of Hermas* and witnessed in Constantine's deferral of baptism to his deathbed attests to the general mediocrity of Christian lay behavior as the rule. They were all no doubt good folks, just not heroic like Jesus or the martyrs. As Stark (*The Rise of Christianity*) shows, the growth rate of Christianity seems to have matched that of analogous modern 'new religions' like Mormonism and the Unification Church. One reason it expanded was its narrowness. Unlike members of other faiths, Christians insisted that theirs was the only way, so if you joined Christianity you left your other affiliations behind, whereas others could and did belong to several movements at once, which naturally watered down devotion to any one of them.

Another way it grew was that Christianity provided a constant safety zone for assimilating Hellenistic Jews who wanted to slough off parochial Jewish ethnic markers like circumcision (already Paul is telling the Corinthian men not to undertake the epispasm operation to "undo" circumcision — ouch!) yet without abandoning the biblical tradition. Yet another growth factor was Christianity's opposition to abortion and infanticide, both quite common among pagans. This meant there were many more Christian women surviving to adulthood, perforce marrying pagan men and converting them. And of course the sterling conduct of Christians, ministering to the sick and destitute in times of plague and famine while pagan priests headed for their countryside villas, like Prince Prospero in Poe's *Masque of the Red Death*, must have attracted many of those helped — and justifiably so! Christianity has much to be proud of in all this. But we don't need any overt miracle to explain it.

As for the unlikelihood that a great number should have welcomed a new faith that offered moral guidance and discipline, I don't see a problem — unless one already takes for granted a doctrine of total depravity.

Intolerance of Intolerance

Christianity began in the Hellenistic age of cosmopolitan tolerance. It was common for members of various religions to regard all the gods as the same, just wearing different names from nation to nation. Even some Jews, like the writer of the *Epistle of Aristaeus*, regarded Jehovah and Zeus as the same. One result was that anyone might join several different religions or cults simultaneously. So mustn't Christianity have disgusted Roman society because of the new faith's exclusivism?

Mustn't the preaching of Jesus as the only way to heaven have appeared a piece of tasteless bigotry? Surely no one would have found such a faith attractive, would they?

Actually, it was a mixed bag. As I have just said, à la E. R. Dodds (*Pagan and Christian in an Age of Anxiety*) and Rodney Stark, exclusivism was also a factor accounting for Christian expansion. The same thing is evident in the modern day in Dean M. Kelly's famous book, *Why Conservative Churches Are Growing*: people feel they are getting the red meat of authentic Christianity with evangelicalism, not the vapid tofu of liberalism, so they flock to the clear notes of the fundamentalist/orthodox trumpet.

On the other hand, what Holding notes about the guardians of the social order being enraged by this, or even some of the people, is true too: there were plenty of lynch mobs before Diocletian and Decius declared open season on Christians. But not everybody reacted the same way. And much of the reaction was conducive to Christian growth — even the persecutions! For, as Tertullian said, the blood of the martyrs was the seed of the church. And then what if significant elements of the establishment embrace the new faith? Things change rapidly.

"Jews, too, would be intolerant to the new faith. Jewish families would feel social pressure to cut off converts and avoid the shame of their conversion. Without something to overcome Roman and even Jewish intolerance, Christianity was doomed." But Christianity appealed to Hellenistic Jews and to Gentile God-fearers precisely because it offered Jewish morality, added to something like Mystery Religion salvationism (and this independent of the question of whether its symbolism and soteriology were borrowed from these faiths. Let's assume for the sake of argument that they weren't), and freedom from what Gentiles and assimilating Jews regarded as the burden of the Law. As Stark (chapter 3) shows, Hellenistic Jews found Christianity a bonanza!

No doubt Ebionite Jewish Christianity did eventually dry up on the vine for the reasons Holding gives: Non-Christian Jews came to associate the name Jesus with what appeared to them a new Gentile cult but wanted nothing to do with Torah-Christianity, either. The plaintive pleas of the latter, "But we're not like them! We're like you!" fell on deaf ears. Meanwhile,

Gentiles faced with the choice of Law-free Christianity or Torah Christianity would surely choose the former, not so much because they were lazy, but because it seemed less inauthentic for them. Why should you have to adopt alien cultural markers to become a Christian?

An Omniscient Public

Holding next cites Acts 26:26, "For the king knoweth of these things, before whom also I speak freely: for I am persuaded that none of these things are hidden from him; for this thing was not done in a corner." Here Paul is making his defense before King Herod Agrippa II.

> The NT is filled with claims of connections to and reports of incidents involving 'famous people.' [For instance,] Herod Agrippa [I]... "was eaten of worms" as Luke reported in Acts 12:20-23. Copies of Acts circulated in the area and were accessible to the public. Had Luke reported falsely, Christianity would have been dismissed as a fraud and would not have 'caught on' as a religion. If Luke lied in his reports, Luke probably would have been jailed and/or executed by Agrippa's son, Herod Agrippa II... because that was the fellow Paul testified to in Acts 25-26... And Agrippa II was alive and in power after Luke wrote and circulated Acts.

No, sorry. For one thing, Luke's account of the first Agrippa's death sounds remarkably like that in Josephus (*Antiquities* 19:8:2) as well as the tale of the worm-devouring death of Antiochus Epiphanes in 2 Maccabees 9:9. For another, there are many reasons to think that Acts stems from the second century, and many scholars think so. Merely mentioning that opinion does not make it true. It does mean, however, that the reader is not entitled to take Holding's assertion of Luke's contemporaneity with Herod Agrippa II for granted either. To paraphrase C. S. Lewis, Agrippa "was dead and couldn't blow the gaff." It is typical of the Hellenistic novels to have fictional heroes interact with famous historical figures, just as in such novels today. Does Holding imagine that the spurious letters between Paul and Seneca must be authentic because otherwise somebody would have definitively put the hoax to rest? Look how hard it is to lay the ghost of Nicholas Notovitch's bogus *Unknown Life of Jesus Christ* which keeps getting revived after the public has forgotten both it and the refutations it garnered in earlier generations.

"People outside the area of Lystra may not have known enough about what happened in Lystra, or wanted to check it, but Christianity was making claims at varied points across the Empire, and there were also built in 'fact checkers' stationed around the Empire who could say something about all the claims central to Jerusalem and Judaea — the Diaspora Jews." Thus Acts' stories must be true. But this is unrealistic and anachronistic — fact checkers? No doubt there were local skeptics who, as in the case of Sabbatai Sevi's miracle reports, denied anything was really going on, but who listens to them? Not the true believers. Like Holding himself, they will mount any argument so as not to have to take threatening factors seriously. Rastafarians refuse to believe Haillie Selassie died. Premies refuse to believe their Satguru's mom fired him. Also, does Holding expect us to accept that the temple of Diana in Ephesus collapsed at the preaching of John because it says so in the *Acts of John*?

> The NT claims countless touch-points that could go under this list. An earthquake, a darkness at midday, the temple curtain torn in two, an execution, all at Passover (with the attendant crowds numbering in the millions), people falling out of a house speaking in tongues at Pentecost... — all in a small city and culture where word would spread fast.

Word spreads fast — word of what? Events and non-events. Rumors spread as fast as facts, faster even. And besides, a little event called the fall of Jerusalem supervened between the time described and the writing of the gospels and Acts. Any witnesses pro or con were long dead and unavailable.

"In short, Christianity was highly vulnerable to inspection and disproof on innumerable points — any one of which, had it failed to prove out, would have snowballed into further doubt, especially given the previous factors above which would have been motive enough for any Jew or Gentile to say or do something." Oh please! If such claims were even made in the time of apostolic contemporaries, we have no way of knowing they were not as thoroughly and adequately refuted as the claims of Joseph Smith were. Christian tradition and documents would hardly inform us of the fact. And once Jerusalem fell, as it had before the New Testament was written, all hope of corroboration is sheer fantasy.

Sticks, Stones, and Names

Holding mounts a version of the argument from martyrdom that is slightly more nuanced than the usual one, and for that we may give him credit. He admits that we have no reliable information as to the possible martyrdom of any specific early Christians. Most of the supposed data come from apocryphal, legendary sources like the fanciful *Acts of Paul*. But, following Robin Lane Fox, Holding widens the scope of social ostracism to which early Christians were subjected: "rejection by family and society, relegation to outcast status. It didn't need to be martyrdom — it was enough that you would suffer socially and otherwise." But this sword cuts both ways, if you are trying to determine its likely effect on the growth and consolidation of membership in a new religion. Such ostracism, when not spontaneously forthcoming at the hands of outsiders, is famously cultivated (even simulated) by cults that seek to cement the loyalty of new members by isolating them from natural family and old friends so they will bond more strongly with "brothers and sisters in the faith." This is why cult deprogramming was such a waste of time — it only drove the victim into the arms of the cult more deeply than ever.

As for outright persecution, *e.g.*, lynchings, seizure of property, just observe how the censured and persecuted Mormons reacted to such hardships — by succeeding fabulously! "It is quite unlikely that anyone would have gone the distance for the Christian faith at any time — unless it had something tangible behind it." Or, unless they *believed* it did, which no one doubts, and which is all Holding can ever show.

Monolithic Monotheism?

Holding has already expressed his reluctance to credit any ancient believing in a crucified god. But what about the general belief that Jesus was God incarnate? Would that notion have proven so repugnant to ancient Jews and Gentiles that none of them could have seriously entertained it — unless irrefutable evidence for the resurrection (how is this a proof for the Incarnation?) forced one to accept it?

Holding, like C. S. Lewis and so many others who use the same argument, is stuck on the discredited notion that something like second-century rabbinic orthodoxy prevailed or even existed in the first centuries BCE and CE. A lot of weird stuff was going on in the Holy Land and elsewhere that would later be forced out under the post-70 hegemony of the rabbis. One might as well ignore the diversity of theologies in Islam and conclude that the Fatimid Caliph al-Hakim was Allah incarnate, as the Druze maintain, or that Ali already was God in the flesh, as many Shi'ite sects believe today. How could such beliefs have arisen in the context of absolutely and fiercely monotheistic Islam? Well, it turns out it wasn't so monolithic, and neither was first-century Judaism.

"And it would be no better in the Gentile world. The idea of a god condescending to material form, for more than a temporary visit, of sweating, stinking, going to the bathroom, and especially suffering and dying here on earth — this would be too much to swallow!" But exactly such was believed of the various demigods, like Asclepius, Pythagoras, and Apollonius. Besides, many early Christians did not believe in a genuine incarnation, but were Docetists, and it is far from certain that Paul was a real incarnationist, with his talk of Christ taking on the *likeness* of human flesh, the *form* of a servant, *etc*. I for one do not take for granted that orthodox definitions of incarnation can be assumed for the earliest Christians.

Armchair Radicalism

"'Neither male nor female, neither slave nor free.' You might be so used to applauding this sort of concept that you don't realize what a radical message it was for the ancient world. And this is another reason why Christianity should have petered out in the cradle if it were a fake." It is a notorious matter of debate even among 'literalist' evangelicals whether statements like the one Holding quotes meant any more than that all the listed categories had equal access to salvation, or whether they also denoted the abolition of traditional social distinctions among Christians. We don't know how progressive a face early Christians presented to their contemporaries. Besides, some of the pre-Socratic Sophists had already preached male-female equality, as did the Pythagoreans and Stoics. Moreover, Christians were by no means, except for Marcionites and Gnostics, quick to implement texts like the one just quoted from Galatians 3:28, as the Pastoral Epistles show.

"Note that this is not just to those in power or the rich; it is an anachronism of Western individualism to suppose that a slave or the poor would have found Christianity's message appealing on this basis." On the contrary, part of the appeal of such 'cults' is that they offer esteem and honor to someone in the eyes of his brethren that he cannot achieve in the secular world. A slave could be a Christian leader.

"Christianity turned the norms upside down and said that birth, ethnicity, gender, and wealth – that which determined a person's honor and worth in this setting – meant zipola." This is characteristic of all sectarian movements in their infancy. It is partly Know-Nothingism – because education is disparaged – and partly true egalitarianism, of course. But hardly unusual for a new religious movement. Buddhism, too, repudiated caste and succeeded. Is it the only true religion, too?

> The group-identity factor makes for another proof of Christianity's authenticity. In a group-oriented society, you took your identity from your group leader, and people needed the support and endorsement of others to support their identity... Moreover, a person like Jesus could not have kept a ministry going unless those around him supported him. A merely human Jesus could not have met this demand and must have provided convincing proofs of his power and authority to maintain a following, and for a movement to have started and survived well beyond him. A merely human Jesus would have had to live up to the expectations of others and would have been abandoned, or at least had to change horses, at the first sign of failure.

This is outrageous special pleading. What about the Buddha, John the Baptist, Martin Luther King, Gandhi, and many others who were let down temporarily or permanently by their followers? And if there were anything special about such persistence, you needn't posit an incarnation. It would be adequate to say Jesus was strengthened by God. Were the indefatigable Paul and Peter God incarnate, too?

"If Christianity wanted to succeed, it should never have admitted that women were the first to discover the empty tomb or the first to see the Risen Jesus. It also never should have admitted that women were main supporters (Luke 8:3) or lead converts (Acts 16)." Similar traditions stem from the ritual mourning of women devotees of Tammuz (Ezekiel 8:14), Attis, Baal (Zechariah 12:11), *etc.* They are not *supposed* to be "evidence for the resurrection" any more than the Oberammergau Passion Play is. And plenty of Mystery cults gave leadership roles to women. That's part and parcel of sectarianism and its first-generation rejection of mainstream norms.

Holding appeals to the bumpkin status of Jesus, John, and Peter (Acts 4:13), and even of the early Christians generally, as another factor militating against the success of the new faith. On the contrary, the supposed illiteracy of prophets and founders is part of apologetic rhetoric, used of Jesus, Peter and John, Muhammad, and Joseph Smith so as to argue they must have been incapable of making this stuff up — "Flesh and blood hath not revealed it to thee, but my father in heaven." It is a common, predictable, and fictive topos, much like the common rhetorical trope that Paul uses in 1 Corinthians 2:1–2, the claim to have renounced or to be inept at clever rhetoric, to throw readers off the track and set them up to fall for it.

Besides, how would Christianity's being 'real' or 'fake' as to miracle claims have anything to do with the success or failure of its progress in society decades later? Wouldn't we have to look to the strengths of the movement at the time? Or are we to picture the Holy Ghost hypnotizing people as they heard the gospel? If instead Holding means they found ancient Christian apologetics so compelling, then he must reproduce them for us to be convinced by. He can't adopt the approach of the Catholic Church, a call for "implicit faith," second-hand *faith in the faith* of the early Christians.

Standing Up for Jesus

"[Bruce] Malina and [Jerome] Neyrey note that in the ancient world, people took their major identity from the various groups to which they belonged. Whatever group(s) they were embedded in determined their identity. Changes in persons (such as Paul's conversion) were abnormal. Each person had certain role expectations they were expected to fulfill. The erasure or blurring of these various distinctions... would have made Christianity seem radical and offensive." Right! Of course! That's what happens when people join new or different religions. Not everyone has the guts to do it (though many have long felt alienated, and have silently waited for some new option to present itself). Holding seems to be arguing that no one converts to new religions except by a miracle of God.

Holding, then, insists that ancient people, much more part of a group-mentality than we are, would not have been likely to break with family and convention to join a new sect. I doubt this, in view of the cosmopolitan character of the Hellenistic Roman Empire when it would have been scarcely less difficult than it is today to run into members of other religions. There was already beginning to be what Peter Berger calls a "heretical imperative" to choose for oneself. But this was probably less true for Palestinian Jews. And yet some did break with their ancestral creeds to join Christianity. Or did they? Remember, Christianity would have begun among Jews. "Faith in Jesus" may not even have amounted to a sect allegiance any more than did Rabbi Johannon ben-Zakkai's controversial belief in the messianic claims of Simon bar-Kochba.

But let us admit that the earliest Christians, as well as other venturesome souls who went out on a limb and joined a new sectarian group, had a lot of guts. All honor to them! But is this miraculous? I know Holding is ultimately trying to say that the evidence for the resurrection must have been pretty darn compelling to prompt such wrenching changes. But it isn't in our day, nor is it even the reason most people give for such conversions. And even supposing there were a few eyewitnesses of the resurrection, assuming it happened, how many of the early conversions can they have accounted for? And then, once you look at the next generation of second- and third-hand converts, the air is out of the tire. "Hey Crispus! I heard this really convincing guy talk about a vision he had!" That is lame. "I guess you had to be there." I see early conversions as motivated by something else than clincher apologetics. "Have you believed because you have seen? Blessed are those who have not seen yet believe" (John 20:29). "Without having seen him you love him; though you do not see him now, you believe in him and rejoice with unutterable and exalted joy" (1 Peter 1:8).

Every Idle Word

In the ancient world, we are told, everybody kept an eye on everybody else. Little escaped a neighbor's scrutiny. Surveillance and gossip were rife — much like today! "So now the skeptic has another conundrum. In a society where nothing escaped notice, there was indeed every reason to suppose that people hearing the Gospel message would check it against the facts — especially where a movement with a radical message like Christianity was concerned." All salvationist sects required repentance and new birth. Jews required righteousness. What was so radical about it? "The empty tomb would be checked." Maybe it was, and maybe it was found occupied, and maybe Christians with their will to believe found it as easy to ignore it as Creationists do the fossil record. Many people, after all, did not come to faith. Maybe this is why. We, at any rate, are in no position to check it out. And Holding begs the question by supposing that the earliest Christians even told such a story.

I agree with Burton L. Mack (*A Myth of Innocence: Mark and Christian Origins*; *The Lost Gospel: The Book of Q and Christian Origins*; and *Who Wrote the New Testament?*) and others who suggest that the empty tomb story is a late addition to the preaching.

"Matthew's story of resurrected saints would be checked out." Two generations later? Not likely. Besides, who would be reading/hearing this story but the members of Matthew's church in Antioch? "Lazarus would be sought out for questioning." What, sixty or seventy years after event? He would be dead again by that time, supposing he was ever a historical character at all, and not just borrowed from the Lazarus of the Luke 16 parable. "Excessive honor claims, such as that Jesus had been vindicated, or his claims to be divine, would have been given close scrutiny." By whom? It is a safe bet Malina and his Social Science colleagues do not mean to depict the ancients as mirror-image apologists as Holding does.

"And later, converts to the new faith would have to answer to their neighbors." How many hearers of the resurrection preaching, which may not at first have included the empty tomb anyway, would have been in any position at all to "check it out"? "Master, I'd like several months off so I can travel over to Palestine and see if I can verify a story I heard from some street corner preacher, that a man rose from the dead over there fifty years ago. I'm hoping I can find his tomb, or maybe somebody who saw it a few days after the execution." And if we are thinking of hypothetical hearers of empty tomb claims in CE 34 or so, what makes Holding think they would be any more inclined to "check it out" than anybody in our day who heard Oral Roberts claiming he had witnessed a King Kong-sized apparition of Jesus in Tulsa one night?

Besides, Holding's whole argument is misguided — as if one could adjudicate historical questions of what did happen by appealing to general tendencies of ancient temperaments and what 'would have' happened. You can't just squeeze history out of peasant sociology, as Crossan does. He and Malina and the crew all tend to reduce Jesus to a mere instantiation of current trends, mores, *etc.*

"I Believe Because It Is Absurd"

"Scholars of all persuasions have long recognized the 'criteria [*sic*] of embarrassment' as a marker for authentic words of Jesus. Places where Jesus claims to be ignorant (not knowing the day or hour of his return; not knowing who touched him in the crowd) or shows weakness are taken as honest recollections and authentic (even where miracles stories often are not!)." Surely, Holding reasons, the framers of a merely concocted religion would take more care to make their imaginary savior deity look good! Hence no one would take the gospel Jesus seriously — unless they had to.

As usual, Holding grossly oversimplifies the historical situation. As John Warwick Montgomery observed, every gospel saying must have been offensive to somebody here or there in the early church. What offended Matthew (Jesus declining to be called 'good,' for example) did not offend Mark, and we may be able to suggest reasons Mark would have created it. At least no criterion of embarrassment will shield it.

Other embarrassing sayings may yet be damage control, fending off something yet more embarrassing. Certainly Paul W. Schmiedel [1851–1935] was naïve in thinking no Christian would ever have fabricated Mark 13:32, where Jesus says he does not know the time of the end. Obviously the point is to correct the impression of the immediate context that he *did* claim to know and that he was *wrong* — as C. S. Lewis ("The World's Last Night") admitted. For Jesus to disclaim knowledge was better than having him mistaken.

Junior Detectives

Encouraging people to verify claims and seek proof (and hence discouraging their gullibility) is a guaranteed way to get slammed if you are preaching lies. Let us suppose for a minute that you are trying to start a false religion. In order to support your false religion, you decide to make up a number of historical (*i.e.*, testable) claims, and then hope that nobody would check up on them. What is the most important thing to do, if you have made up claims that are provably false? Well, of course, you don't go around encouraging people to check up on your claims, knowing that if they do so you will be found out!

Once a student in a class of mine insisted that the CEO of Proctor and Gamble had admitted on the *Donahue* TV show that he was a Satanist and that the corporate logo was Satanic symbolism as well. I told my student that this was an urban legend. Next time he brought in the crudely copied hand-bill he had read. It offered a New York City phone number and urged the reader to call and ask for the transcript of the show for such-and-such date. I called it. There was no connection at all with *Donahue*. The hoaxer had evidently assumed that the mere provision of this (fake) information would be so convincing as to deceive the reader into thinking just as my student did and just as Holding does.

When the reader of 1 Corinthians 15 reads that Paul challenged him to go and ask the 500 brethren about their resurrection sightings, something Paul knew well the Corinthians would never have the leisure to do, he may be impressed, but Paul was taking no risks. The mere challenge in such a case functions as sufficient proof. *Note that he provides no clue as to the names or locations of these supposed witnesses.*

In the late Syriac hagiography, *The Life of John Son of Zebedee*, the apostle similarly invites his hearers to check out the story of Jairus' daughter, resurrected by Jesus. The idea is that the reader will understand that once upon a time the facts could have been checked out, even though it is too late for him personally to do so. This all proves nothing and indeed invites suspicion of imposture where it might not have arisen otherwise.

Holding imagines, with the eye of faith that calls thing which are not as though they were, that "Throughout the NT, the apostles encouraged people to check seek proof and verify facts: 1 Thessalonians 5:21 [says to] 'Prove all things; hold fast that which is good'." But this text refers, in context, to prophetic utterances which should not be dismissed out of hand but scrutinized, as in 1 Corinthians 14:29.

"And when fledgling converts heeded this advice, not only did they remain converts (suggesting that the evidence held up under scrutiny), but the apostles described them as 'noble' for doing so: Acts 17:11 [says] 'These were more noble than those in Thessalonica, in that they received the word with all readiness of mind, and searched the scriptures daily, whether those things were so'." But this is only a much later description of a dubiously historical scene and in any case means only "See? The smart people agree with us!" And if Luke means us to take as representative the fanciful scripture 'proofs' he has the apostles offer elsewhere in the book, we can hang it up right now.

Stigma and Dogma

"Christianity, as we can see, had every possible disadvantage as a faith… I propose that there is only one, broad explanation for Christianity overcoming these intolerable disadvantages, and that is that it had the ultimate rebuttal — a certain, trustworthy, and undeniable witness to the resurrection of Jesus, the only event which, in the eyes of the ancients, would have vindicated Jesus' honor and overcome the innumerable stigmata of his life and death. It had certainty that could not be denied; in other words, enough early witnesses [*as in the 500!*] with solid and indisputable testimony (no 'vision of Jesus in the sky' but a tangible certainty of a physically resurrected body)." Finally we are reduced to this: It was plenty convincing to those in a position to know the inside story, so you ought to be convinced, too! Sorry, but I can only look at the meager fragments of evidence that survive, and they do not look promising.

If Holding deems the evidence for the resurrection to be so strong, then what is the point of all this business of "disadvantages" and so forth? Why beat around the bush rather than getting to the real business at hand? It is not as if he is shy to discuss the evidence in its own right, but the argument considered here is not only fallacious; it is wholly superfluous even if he could be shown to be right in his other arguments for the resurrection.

Glenn Miller's
"Were the Gospel Miracles Invented by the New Testament Authors?"

Strike Up the Band

When I was cutting my teeth on the polemical literature of evangelical apologetics, the leading authors in the field (at least of historical apologetics) included F. F. Bruce, John Warwick Montgomery, and Josh McDowell. They formed a diverse group: Bruce a member of the Plymouth Brethren and a sophisticated New Testament scholar, Montgomery a Lutheran Theology professor, and McDowell a Campus Crusade for Christ evangelist largely derivative of others like Bruce, Montgomery, and still earlier apologists like Wilbur Smith and Paul Little. My study of apologetics eventually pointed my way out of evangelical Christianity altogether, and I documented my case in a book, *Beyond Born Again*. I entered the lists of debates on biblical accuracy and the historical Jesus only some years later, in the late 1990s, and by then a new generation of apologists (I suppose, the generation I had once planned on being a part of!) had taken the stage, including William Lane Craig, Ravi Zacharias, Craig Blomberg, Glenn Miller, Gary Habermas, and Greg Boyd. As I began to delve into their pages, I wondered if any of them had come up with anything new. I hoped I should be open-minded enough to be convinced if they proved to be convincing. To tell the truth, I can only say I was amazed that their case had not advanced by an inch. As one, these new defenders of the faith alike hauled out the same old arguments, just as lame as they ever seemed to me. One supposes they were trotting out the same shelf-worn wares to young audiences unfamiliar with them. I think of the NBC slogan to promote their summer reruns: "If you haven't seen it, it's new to you!" Glenn Miller is typical of these very bright writers and debaters in that his work is a galling waste of time and talents that, freed from the blinders of dogma, might be better applied to genuine biblical criticism. But then again, many of today's critics began as would-be apologists, and, like me, decided "if you can't beat 'em, you might as well join 'em." Maybe Glenn Miller will eventually see it our way, too.

Miller has certainly done his homework in his essay "Were the Gospel Miracles Invented by the New Testament Authors?" (http://www.christian-thinktank.com/mqx.html). And yet I find myself thinking that, like his less sophisticated brethren, he still tends to dismiss critical approaches to the gospel material by amassing *a priori* arguments, as if to disqualify critics' arguments in advance instead of having to deal with them head-on. This is not at first evident, nor am I suggesting he means to do this, for Miller does try to dissect and to address critical theories in great detail. But, for instance, with regard to the claim that the gospels are myth, he lets formal categories get in the way of analyzing the gospels, asking if the gospels meet this and that possible definition of "myths," and demonstrating that they do not. When he is finished, I am left with the distinct impression that the issues are a bit more subtle than that. To wit...

Myth Perceptions

I am delighted to see Glenn Miller bring into the discussion the fascinating book by Classicist Paul Veyne, *Did the Greeks Believe their Myths?* (1988). Veyne (pp. 17–18, 88) says they did not believe them in the same sense that they believed in the factual reality of recent, datable historical events. Instead, they vaguely pictured the 'events' of myth as having happened somewhere in the distant past, something like the notion of *Heilsgeschichte* as used by Rudolf Bultmann (*Jesus Christ and Mythology*) and Gerhard von Rad (*Old Testament Theology*). No one would have thought to ask when in history this or that exploit of Apollo occurred. It happened 'once upon a time,' in an altogether different mental category. Miller rightly points out that the gospels do not fall under this category of myth for the simple reason that the foundational saga of Christianity is set in the era of Herod Antipas and Pontius Pilate. True enough.

But that is not the whole point. We still have to reckon with the relationship and the difference between myths and legends. As Jaan Puhvel (*Comparative Mythology*, 1989, p. 2) sums it up, there are two stages of evolution in the transmission of fantastic tales in antiquity. The earlier stage is that of myth proper, raw myth as I like to call it. The protagonists are the gods themselves. The stories happen 'once upon a time' or at the dawn of time. There may be Trickster animals who, it is taken for granted, may speak with human beings. The Yahwist's Eden story would be such a myth.

The subsequent stage is when myth becomes legend through a transformative retelling: the old stories are set into historical time. Gods and Tricksters become mortals, albeit supernaturally endowed mortals, epic heroes, culture heroes. The Hercules stories would fit in here. Hercules was originally simply the sun. But he has gone a good way toward historicization. His rays have become his poison arrows and the mane of the Nemean Lion, which he strips off and wears. The houses of the Zodiac have become his twelve labors, *etc*. Later still, as Veyne notes (p. 32), Herodotus tries to establish when in history Hercules would have, or must have, lived. Plutarch does the same with the grain and desert deities Osiris and Set, making them royalty in ancient Egypt.

The whole trend toward 'Euhemerism' as far back as the Sophist Prodicus partakes of the same process, albeit at a more reflective stage. (Euhemerus assumed that behind all mythic characters lay historical figures, a general behind a war god, a doctor behind a healing god, *etc*.) Though Euhemerists imagined historical individuals had been mythicized, the truth was that they themselves were historicizing mythic and legendary characters.

Much of the Old Testament appears to me to represent this historicized stage. Jubal, elsewhere attested as the Canaanite god of music, has become the culture hero who invented the lyre and pipe. Gad, known as the Near Eastern god of luck, has become a tribal patriarch. Baal has become Abel. Joshua the son of Oannes/Dagon has become Moses' successor. Several sun gods have become patriarchs, ethnic stereotypes, and heroes:

Samson, whose name simply means 'the sun,' Nimrod, Elijah, Moses, Isaac, Esau, and Enoch. Abraham, Elisha, and Jacob were at first moon gods (Ignaz Goldziher, *Mythology among the Hebrews and Its Historical Development*, 1877, reprinted 1967, pp. 32, 104–161*ff*). Ishtar Shalmith becomes 'the Shulammite' (Song of Songs 6:13). Eve/Hebe, like her Greek sister Pandora, begins as the Great Mother, but she is demoted to a primordial Lucy Ricardo. And so on.

Sometimes attempts to fix a historical period, *à la* Herodotus, were not stable; there was more than one attempt. For instance, Cain is set in various historical periods, which is why one episode, where he marries a wife (Genesis 4:17), presupposes a populated earth, while another (Genesis 4:1) makes him the first son of Adam and Eve. Ezekiel, who lived during the Babylonian Exile, thinks of Daniel as a figure of great wisdom sharing the remote antiquity of Noah (Ezekiel 14:14, 20), while the later Book of Daniel places Daniel himself in the Exile, contemporary with Ezekiel.

This is the distinction we must draw when we approach the gospels as deposits of myth. They appear now in a historical setting, but the issue is whether they are perhaps historicized myths. For instance, George A. Wells (*The Jesus of the Early Christians* and others) and Earl Doherty (*The Jesus Puzzle*), the great Mythicists of our time, argue that the earliest Christians, whose beliefs are on display in the early Epistles, worshipped a savior who had either (*à la* Wells) lived in the mythic long ago, or (as *per* Doherty) had never lived on earth at all, but died and rose in a heavenly world, that of the Gnostic Archons. Similarly, Barbara G. Walker (*The Women's Encyclopedia of Myths and Secrets*, articles "Jesus Christ" and "Mary Magdalene") reads the gospels as historicizations of very ancient nature-religion myths, the kind we read of in James Fraser's *The Golden Bough*. It would have been a subsequent development for Christians to attempt to fix a historical period for Jesus, for church-political reasons well explained by Arthur Drews (*The Christ Myth*, 1910, reprinted 1998, pp. 271–272; *cf.* Elaine Pagels, who makes the same point in connection with the objectification of the resurrection in *The Gnostic Gospels*, 1979, pp. 3–27). This would account for the varying attempts to do so.

The Talmud and various Jewish-Christians place Jesus 100 years BCE (G. R. S. Mead, *Did Jesus Live 100 BC?*). Irenaeus (*Against Heresies* 2:22:6) thinks Jesus was crucified in Claudius' reign, which he harmonizes with the gospels by making Jesus nearly fifty years old at his death. The Gospel of Peter (1:2) holds Herod Antipas responsible for his death, while Mark blames it on Pilate. If Jesus were a person of recent historical memory, how can we explain such uncertainty? It would fit better with a trend toward historicizing a mythic figure.

Alan Dundes ("The Hero Myth and the Life of Jesus," in Robert A. Segal, ed., *In Quest of the Hero*) similarly shows how extensively the gospel life of Jesus parallels the standard mythic hero structure, implying that myths have been historicized (or that a historical character has been mythicized, the facts getting lost in the haze of hero-worship). And this is where we ought to see the relevance of *mythemes* from the sacred kingship ideology (see Sigmund Mowinkel's *The Psalms in Israel's Worship* and *He That Cometh*, as well as Aubrey R. Johnson, *Sacral Kingship in Ancient Israel*; Ivan Engnell, *Studies in Divine Kingship in the Ancient Near East*, and the many works of Geo Widengren.). Miller mentions this, then discounts it. He says that this ancient myth of civic and cosmic renewal may have fit ancient Babylonian and Canaanite monarchies (actually, Hellenistic ones, too) but it does not fit with a figure like Jesus. To apply it to Jesus is to rip it out of the only historical context in which it made sense.

Again, I don't agree, because we need only remind ourselves that the messiah was the sacred king, albeit demystified to some extent by the rabbis once Judaism had embraced monotheism some time after the prophets introduced it. Originally the king of Judah was a god on earth (Psalm 45:6; Isaiah 9:6), or the son of one (Psalm 2:7), or of Yahweh and Shahar (Psalm 110:3, "from Dawn's womb"). Such a king ritually reenacted the mythic victory of the god whose vicar he was, the victory and resurrection of Baal, Marduk, Dumuzi, *etc.* This was how the god had, in primordial times, secured his kingship (Psalm 74:12–17; 89:5–14), and how in historical times, the king renewed his own heavenly mandate. Once the tree of Jesse was chopped down by Nebuchadnezzar in 587 BCE, these myths were officially set aside, waiting, along with kingship itself, to be renewed. When Jesus was understood as King of the Jews, no wonder it all came flooding back in. (This, whether Jesus was a historical or originally a mythic figure: the messiah association would have placed him within this conceptual world.)

Near Myth

A related issue: Miller notes that genuine Christian myths, which he says do not exist in the gospels, might be expected to portray Jesus wrestling with Zeus, chatting with Marduk, *etc.* But are we not on pretty much the same unstable ground when Jesus is shown trading scripture quotes with the very Devil and the latter miraculously teleports him all over Palestine (Matthew 4:1–11; Luke 4:1–13) — or when *demons* (not just demoniacs) threaten to blow his cover (Mark 1:34)? Miller may object that the miraculous and the mythic are not the same thing. But here we begin to see why they are. Myth, as Bultmann said so well, is the representation of the transcendent in objectifying terms (Bultmann, "New Testament and Mythology," in Hans Werner Bartsch, ed., *Kerygma and Myth*, pp. 10–11, 35, 44; Bultmann, *Jesus Christ and Mythology*, 1958, pp. 19–20).

Miller resorts to the old apologists' contention (maintained by his present-day colleagues, and given new impetus recently from the unlikely quarters of G. W. Bowersock, *Fiction As History: Nero to Julian* (Sather Classical Lectures, Vol 58) and Jonathan Z. Smith [see his article "Dying and Rising Gods" in Mircea Eliade, ed., *Encyclopedia of Religion*]) that relevant myths like that of the dying and rising gods and later novelistic reflections of them in the Hellenistic Romances (see B. P. Reardon, ed., *Collected Ancient Greek Novels*; Reardon, *The Form of Greek Romance*; Tomas Hägg, *The Novel in Antiquity*; Niklas Holtzberg, *The Ancient Novel: An Introduction*; J.R. Morgan and Richard Stoneman, eds., *Greek Fiction: The Greek Novel in Context*) were borrowed from the Christian gospel by pagan imitators, that the direction of influence was opposite that usually claimed by critics.

But, as I have argued in detail elsewhere (*Deconstructing Jesus*, 2000, chapter 3), this is ruled out at once both by specific pre-Christian evidence of beliefs in the resurrection of Osiris,

Baal, Tammuz, and Attis and by the simple fact that the second-century Apologists admitted that the pagan versions were the older — the result, as they desperately reasoned, of Satanic counterfeiting *in advance*. No one would mount such an argument if there had been any reason to think the pagans had borrowed them from Christians. Bowersock's derivation of the 'apparent death' element of the novels from the Christian gospels seems to me even more outrageous — nothing but special pleading. The religious roots of the novels and their tales of the providence of the gods are plain; so plain, in fact, that some scholars regard the novels as popular religious propaganda for the cults mentioned in them. That may or may not be, but I find no hint of Christian influence. What I think we *can* see, as I have argued elsewhere ("Implied Reader Response and the Evolution of Genres: Transitional Stages Between the Ancient Novels and the Apocryphal Acts," *Hervormde Teologiese Studies*, 53/4, 1997), is just which pagan elements in the novels were seized upon by Christian readers and lifted for reinterpreted use in their own version of the genre, the *Apocryphal Acts of the Apostles.*

Did pagans never charge Christians with concocting a purely mythic Jesus, as Miller asserts? Of course they did, as the Apologists of the early church themselves attest, as they replied to skeptics who rejoiced, as today, to list all the parallels between Jesus, Hermes, Apollo, *etc.* Miller points to skeptics like Celsus and the rabbis who were willing to grant a historical Jesus who performed miracles. On this basis, Miller claims, early opponents of Christianity viewed it not as myth but as magic — charlatanry. But clearly both criticisms were in the air. Nor can one read 2 Peter 1:16 as anything but a rebuttal to some who were charging precisely that the gospel episodes were "*mythoi*" in some sense recognized by the ancients, though the intention here is apparently 'myth' as 'hoax and imposture,' a different issue, treated elsewhere by Miller. But then again, the pagans who made such charges probably viewed the traditional Greek myths as humbug and priestcraft *à la* Bel and the Dragon.

Miller does not seem to want, despite some comments, to deny that ancient pagans considered gospel events to be myths. His point is that Christians in rejecting such criticism showed *they* did not take the same stories as fictive. But this later Christian reading doesn't tell us one way or the other how the gospel tradents and writers intended their work. Why may they not have understood the gospels as Origen did? As filled with "thousands" of historical impossibilities, all planted there to lead the reader deeper, into the real allegorical meaning?

It seems to me that Miller's verdict on mythology in the gospels would come out a bit different if he compared them with the form-critical categories of Herman Gunkel in his great Genesis commentary. Though, as we now read them, the gospel stories are legends, *i.e.*, historicized myths, we can still see what Miller denies, namely didactic intent, as when Peter walks on water, founders, and is rescued by Jesus, surely a comment on the Christian duty to keep one's eyes fixed on Jesus in the midst of life's storms.

Ceremonial etiologies abound, as in the feeding stories and the Emmaus epiphany, which have long been read (correctly, I think) as Eucharistic stories. The 'Suffer the little children' pericope is, *à la* Oscar Cullmann (*Baptism in the New Testament*, Studies in Biblical Theology # 1, pp. 76–79), a piece of infant-baptismal liturgy. The various stories in which this or that apostle or kinsman of Jesus comes in for a drubbing are surely to be seen as analogous to the ethnological myths of the Old Testament, memorializing and accounting for national and tribal rivalries in the story-teller's day by using the ancient personages as political cartoon symbols for the latter-day factions.

Miller says that historians seem agreed these days that the gospels are intended as something on the order of ancient hero biographies. Indeed so. But this says nothing about the historicity of their contents. Do the miracles of Pythagoras in his various biographies, much less those of Apollonius of Tyana, guarantee their accuracy? Maybe all Miller means is that the episodes in them would not have been intended by the biographers as fiction. But again we cannot read their minds. After all, Mason L. Weems, the first biographer of George Washington, admitted he concocted incidents like boy George throwing the silver dollar across the Potomac and admitting to having chopped the cherry tree because he thought they epitomized the character of his subject more than any actual facts. These tall tales appeared in his *Life and Memorable Actions of George Washington*, published in 1800, a single year after Washington's death.

Fear of Fiction

I believe that conservative/evangelical/apologetical approaches to the historicity of the gospels (or lack of it) are severely hampered, if not altogether thrown off course, by an unexamined presupposition, namely that if a gospel narrative, with the exception of Jesus' parables, were to be judged fictional, that would make it a hoax and a scam. Indeed, I once had a student who did not make an exception of the parables. When I ventured as a commonplace observation that Jesus was making up stories to get his point across, this lady, eyes flashing, informed me that I was calling Jesus a liar and would face his ire on the Day of Judgment! I do not mean to caricature the mainstream conservative position, but my anecdote does seem to me to put a finger on the unsuspected arbitrariness of the conservative position. Why should one insist that any narrative, even one *about* Jesus if not told *by* Jesus, must be historical, or else it is a lie?

I argue in an essay of some length ("New Testament Narrative as Old Testament Midrash" in Jacob Neusner, ed., *The Midrashim: An Encyclopedia of Biblical Interpretation in Judaism,* Brill, 2005) that virtually every single gospel narrative can be shown with real plausibility to have been rewritten, with no factual basis, from (in most cases) the Septuagint and (in a few cases) from Homer. Acts adds Euripides' *Bacchae* and Josephus. Though I will shortly consider Glenn Miller's arguments that the early gospel tradents and evangelists *could* not or *would* not have created fictive Jesus material, let me first register my vote that it seems like they *did*. I am reminded of a favorite *hadith* about the great evangelistic preacher Charles Haddon Spurgeon. Once an admirer asked Spurgeon, a Baptist, if he believed in infant baptism. His reply: "*Believe* in it? Why, man, I've *seen* it!"

I see a number of features in the gospel texts implying that their writers were not trying to write factual histories. Most obvious is the simple fact of their creative redaction of each other's previous texts. No one can compare Matthew or Luke, much less John, with Mark and come away thinking that the evangelists did not feel utter freedom in retelling the story, rewriting the supposedly sacrosanct teaching of Jesus, the events of the Passion, *etc.* They wrote, rewrote, and edited in such a way as to suggest that they understood themselves to be amending sacred texts, not "falsifying historical records." They were doing what the liberal revisers of the New RSV or the Revised English Bible or the Inclusive Language New Testament did when they added "and sisters" to Pauline salutations, changed male singulars to inclusive plurals, *etc.* They did not mean to tell naïve readers that the ancient writers actually wrote this. They were instead approaching an instrument of liturgy and instruction and trying to sharpen or update it. So were the evangelists. This is why Luke changed Mark's thatched roof (implicit in Mark 2:4) to a tiled roof (Luke 5:19), for the ease of his readers. This is why scribes added "and fasting" onto Mark 9:29. Sad experience showed that deaf-mute epileptics did not necessarily respond to the treatment of simple prayer after all, so the text had to be updated. They were interested in the text of a sacred book, not the question of exactly what Jesus had said one day.

And the same would be true in the New Testament rewriting of the Old Testament narratives. They were not trying to fake or fabricate a spurious history of Jesus in order to deceive people. No, they were trying to create a Christian version of the Jewish Scripture. It would have Christian versions of familiar Bible stories. We simply do not face the alternative of "hoax or history," which is a blatant example of the bifurcation fallacy.

How do the evangelists deal with the resurrection? In such a manner as to suggest that it is some sort of spiritual reality rather than a concrete piece of history. For example, when the Lukan Jesus reveals himself to the disciples in the breaking of the bread – and vanishes into invisibility (Luke 24:30–31) – surely we are to learn the lesson that we meet the Risen One invisibly present at the communion table. The 'literal' point is a *figurative* resurrection.

In John's 'Doubting Thomas' story (John 20:24–29), Jesus speaks to Thomas, who obviously stands for the reader, not lucky enough to have been on the scene, and he speaks an aside to the audience: "Blessed are those who have not seen and yet have believed." This is a stage whisper, as when a character in a movie, *e.g.*, Ralphie in *A Christmas Story*, turns to the audience and winks. We know we are watching fiction.

The same is true of Matthew's farewell of Jesus to the disciples after the resurrection (Matthew 28:20). The missionaries who will carry the gospel to the nations are not the twelve, long dead in any case, but the eager missionaries from the evangelist's own community, probably in Antioch. And when he promises them his invigorating presence until the close of the age, instead of an ascension, we ought to recognize a seamless transition between the literary character of Jesus and the experience of the reader. It is well portrayed at the end of the movie version of *Godspell*, when the disciples carry the body of the slain Jesus around the corner, and then from around all city corners streams a flood of new Christians. *That* is how Jesus rose, and Matthew knew it.

How could Luke think nothing amiss when he has the ascension of Jesus take place on Easter evening in his gospel (24:1, 13, 33, 36, 44, 50–51), but forty days later in Acts 1:3 —unless he was not even trying to record "the way things happened"? The same is true for his three versions of Paul's conversion (Acts 9:1–19; 22:4–21; 26:9–20). They contradict themselves intentionally, for sound literary reasons, in order to defamiliarize the story so that it sounds fresh each time.

Mad Rush to Midrash

Glenn Miller, in another admirably erudite discussion – this time of Jewish midrashic and haggadic techniques – seeks to rebut the claim made by some New Testament scholars that in freely amplifying Jesus stories, the evangelists/tradents were simply following in the footsteps of the rabbis. Miller's first objection to this claim is that midrashic exposition is a later development, after the first century. Hence it would have been unavailable as a precedent or guideline for Christian creation of edifying fiction. Second, *midrashim* were expositions only of specific scriptural texts, and those only from the Pentateuch. Other ancient Jewish expansions of scripture, he tells us, rarely involved ascribing miracles to biblical heroes and even downplayed such motifs.

First, let me say that in every case of a gospel tale seeming to be a rewrite of a tale of Elijah/Elisha, Moses, David, *etc.*, we can easily determine what specific text of the Septuagint the Christian writer was using as a springboard (see Randel Helms, *Gospel Fictions*; Thomas Louis Brodie, *Luke the Literary Interpreter: Luke-Acts as a Systematic Rewriting and Updating of the Elijah-Elisha Narrative in 1 and 2 Kings*, Ph.D. dissertation, 1981). I do not think the Jesus stories are cut from whole cloth. Just as Miller says the rabbis employed traditional material to expand on a biblical passage, so I am saying the Christian gospel scribes used the Old Testament (and Homer, Euripides, *etc.*).

Sometimes they were expanding on earlier gospel material, as Heinz Joachim Held ("Matthew as Interpreter of the Markan Miracle Stories," in Günther Bornkamm, Gerhard Barth, and Hans Joachim Held, *Tradition and Interpretation in Matthew*, 1963, p. 165–300) shows Matthew retooled Markan miracle stories to make them into churchly lessons of faith and prayer. Similarly, Matthew (27:19) posits Mrs. Pilate's nightmare to account for the otherwise puzzling urgency of Pilate in Mark's gospel to get Jesus off the hook. To satisfy reader curiosity over the amount of money Mark said Judas received, Matthew (26:15; 27:3–10) went to Zechariah 11:12–13, and so on.

Miller will deny that any of this is technically *midrash*, since Elijah and Elisha are not the Pentateuch and the Septuagint is not the Massoretic Text. But so what? To use the term 'midrash' for what the gospel creators were doing is to borrow a term that sheds light, at least because of close similarities with what the familiar term denotes. Miller likes to point out how the gospel stories do not fit the precise conventions of Greek myth or Hebrew midrash, as if that meant the categories are not appropriate or helpful. In this he resembles, I think, those literary critics blasted by Wayne Booth who condemn genre transgressions as the mark of a bad example of a would-be member of the genre in question (*The Rhetoric of Fiction*, 2nd ed., 1983, p. 31). Booth, along with Tzvetan Todorov ("The Typology of Detective Fiction," in his *The Poetics of Prose,* pp, 42–52), notes that genres evolve precisely by means of 'transgression' of genre conventions. What we are seeing in the Christian rewriting of Septuagint stories as Jesus stories is something like a mutant strain of what was happening over in the cousin religion of Rabbinic Judaism. An apple is not an orange. Neither is a tangerine, but it is helpful to compare a tangerine to an orange if you are trying to describe a tangerine. It is more helpful than comparing it to an apple or saying that, since it is like nothing else exactly, it does not exist.

Again I say that Glenn Miller appears content to wield *a priori* considerations as clubs to bludgeon critical analyses of the gospels. In order to establish and define the Jewish practice of expositional Bible expansion, he is happy to marshal numerous fine analyses of Josephus, the *Book of Jubilees*, the Pseudo-Philonic *Biblical Antiquities*, and so forth. How does he know what they did with the Bible? It is because of (someone's) inductive study of their treatment of the underlying biblical texts. He does not start with what they must have or should have done. But when we get to the gospels, we are warned that their authors cannot have been doing this or that because no rabbis were doing it. I realize he seems at first merely to be saying "Whatever they were doing, it wasn't, *e.g.*, *midrash*." But his larger project is the process of elimination. He will eventually get around to telling us that the gospel creators cannot have been doing anything but telling us the police report. "The facts, ma'am, just the facts."

I would rather begin with a close scrutiny of the gospels to see what they seem to be doing with their sources. I would like to begin with my own comparisons between the gospels and their possible underlying sources. But Miller seeks to head that off at the pass.

For instance, in the case of Dennis R. MacDonald's claim that Mark is dependant upon Homer (*The Homeric Epics and the Gospel of Mark*) Miller laughs him off with the note that, if the gospels really made any use of Homer, surely Celsus would have noticed it and mentioned it. That proves just exactly nothing. It is a strange kind of appeal to authority. MacDonald's work is full of references to ancient reader responses to Homer that make it look ever more likely that Mark's work embodies his own ancient readings of Homer. Maybe Celsus just didn't get it. Whether he did or didn't doesn't save us the trouble of seeing for ourselves if maybe the evidence tends that way. It's always possible that we are only getting MacDonald's readings of Homer this way, but that's what we would have to show on a reading-by-reading basis. We can't just obviate the argument by appealing to Celsus.

Silly Rabbi! Magic Tricks are for God's Kids!

Next Glenn Miller explores the proposal of Geza Vermes (*Jesus the Jew*), and glancingly that of Morton Smith (*Jesus the Magician*). He has the acuity to see that the two books are related, as some seem not to. Vermes sees the historical Jesus as resembling certain charismatic Jewish holy men of the immediate pre- and post-Christian centuries, including Honi the Circle-Drawer and Hanina ben-Dosa, famous legendary rain-makers. Smith shows how the gospel Jesus fits the pattern of Hellenistic magicians at many points. But Miller is, I think, asking a slightly different question from the one Vermes and Smith want to raise. Miller wonders whether the gospel writers or story-tellers fabricated miracles and ascribed them to Jesus in order to conform him to the desirable stereotype of such a wonder-worker, whereas Vermes and Smith are talking about a possible historical Jesus who, as Bultmann said, must have done deeds he and his contemporaries understood as miracles (*Jesus and the Word*, 1958, p. 173).

Miller rightly notes the disdain and suspicion of the early rabbis regarding claims of contemporary miracles. Even when, as in the case of the famous heretic Eliezar ben Hyrkanus, the miracle-worker was acknowledged to be a righteous man, and even when some of his halakhic rulings were considered valuable, such figures were marginalized, as Jacob Neusner shows (*Why No Gospels in Rabbinic Judaism?*) because they had become centers of religious attention in their own right. Venerated sages with unexceptionable opinions tended to be merged almost anonymously into the mass of 'our rabbis' on the assumption that the Truth of the Torah is no one's pet theory or doctrine. Miracles would function as credentials for innovations (or heresies as the mainstream would view them). The notion of there being no new prophets or new miracle workers was a doctrine aimed at protecting the conventional orthodoxy, preventing the boat from getting rocked and capsized. Such a doctrine does not tell us that in fact there *were* no prophets or miracle-workers, but rather the opposite: the establishment wanted nothing to do with them. The situation is precisely parallel to that of Dispensationalists and Calvinists *vis-à-vis* the Pentecostal/Charismatic movements in our own day.

This is relevant in a way I am not sure Miller grasps. As Neusner sees, there are no gospels in Rabbinic Judaism for the reasons already mentioned, and he explains the existence of Christian gospels about Jesus by the fact of Christian devotion to Jesus, in principle like that of their followers to Eliezar ben Hyrkanus and others, bringing the new movement to a crossroads in which Jesus assumed the centrality hitherto assigned to the Torah. The lack of Rabbinic 'gospels' about charismatic sages Miller seems to take to denote a purely historical conservatism, and he infers that the gospels with all their miracles of Jesus must represent, instead, simple historical reporting by people who must have had a similar conservative historiographical (not theological) disdain for bogus miracles. The difference was, they found to their surprise that there were loads of miracles to record.

I think that is the whole trend of all Miller's individual analyses gathered here. But Neusner shows us how miracle stories garnishing the lives of sages marked them off as loose cannons outside the canon. Figures like Jesus were spinning off the Jewish axis on a tangent. Miracle-ascription is a theological-symbolic function of this dynamic.

Even the cases he cites, Vermes's cases as well, represent a degree of 'rabbinization' (as William Scott Green calls it, "Palestinian Holy Men: Charismatic Leadership and the Rabbinic Tradition," *Aufstieg und Niedergang der Römischen Welt* 2.19.619–647) — a later attempt to draw some of these figures back into the mainstream, and undoubtedly the key feature (rightly spotlighted by Miller) of their asking God for the miracle instead of being the immediate authors of it themselves, is meant to subordinate them to God, and to orthodoxy. Originally they would have been more on the order of shamans, working miracles by their own power. Interestingly, in Islamic tradition, where Jesus has again become a mediator of God instead of a God in his own right, there is a rainmaking story in which Jesus has someone else call upon the Father to be heard for his righteousness. Just the kind of distancing we miss in the gospels.

As for Morton Smith, I am at a loss to understand how Miller can dismiss so casually the parallels in technique that Smith and others (see John M. Hull, *Hellenistic Magic and the Synoptic Tradition*) adduce, *e.g.*, the use of spit and clay to heal (Mark 7:32–35; 8:22–26; John 9:6–7) as gestures of imitative magic.

The biggest surprise to me in this section of Glenn Miller's essay is this statement: "The mass of later [rabbinical] miracle stories are generally considered to be deliberate *fabula*, designed for teaching, preaching, and illustration (like a colorful parable might be)." Bingo! This, applied to the gospels, is form criticism in a nutshell. Why is it so hard to imagine that the gospel miracle tales may belong to the same species? Because they are somewhat earlier? What does that have to do with it? We may not be able to show that the gospel writers would have gotten the idea from hearing such rabbinical *fabulae*, but is that really important? I should think the relevant point is whether rabbinical literature offers us helpful historical parallels and literary analogies, not whether they enable us to trace out genealogical trees.

True Romance

I must say I reject almost completely what Miller says in his section about the Hellenistic Romances and their possible relation to gospel origins. With Bowersock, Miller (for obvious reasons) wants desperately to date the novels as late as he can and make them dependent upon the gospels or Christian preaching. But as he himself admits, three of the five major Greek novels may date from the mid-first century CE to the middle of the second. While we need not assume any gospel writer read and copied scenes from any of these novels, the closeness in time is easily enough to posit the likelihood of shared fictive themes. Just compare the empty tomb scenes in John's Gospel and Chariton's *Chaereas and Callirhoe* and tell me if they are not astonishingly similar. I don't care who borrowed what from whom. The point is that such narrative features are shown not to require a historical origin or to represent historical reporting.

When you keep in mind the recurrence in the novels of premature burial in a rich man's tomb, escape from the tomb thanks to the appearance of tomb-robbers, the crucifixion of the hero (not just endangerment, mind you, but actual crucifixion!) and his escape, and the reunion of the hero and heroine in a scene where each first assumes the other must be a ghost — well, I just don't see how you can dismiss the novels as irrelevant to the gospels. The types of plots are different, granted, but Philostratus' *Life of Apollonius of Tyana* is another case of a novel sharing the gospel plot outline, with an annunciation, miraculous conception, itinerant wandering, healings and exorcisms, confrontation with a tyrant, miraculous deliverance, ascension into heaven, reappearance to assure the faithful, *etc.*

It will not do to dismiss Philostratus as a gospel imitator, since the resemblances, though many and striking (which is my whole point, of course) are not similar enough to imply borrowing, unlike, *e.g.*, the fish miracle of John 21 which must be directly based on a similar Pythagoras story. Philostratus' work is third-century, but Apollonius lived in the first, and some of his legends presumably stem from that period, too.

Besides, as I argue in two chapters of my *The Widow Traditions in Luke-Acts*, we can find traces in one of Luke's sources of a Joanna story very similar to the conversion stories of celibate women in the *Apocryphal Acts*, which all scholars admit are derived from the Romance genre.

Miller refuses to recognize any reflection in the gospels of the important contemporary trend of Homeric rewrites. I just can't see how one can sweep away the books of Dennis MacDonald on this subject. I am not convinced by all of the cases of Homeric borrowing he finds in Mark, but to dismiss them all is like a Creationist saying that God didn't actually cause one species to evolve from another: he just created them to *look* as if they did!

Does Miller not feel the need to respond to the powerful case Richard I. Pervo makes (in his wonderful *Profit With Delight:*

The Literary Genre of the Acts of the Apostles) that the canonical Acts have much more in common with both the *Apocryphal Acts* and the Romances than scholars have been willing (for reasons of canon-apologetics) to admit? I think he has carried the day. I can only say that in the deliberations of the Acts Seminar of the Westar Institute, we find no paradigm for the study of Acts so illuminating as that it is historical fiction. By saying so, I do not mean to invoke authority. No, I mean that it is only close scrutiny of the text itself that will enable us to form judgments, not *a priori* assertions about what would or would not have been possible for ancient writers. Neither the Acts Seminar nor Glenn Miller can save the interested individual that trouble.

Crucial to this section and the next, on Divine Men, is a strategic error, the failure to grasp the nature of an ideal type, a textbook definition or category that groups recurrent features of various phenomena, setting aside their differences. One may dispute the aptness of such an ideal type and propose a better one. But to do so would require one to show not that the differences between the specific cases are greater than the similarities (that will almost always be true), but that the most important features of the phenomena match those of the members of some other class, some other type, and have thus been misclassified. Because the gospels and Acts are different at several points from the novels does not mean they do not at least overlap them as cousin genres, close enough to share themes or to have influenced one another.

Simply Divine

Because some 'divine men' (a category of ancient wonder-workers into which Jesus is often placed) specialize in this rather than that type of miracle, some do more miracles than others, or because divinity is predicated of Moses and Pythagoras in somewhat different senses hardly means these figures, as portrayed in Hellenistic literature, do not all qualify as divine men. You can't tell me that such differences – which surprise no one – outweigh the recurrence of numerous themes such as those compiled by Charles H. Talbert in his *What Is a Gospel?* Does it mean nothing for Pythagoras, Apollonius, Alexander,

Plato, Jesus and others to share miraculous nativities and so many other features such as Talbert surveys? We might as well join apologist Leon Morris (*Apocalyptic*, 1972) in denying that the Revelation of John belongs with other apocalypses like 4 Ezra because they are not exactly alike at every point. Sorry, Leon, there is a larger genre of apocalypses. And sorry Glenn, there is a larger category of *aretalogies*.

The ancients did not seem to have any trouble lumping such figures together, as when Celsus recalls the divine men he saw in action in his Near Eastern travels: "I am God or God's Son or a divine spirit! I have come, for the destruction of the world is at hand! And because of your misdeeds, O mankind, you are about to perish! But I will save you! Soon you will see me ascend with heavenly power. Blessed is he who now worships me! Upon all others I will cast eternal fire, on all cities and countries... But those who believe in me I will protect forever." (quoted in Origen, *Contra Celsum* 7:9). This sounds very much like Jesus as portrayed in the gospels. And Celsus' statement raises the possibility that the divine man category might be not only a literary type but a social-religious type, a mystagogue, cult leader, Bodhisattva, what have you. Jesus may well have been one of them. Marcus Borg (*Jesus: A New Vision*) certainly thinks so.

On the other hand, D. F. Strauss (*The Life of Jesus for the People*, 1879, vol. 1, pp. 359–360) pointed out what is implicit in the comparison with the Celsus passage: if the historical Jesus really went about making such bombastic boasts (as in the Gospel of John), we would be hard put not to dismiss him as a self-important megalomaniac, a deluded kook. Such extravagances would, however, make sense as the poetry of worship and exaltation placed upon the lips of Jesus as the literary incarnation of Christian devotion.

Is there really so little, as Miller thinks, in common between Jesus and Asclepius, or as they used to call him, *the Savior*? Asclepius was a son of a god and a mortal woman and had walked the earth as a mortal, albeit a demigod. He healed many and finally raised the dead. One may say he healed using conventional means, but then so did Jesus when he employed spit, clay, gestures, *etc.* Zeus struck him dead for blasphemy when Asclepius raised the dead, but then he raised Asclepius himself up on high to become one of the Immortals.

From heaven he would frequently appear to his suppliants on earth. The healing shrines dedicated to him are brimming with testimonial plaques, many quite fanciful, allegedly placed there as votive offerings by satisfied customers. And many of the stories have the same component features as the gospel miracle stories, including the case history, skepticism of the suppliant or of the bystanders, inability of the disciples, *etc.*

There is no reason to say that the gospel writers or tradents borrowed from Asclepius; it is just the same kind of thing. Even the fact of the Asclepius healings occurring in the shrines after the ascension of the god coincide with the form-critical theory that the gospel miracles stem from the practice of the early church. It just happens that, like medieval Elijah stories set in the prophet's time but used in ritual exorcism (see Raphael Patai, *The Hebrew Goddess*, 1978, pp. 188-190), the gospel stories depict Jesus in his natural habitat, though, like Asclepius, it is really the Risen Savior who is doing the healing — among early Christians.

Ideal types are not Procrustean boxes into which phenomena must fit or be forced to fit. Rather they are yardsticks distilled from common features, yardsticks employed in turn to measure and make sense of the features the phenomena do *not* have in common. The differences are just as important as the similarities, which is why it is needful to study the various phenomena (in this case, ancient miracle-workers and inspired sages) each in its own right. Each is unique, but what they have in common with the other recognizable members of the same class will help us understand where they differ and why.

Thus it is not helpful in studying the gospels to cross 'divine men' off the list for gospel study either because the proposed members of the class are not all alike (as Jack Dean Kingsbury wants to do in *The Christology of Mark's Gospel*) or because there are also other elements besides that of the divine man in the gospels. Theodore J. Weeden (*Mark: Traditions in Conflict*) shows how Mark both presupposes and critiques the Christology of Jesus as a *theios aner* — a divine man.

Here and in other sections, Glenn Miller's way of putting his questions seems to presuppose that early Christian preachers were some sort of marketing agents: "How can we make Jesus salable to our contemporaries? They like charismatic rabbis?

Let's roll out Rabbi Jesus! They like sacred kings? Let's give 'em what they want! And miracles — you've been doing some work on this, haven't you, Harvey?" It is easy to dismiss such a picture of the disciples.

I sense lurking here a version of the old hoax-or-history bifurcation. It's *not* as simple as the first Christian story tellers either cynically faking things – like Bill Clinton's policies based on focus groups – or else being Pulitzer Prize-winning reporters. As with modern urban legends, we usually cannot tell or even guess where rumors and miracle legends originate. It is no easier than discovering who was the first to use a particular cliché or to tell a particular joke. Herder and the early form critics tried to take this into account when they spoke of the "creative community" standing behind the gospels and other popular traditions. Harald Riesenfeld (*The Gospel Tradition*) and Birger Gerhardsson (*Memory and Manuscript*) tried to vindicate gospel accuracy by (gratuitously) positing that the gospel traditions all go back to rabbinical-type disciples memorizing the maxims of Jesus and handing them on. But this is to beg the question, since we just do not know who originated any single gospel pericope, or whether they stemmed from memory or imagination. Sure, *if* the gospel traditions stemmed from a circle of eager memorizers, we would be entitled to regard them as accurate, but that is just the point at issue.

Dead Prophets Society

Did early Christians customize Jesus to make him another Elijah, Elisha, or Moses? Glenn Miller says no. I am not so sure. Paul Achtemaier's article "Miracle Catenae in Mark" (*Journal of Biblical Literature* 91, 1972, pp. 198–221) shows us a collection of Northern Israelite, non-Davidic (hence nonmessianic) miracle stories where Jesus is modeled upon Elijah, Elisha, and Moses. Mark (8:28) probably has the disciples say "Some say you are Elijah" because it is a current opinion among Jesus-believers in his day, presumably in Caesarea Philippi (Mark 8:27), and it is a belief that Mark rejects.

At any rate, it seems very hard to deny that the Elijah/Elisha miracles were the sources of many Jesus miracle stories.

To point out minor differences does not change this. No one is saying the gospel writers Xeroxed them. Again, I refer readers to my article "New Testament Narrative as Old Testament Midrash."

Similarly, it seems hard to deny that Luke has based his Jesus nativity story on, among other things, Pseudo-Philo's version of Moses' nativity, while Matthew has based his on Josephus' Moses nativity. See my *The Incredible Shrinking Son of Man*, pp. 59, 63.

But did early Christians perhaps fabricate miracles so as to make Jesus look like other recent 'sign prophets' (Theudas the Magician, *etc.*)? With Miller, I see no particular reason to think so. I have nothing to dispute at this point. Similarly, as to whether early Christians clothed Jesus in the robes of a miracle-worker so as to make him fit messianic expectations, I doubt it. The data are unclear (to me, anyway) whether anyone expected a messianic miracle-worker. If you expected a new Elijah or a new Moses, you weren't expecting a messiah, which is Davidic. I do, however, think that Mark's artificial Messianic Secret motif presupposes that, given the delay of the Parousia, some Christians had retrojected Jesus' messiahship (at first a role he should play only as of his second advent) into his earthly career and retroactively took his miracles to be proof of his messiahship. But this has nothing to do with Jewish expectations.

Archetype Casting?

In my view, Miller's attempts to dismiss the very existence of pre-Christian myths of sacred kings and dying and rising gods are just ludicrous. This is an old apologetical tactic, and a desperate one. Still, they will not give it up for obvious reasons. Again, I have dealt with this at some length in *Deconstructing Jesus*. Suffice it to say here that we have not only a misrepresentation of the evidence but also the attempt to discount Ideal Types by misunderstanding them as collections of exactly identical phenomena. This error is only compounded when Miller seeks to evade the force of the claim that the gospel life of Jesus fits the outlines of the Mythic Hero Archetype. Miller thinks to debunk the whole idea because there are somewhat different scholarly versions and descriptions of it, as if that meant anything; and because warrior hero myths don't fit it, as if that were somehow relevant; and because not all hero stories contain every single feature of the Ideal Type. Again, he does not want to know what an Ideal Type is. And Jesus certainly does fit this one, as well as the sacred king mytheme and the dying and rising god myth. Here we are dealing with special pleading, the stock in trade of the apologist.

I will agree, however, that performing miracles has little to do with any of these archetypes or categories. That is not their relevance.

I will also readily agree that there is no reason at all to suggest that early Christians unwittingly fabricated resurrection stories as a way of dealing with their own feelings of grief and guilt at Jesus' passing. I will not grant that there ever were such experiences. I believe the stories, and even the 1 Corinthians 15:3–11 list, are the product of dogmatic belief and mythic assimilation, not of historical memory.

Again, I agree with Miller that it is unfruitful to suggest that early Christians might have unconsciously exaggerated and turned into miracles various mundane events, *à la* the more ridiculous theories of the eighteenth-century Rationalists, and the preposterous theory of the pathetic Jerome Murphy-O'Connor about the Transfiguration stemming from Jesus' beaming smile of relief! That's all a blind alley.

Historie versus *Bullgeschichte*

We finally come, as we knew we must, to the same old stuff, how there was not sufficient time for legends to form between Jesus and the writing of the gospels, about how the business of the apostles of Jesus was to make things easier for future evangelical apologists by keeping a close eye on the Jesus tradition with the same zeal as modern fundamentalists who club any new piece of theology to death the moment it rears its ugly head. That some New Testament writers claim to be guarding tradition, *e.g.*, in the Pastorals which are late and post-Pauline anyway, means nothing, since on the one hand they were probably (if the absence of Jesus sayings and the presence of 'faithful sayings' are any guides) talking about creedal summaries such as we find in Tertullian, Irenaeus, and the Apostles Creed. Even if they weren't, the apologist begs the question of ancient standards of accuracy. Josephus, as Miller knows too well, freely rewrites and adds material to the Old Testament in his *Antiquities* even though he says he will add or subtract nothing. He no doubt thought he was keeping his promise.

I will consider in just a moment the interesting business in Miller about tendencies within and beyond the canonical gospels. He argues that we do not find further embellishment of gospel miracles beyond the canon, so we have no reason to posit it having occurred within the canon either. First, though, let me note the implication of his argument for the kindred topic of the sayings of Jesus. In non-canonical works we find a great profusion of dialogues, aphorisms, parables, revelation discourses, *etc.*, falsely attributed to Jesus. Shouldn't Miller be ready to admit that we may follow this trajectory back into the New Testament texts precisely as critical scholars do, bracketing numerous 'Jesus sayings' in the canon as redactional compositions, prophetic coinages, *etc.*?

Now what about the lack of further miracle embellishment between the canonical and the apocryphal gospels? Miller mentions the miracle in the *Gospel of Philip* where in the dye-works of Levi Jesus pours in various dyes and the clothes all come out white. This ought to count, and it has probably been inspired by the reference in the Transfiguration story about Jesus' garments becoming white like no mortal fuller could dye them.

In the *Gospel According to the Hebrews* Jesus relates how he was grasped by the hair by his Mother the Holy Spirit and whisked away to Mt. Tabor. In the *Gospel According to the Ebionites,* when Jesus is baptized, the visionary and anointing scene receives the addition of a fire kindled on the water. In *John's Preaching of the Gospel*, a section of the *Acts of John*, we read that Jesus appeared in constantly shifting forms to James and John when he called them to be fishers of men. The point is apparently to account for their readiness to drop everything and follow him. The same source has Jesus change consistency from the insubstantiality of mist to the hardness of iron. (Miller seems to feel he is entitled to discount material from Gnostic sources, which this might be, unless it is simply popular hyper-spirituality, informal Docetism. I'm not sure why this material would be less relevant.)

The *Toledoth Jeschu* is probably based on a Jewish gospel (Hugh J. Schonfield, *According to the Hebrews*), seeing that it seems to show way too much serious Jewish-Christian character for a mere polemical hack-job. And this gospel has Jesus sit upon a millstone in the sea without sinking. (Possibly this miracle has grown from a dim-witted reading of Mark 4:1, "he got into a boat and sat in the sea.")

Syrian monastic traditions of Jesus, preserved by Sufi writer al-Ghazzali (*Revival of the Religious Sciences*) has Jesus awaken the dead to account for their fate. He brokers a rain-making miracle by finding a sinless man and asking him to pray for it.

The resurrection of Jesus is elaborated in a spectacular manner in the *Gospel According to Peter*, where the Risen Christ emerges from the tomb having grown to gigantic stature, "overtopping the heavens." And in the *Gospel of Nicodemus/Acts of Pilate* the Risen One appears to half a thousand Roman soldiers. The *Gospel According to the Hebrews* adds a resurrection appearance to the high priest's servant and supplies one to James the Just (barely mentioned in 1 Corinthians 15), elaborating the story, since it retroactively places James at the Last Supper, a disciple already.

I'm not sure why Miller sees such a gap between stories of the mature Jesus and the adventures of Jesus in the Infancy Gospels. These, as a category, would have been later than stories of the mature Jesus for the simple reason that the belief in his miracle birth, which invited speculation about how his divine nature would have manifested itself in the early years, was also secondary. Stories of the young god Jesus saving the day when doltish adults had failed already become evident in Luke 2:41–51 (the visit to the temple at age 12) and in John 2:1–11 (the Cana story which, as Raymond E. Brown [*The Birth of the Messiah*, 1977, pp. 487–488] noted, must have begun life as a tale of Jesus the miracle-working lad). They blossom in the later Infancy Gospels. Why this does not count as an ongoing heightening of the miraculous in the Jesus story, I don't know.

Can we indeed not discern any cases within and among the canonical gospels where miracles have been added or made more spectacular? How about these? Mark knows of no miracle birth. Matthew and Luke must alter Mark to add such a miracle (though they have different stories of it). Mark has no resurrection appearances, but Matthew, Luke, and John add some. Mark 15:33 has darkness at the crucifixion, but Matthew 27:51–53 adds an earthquake, exploding boulders, and the resurrection of many local dead saints. In Mark 16:5, there is only a young man at the empty tomb, possibly an angel. But Matthew 28:2–5 makes him definitely an angel and has him swoop down and move the stone in plain sight of the women. He has added tomb guards (27:66) to witness the feat and to faint in astonishment (28:4). Matthew also adds a cameo appearance of Jesus himself on the scene (28:9–10), *contra* Mark and Luke. Luke and John have two men (Luke 24:4) or angels (John 20:12).

At the arrest, John 18:5–7 has Jesus flatten the arresting party with a word, though they get up, brush themselves off, and proceed as before! Luke has misunderstood an underlying "Let it be restored to its place," which Matthew and John thought meant the disciple's sword (Matthew 26:52; John 18:11), but which Luke thought must refer to the severed ear! So Jesus now glues it back on (22:51).

In Mark 6:48 and John 6:19 only Jesus treads the waves, but Matthew 14:28-29 adds Peter. Likewise, Matthew (20:29–34) doubles Bar-Timaeus (from Mark 10:46–52) as well as the Gerasene demoniac (Mark 5:1–20 vs. Matthew 8:28–34). The cursing of the fig tree in Matthew 21:18–19 and Mark 11:12–14, 20 may have grown from the parable of the barren fig tree in Luke 13:6–9; 17:5–6. The raising of Lazarus in John chapter 11 probably comes from the parable in Luke 16:19–31, where Dives asks Abraham to send Lazarus back among the living.

Mark 5:22–24a, 35–43//Matthew 9:18–26 (Jairus' daughter) and Luke 7:11–17 (son of the Widow of Nain) have stories which are like other ancient tales where a miracle-worker, a doctor, *etc.*, awakens someone from a seeming death and saves the person from premature burial. John's gospel removes any ambiguity about Lazarus' resurrection by having him dead four days by the time Jesus arrives (John 11:17). In Jesus' own case,

John (20:20, 25, 27) changes Jesus' display of corporeal feet and hands (as in Luke 24:39) to that of wounded *side* and hands, so as to prove Jesus had really died and risen, not merely escaped death, as in the novels.

Mark juxtaposes two explanations of why Elijah had not publicly appeared, preceding Jesus, which ostensibly he should have if Jesus was the Messiah. One (Mark 9:13) says John the Baptist figuratively fulfilled this prophecy. The other (Mark 9:4) had Elijah himself appear after all, just in private, on the Mount of Transfiguration. No one would have concocted the John the Baptist version if he already knew of the Transfiguration version, which must imply the Transfiguration, a supernatural event, is the later invention. And in Mark 9:3, it is only Jesus' clothes that shine, whereas in Matthew 17:2, his face does, too.

Mark 1:16–20 has the disciples just drop everything to follow Jesus, but Luke 5:1–11 adds the miraculous catch of fish to provide adequate motivation.

There is no ascension in Mark and Matthew, but there is one in Luke-Acts. Rising bodily into the sky! I should think all of this constitutes a heightening of the miraculous. I'm sure Miller has harmonizations at the ready for all them, like a cocked gun. But harmonizations are by their very nature a way to discount the apparent sense of troublesome data. *Prima facie*, I think these passages point in the direction I have indicated.

Authenticity and Autonomy

Plausibility has worn paper-thin once we reach the section in which Miller tries to turn the authenticity criteria framed by critical scholars against them. One fundamental problem is that he employs the criteria of multiple attestation, dissimilarity, coherence, *etc.*, to *miracle stories*, whereas they are designed to apply instead to *sayings*, as, *e.g.,* Norman Perrin states explicitly in one of the quotes from him Miller includes. Let's see why this does not work. Yes, Miller quotes others, like Craig Evans and John Maier, who apply the criterion to miracle stories, but the trouble is: these men are axe-grinding apologists, too.

Miller plays a shell game (whether intentionally or not) in that he takes the supposedly important feature of the autonomy of Jesus' miracles (*i.e.*, he doesn't need to call upon God to get him to perform them) as the litmus test by which to see if the gospel miracles are dissimilar (not like other miracle stories from the culture), and, guess what, they are! Jesus doesn't invoke Solomon as Josephus' exorcist Eleazer does (*Antiquities* 8:2:5). But Apollonius does not invoke powers or names. He just does the trick, like Jesus does. So does the ascended demigod Asclepius. And Pythagoras.

Besides, I suspect the godlike "unbrokered" (to use John Dominic Crossan's favorite piece of pet vocabulary) quality of Jesus' miracles is a product of the Christologizing of the original stories which would have featured him using standard exorcistic technique. The adjuration element – which is where the authority would have been invoked – is now frequently placed in the mouth of the demon instead, because the exorcisms have been readjusted to Christology. We see precisely the same thing going on in Matthew's and Luke's omission of Jesus' spit-and-polish healing techniques from Mark. John saves the use of clay for healing the blind man in chapter 9 because he wants to use it as a symbol equivalent to Acts 9:18's "something like scales" which fell from the newly converted Paul's eyes.

Again, if we bracket both Q's and Mark's deflective questions or conditions from the Beelzebul pericope (Mark 3:23: "How can Satan cast out Satan?" Matthew 12:27–28//Luke 11:19–20: "If I cast out demons by Beelzebul, by whom do your protégés cast them out? Ask them what they think of your reasoning! But if I cast them out by the Spirit/finger of God, then the Kingdom of God has come upon you"), we are left with an original in which Jesus defends his magical practice of binding the strong man Beelzebul in order to force him to part with his goods, his possessed victims.

But Q and Mark, like Philostratus, were disinclined to let their hero any longer be seen as a magician. As Käsemann said ("The Problem of the Historical Jesus" in Käsemann, *Essays on New Testament Themes*. Studies in Biblical Theology # 41, 1964, p. 28), the evangelists have probably altered the exorcism stories as a bit of retrospective "realized eschatology," putting already into the time of the ministry the envisioned day of

Philippians 2:10–11, when all infernal powers should swear grudging fealty to the Lord Jesus.

Miller does eventually go the whole way and tell us that Jesus' miracles are not, even in broad outline, much like any others claimed for other figures in the Hellenistic world. Well, this is just patently absurd. I invite you to read, among many collections of such ancient tales, the miracles chapter of my *The Incredible Shrinking Son of Man*.

How about multiple attestation? Miller is pulling a fast one here, too. It is scarcely enough to show that all types of miracles are attested in every gospel source (Q, Mark, special Matthean, special Lukan, John), distributed evenly among them. If we could say of *sayings* only that their various *forms* are evenly distributed among the gospels, that would bring us no closer to a solution of the authenticity question as it pertains to *any particular saying*. This is not what critics do: they want to know if any particular saying is preserved in more than one place. If we apply this test to miracles, then, on Miller's own showing, there is *one single miracle* that might meet the criterion, namely the Beelzebul controversy and the presupposed exorcism. Mark and Q appear to have preserved different versions of it, as *per* my discussion, just above. But even that vanishes if we accept the judgment of H. T. Fleddermann (*Mark and Q*) that Mark used Q. In all the other cases, any miracle appears in more than one gospel simply because Matthew, Luke, and John all used Mark, and Matthew and Luke also used Q. So much for multiple attestation.

The criterion of embarrassment is, unfortunately, useless, whether by critics or by apologists. As John Warwick Montgomery once said (in *The Altizer-Montgomery Dialogue: A Chapter in the God Is Dead Controversy*, 1967, p. 64), everything Jesus said must have been offensive to someone in the early church, just as (I would add) everything attributed to him must have been useful for some faction of early Christians or it would not have been preserved in the first place. So can we take the 'unseemly' attempt of Jesus to heal the Markan blind man on a second try (Mark 8:23–25) as authentic because later Christology would have omitted it? Well, Matthew and Luke did find it embarrassing, but obviously Mark did not. Changing fashions make the criterion useless.

But the hugest problem here is that *the principle of analogy* discounts the nature miracles of Jesus, everything but psychosomatic healings and psychodramatic exorcisms. When an ancient claim of some event paralleled only in legend and myth occurs in our sources, the only probable judgment we as historians can render is that this one, too, is most likely a myth or a legend (or a misunderstanding).

Hume ("Of Miracles") was right, despite C. S. Lewis's misrepresentation of his argument (*Miracles: A Preliminary Study*). Knowing the ease and frequency with which people misperceive, misunderstand, *etc.*, and keeping in mind the massive regularity of our perceived experience, how can we ever deem a miracle report as probable? We can *never* make such a judgment. We were not there and cannot claim to *know* miracles have never happened, but what are the chances? Not very great. The bare philosophical possibility (which, admittedly, no one can rule out) of a miracle doesn't make any particular report of one probable.

On the other hand, we know very well that one can find today scenes analogous to those in the gospels where people have the demons cast out of them, or think they do. We know there are meetings where people are healed (or believe they are). And we have no reason at all to rule those out for Jesus. At least not *a priori*.

The Devil In the Details

Miller holds that it is a sign of historical authenticity when we find vivid narrative detail, though he admits it is theoretically possible this could be the result of literary polish. For example, the details of John's empty tomb story can easily be matched in Chariton's novel *Chaireas and Callirhoe*. But Miller doubts this is possible for the gospels since we can be sure the early Christians were a bunch of uneducated morons who couldn't have composed such texts. That, he senses at once, is a gratuitous assumption, so he allows that there might have been gifted writers among the early Christians. But they cannot have contributed to gospel production because the gospel traditions were firmly under the control of apostles and their close associates. How on earth does he know this? What is he: Rudolf Steiner?

By the way, this attempt to run down the education of the early Christians is an old piece of apologetics. Jesus, Peter, John, Muhammad, and Joseph Smith must have been inspired recipients of true revelation since they could never have come up with this stuff on their own. Flesh and blood hath not revealed it to them. Sure, and Shakespeare wasn't smart enough to have written all those plays.

Odd details must, Miller assures us, be vestiges of what reporters just happened to remember, preserved because those who heard them would never have left out a single sacred syllable. It might be. But it may just as easily be a sign of incomplete editing. The evangelist may have taken something from another source and left in something that made sense in the original context but no longer does.

For instance, why are other boats said to have launched off along with the one Jesus and the disciples were in at the start of the stilling of the storm story in Mark 4:36? There is no follow-up. Dennis MacDonald argues quite plausibly that the other ships are a vestige of the *Odyssey*, where Odysseus and his men had more than one ship as they headed into their ill-fated adventure with the bag of winds given them by Aeolus.

Similarly, the mention of the exact number of fish in John 21:11, irrelevant in context, must be a vestige of the underlying Pythagorean story, where the miracle was the sage's supernatural knowledge of how many fish had been caught.

Miller pooh-poohs the suggestion that little details and changes in details have sprung up between one gospel and the next as a result of redactional rewriting, to wink to the reader and make a new point. Why didn't the evangelists just add whole new characters and/or speeches? Well, sometimes they did. Stylistically and thematically, much of the material unique to Matthew, Luke, and John appears to be wholesale invention by the evangelists. But the fact remains that when you do what Hans Conzelmann (*The Theology of St. Luke*) and the other redaction critics did, compare very carefully the little differences between one gospel and another based on it, you do begin to discern what look for all the world to be coherent and meaningful patterns of alteration. Are they just accidental?

There is no reason to think so. This willful blindness is a prime example of how apologetics cheats its practitioners out of an appreciation for the riches of critical exegesis.

Miller admits the advocate of gospel authenticity would have trouble if he were to spot anachronisms in the stories or the teachings of Jesus. To my surprise, he simply denies there are any! I refer the reader to my *The Incredible Shrinking Son of Man* where I repeat Strauss *vis-à-vis* anachronisms in the nativities, then go on and show how many teachings ascribed to Jesus presuppose a later period of the church. Miller is dreaming. He is taking massive harmonization for granted.

Magic Mirror

Glenn Miller feels sure that the miracle-working powers and deeds of Jesus are amply and convincingly attested in extra-biblical sources. We must endure the old Josephus routine again. I can only say here that it seems most likely to me that the *Testimonium Flavianum* originated with Eusebius (see Ken Olson, "Eusebius and the *Testimonium Flavianum*," *The Catholic Biblical Quarterly* 61.2 (April 1999): pp. 305–22). Origen had never seen it. As for the Talmud, Celsus, and others who dismissed Jesus as a sorcerer, they do not prove Jesus did supernatural feats. No one has ever shown why such claims need mean more than that the critics of Christianity were replying to the Christian story as it was being preached, not to supposed prior facts to which they still somehow had access. Celsus was in no position to know what Jesus may have done or not done. He could only reply to the claims of miracles made by Christians. And if he believed in magic, there was certainly no problem granting that Jesus performed magic. We should not picture Celsus and the rabbis as members of today's Committee for Scientific Investigation of Claims of the Paranormal, stubborn skeptics *re* supernaturalism. No, these ancient people were themselves believers in supernaturalism of various sorts. So it was nothing for them to take for granted that Jesus had been involved with the supernatural in some form. Celsus was no James Randi.

Miller thinks that the mention in the *Sibylline Oracles* of Jesus (if it is Jesus who is intended; no name is given) multiplying loaves and fish and walking on the water constitutes an independent reference to these two miracles, not derived from the New Testament. Maybe so. But his is not the only way to read it. Margaret Morris argues (in her *Jesus-Augustus*) that the passages in question are not, as usually supposed, Christian fabrications about Jesus, but in fact pagan eulogies of Caesar Augustus, and that the gospel stories have been borrowed from the propaganda of the divine Caesar. I don't claim to know either way.

Similarly, Miller says the version of the Last Supper in the Koran, where Jesus causes a fully laden table to descend for the disciples, represents yet another historically independent version of the miraculous feeding. But surely this story is a garbled mix of the Last Supper and the "bread from heaven" discourse.

I Have a Bridge Over Troubled Water I'd Like to Sell You

Miller takes on Evan Fales and Richard Carrier, who claim that, given the gullibility of people in the ancient world, we would not be entitled to trust the claims even of eyewitnesses to gospel miracles, if we had reason to believe any of these tales stemmed from eyewitnesses. Miller will have none of this. Instead, he assures us, the ancient world was all Bertrand Russell. And if they believed in miracles, then, by golly, they must have passed muster, and we ought to believe in them, too. No one is saying there were no sophisticated thinkers and observers in the ancient world, only that their presence does nothing to obviate the prevalence in any generation of the *Weekly World News* readership. Isn't it interesting how the early Christians were too stupid to write detailed fictions but too smart to accept a wooden nickel when it came to miracle reports? They turn out to be as illusory and polymorphous as the Jesus of the Gnostics was.

In the end, for all his genuine and manifest erudition, Glenn Miller strikes me as one more religious spin-doctor, wasting a fine mind to defend the indefensible — like an O. J. Simpson attorney.

Christ A Fiction

I remember a particular *Superboy* comic book in which the Boy of Steel somehow discovers that in the future, he is thought to be as mythical as Peter Pan and Hermes.

Indignant at this turn of events, he flies at faster than light speed and enters the future to set the record straight. He does a few super-deeds and vindicates himself, then comes home. So Superboy winds up having the last laugh — or does he? Of course, it is only fiction! The people in the future were quite right! Superboy *is* just as mythical as Hermes and Peter Pan. This seems to me a close parallel to the efforts of Christian apologists to vindicate as sober history the story of a supernatural savior who was born of a virgin, healed the sick, raised the dead, changed water into wine, walked on water, rose from the grave and ascended bodily into the sky.

I used to think, when I myself was a Christian apologist, a defender of the evangelical faith, that I had done a pretty respectable job of vindicating that story as history. I brought to bear a variety of arguments I now recognize to be fallacious, such as the supposed closeness of the gospels to the events they record, their ostensible use of eyewitness testimony, *etc*. Now, in retrospect, I judge that my efforts were about as effective in the end as Superboy's. When all is said and done, he remains a fiction.

One caveat: I intend to set forth, briefly, some reasons for the views I now hold. I do not expect that the mere fact that I was once an evangelical apologist and now see things differently should itself count as evidence that I must be right. That would be the genetic fallacy. It would be just as erroneous to think that John Rankin must be right in having embraced evangelical Christianity since he had once been an agnostic Unitarian and repudiated it for the Christian faith. In both cases, what matters are the *reasons* for the change of mind, not merely the fact of it.

Having got that straight, let me say that I think there are four senses in which Jesus Christ may be said to be a fiction. First (and, I warn you, this one takes by far the most explaining): It is quite likely, though certainly by no means definitively provable, that the central figure of the gospels is not based on any historical individual. Put simply, not only is the theological 'Christ of faith' a synthetic construct of theologians – a symbolic Uncle Sam figure – if you could travel through time, like Superboy, and you went back to First-Century Nazareth, you would not find a Jesus living there. Why conclude this? There are three reasons, which I must oversimplify for time's sake.

(1) In broad outline and in detail, the life of Jesus as portrayed in the gospels corresponds to the worldwide Mythic Hero Archetype in which a divine hero's birth is supernaturally predicted and conceived, the infant hero escapes attempts to kill him, demonstrates his precocious wisdom already as a child, receives a divine commission, defeats demons, wins acclaim, is hailed as king, then betrayed, losing popular favor, executed, often on a hilltop, and is vindicated and taken up to heaven. These features are found worldwide in heroic myths and epics. The more closely a supposed biography, say that of Hercules, Apollonius of Tyana, Padma Sambhava, or of Gautama Buddha, corresponds to this plot formula, the more likely the historian is to conclude that a historical figure has been transfigured by myth. And in the case of Jesus Christ, where virtually every detail of the story fits the mythic hero archetype with nothing left over – no 'secular' biographical data, so to speak – it becomes arbitrary to assert that there must have been a historical figure lying back of the myth. There *may* have been, but it can no longer be considered particularly probable, and that's all the historian can deal with: probabilities. There may have been an original King Arthur, but there is no particular reason to think so. There may have been a historical Jesus of Nazareth, too, but, unlike most of my colleagues in the Jesus Seminar, I don't think we can simply assume there was.

(2) Specifically, the passion stories of the gospels strike me as altogether too close to contemporary myths of dying and rising savior gods including Osiris, Tammuz, Baal, Attis, Adonis, Hercules, and Asclepius. Like Jesus, these figures were believed to have once lived a life upon the earth, been killed, and risen shortly thereafter. Their deaths and resurrections were in most cases ritually celebrated each spring to herald the

return of life to vegetation. In many myths, the savior's body is anointed for burial, searched out by holy women and then reappears alive a few days later.

(3) Similarly, the details of the crucifixion, burial, and resurrection accounts are astonishingly similar to the events of several surviving popular novels from the same period in which two lovers are separated when one seems to have died and is unwittingly entombed alive. Grave robbers discover her reviving and kidnap her. Her lover finds the tomb empty – grave clothes still in place – and first concludes she has been raised up from death and taken to heaven. Then, realizing what must have happened, he goes in search of her. During his adventures, he is sooner or later condemned to the cross or is actually crucified, but manages to escape. When at length the couple is reunited, neither, having long imagined the other dead, can quite believe the lover is alive and not a ghost come to say farewell.

There have been two responses to such evidence by apologists.

First, they have contended that all these myths are plagiarized from the gospels by pagan imitators, pointing out that some of the evidence is post-Christian. But much is in fact pre-Christian. And it is significant that the early Christian apologists argued that these parallels to the gospels were *counterfeits in advance*, by Satan, who knew the real thing would be coming along later and wanted to throw people off the track. This is like the desperate nineteenth-century attempts of fundamentalists to claim that Satan had created fake dinosaur bones to tempt the faithful not to believe in Genesis! At any rate – and this is my point – no one would have argued this way had the pagan myths of dead and resurrected gods been more recent than the Christian.

Second, in a variation on the theme, C. S. Lewis suggested that in Jesus' case "myth became fact." He admitted the whole business about the Mythic Hero Archetype and the similarity to the pagan saviors, only he made them a kind of prophetic charade, creations of the yearning human heart, dim adumbrations of the incarnation of Christ before it actually happened. The others were myths, but *this* one actually happened. In answer to this, I think of an anecdote told by my colleague Bruce Chilton. Staying the weekend at the home of a friend, he was surprised to see that the guest bathroom was festooned with a variety of towels filched from the Hilton, the Ramada Inn, the Holiday Inn, *etc.* Which was more likely, he asked: that representatives from all these hotels had sneaked into his friend's bathroom and each copied one of the towel designs? Or that his friend had swiped them from their hotels? Lewis's is an argument of desperation which no one would think of making unless he was hell-bent on believing that, though all the other superheroes (Batman, Captain Marvel, the Flash) were fictions, Superboy was in fact genuine.

(4) The New Testament epistles can be read quite naturally as presupposing a period in which Christians did not yet believe their savior god had been a figure living on earth in the recent historical past. Paul, for instance, never even mentions Jesus performing healings or even as having been a teacher. Twice he cites what he calls "words of the Lord," but even conservative New Testament scholars admit he may as easily mean prophetic revelations from the heavenly Christ. Paul attributes the death of Jesus not to Roman or Jewish governments, but rather to the designs of evil "archons," angels who rule this fallen world. Romans and 1 Peter both warn Christians to watch their step, reminding them that the Roman authorities never punish the righteous, but only the wicked. How could they have said this if they knew of the Pontius Pilate story? The two exceptions, 1 Thessalonians and 2 Timothy, epistles that *do* blame Pilate or Jews for the death of Jesus, only serve to prove the rule. Both can easily be shown on other grounds to be non-Pauline and later than the gospels.

Jesus was eventually historicized, redrawn as a human being of the past (much as Samson, Enoch, Jabal, Gad, Joshua the son of Nun, and various other ancient Israelite gods had already been). As a part of this process, there were various independent attempts to locate Jesus in recent history by laying the blame for his death on this or that likely candidate, well known tyrants including Herod Antipas, Pontius Pilate, and even Alexander Jannaeus in the first century BCE. Now, if the death of Jesus were an actual historical event well known to eyewitnesses of it, there is simply no way such a variety of versions, differing on so fundamental a point, could ever have arisen.

If early Christians had actually remembered the Passion as a series of recent events, why does the earliest gospel crucifixion account spin out the whole terse narrative from quotes cribbed without acknowledgement from Psalm 22? Why does 1 Peter have nothing more detailed than Isaiah 53 to flesh out his account of the sufferings of Jesus? Why does Matthew supplement Mark's version, not with historical tradition or eyewitness memory, but with more quotes, this time from Zechariah and the Wisdom of Solomon?

Thus I find myself more and more attracted to the theory, once vigorously debated by scholars, now smothered by tacit consent, that there was no historical Jesus lying behind the stained glass of the gospel mythology. Instead, he is a fiction.

Some of you, well-versed in the writings of apologists like Josh McDowell, may already be posing objections. Let me try to anticipate a few.

First, am I not arguing in a circle, considering gospel miracles as myths because of "naturalistic presuppositions"? Actually, no. We deem them myths not because of a prior bias that there can be no miracles, but because of the Principle of Analogy, the only alternative to which is believing everything in *The National Inquirer*. If we do not use the standard of current-day experience to evaluate claims from the past, what other standard is there? And why should we believe that God or Nature used to be in the business of doing things that do not happen now? Isn't God supposed to be the same yesterday, today, and forever?

Secondly, the apologists' claim that there was "too little time between the death of Jesus and the writing of the gospels for legends to develop" is circular — presupposing a historical Jesus living at a particular time. Forty years is easily enough time for legendary expansion anyway, but the Christ-Myth Theory does not require that the Christ figure was created in Pontius Pilate's time, only that later on, Pilate's time was *retrospectively chosen* as a location for Jesus. See Jan Vansina, *Oral Tradition as History* on the tendency in oral tradition to keep updating mythic foundational events, keeping them always at a short distance, a couple of generations before one's own time.

Even if there were a historical Jesus and we knew we had eyewitness reports, the apologists fail to take into account recent studies which show that eyewitness testimony, especially of unusual events, is the most unreliable of all, that people tend to rewrite what they saw in light of their accustomed categories and expectations. Thus Strauss was right on target suggesting that the early Christians simply imagined Jesus fulfilling the expected deeds of messiahs and prophets.

Thirdly, it is special pleading to dismiss all similar stories as myths and to insist that this case must be different. If you do this, admit it, you are a *fideist*, no longer an apologist at all — if there is any difference!

But I had better get on with the matter of the various senses in which it might be proper to say that Christ is a fiction. The second one is that the 'historical Jesus' reconstructed by New Testament scholars is always a reflection of the individual scholars who reconstruct him. Albert Schweitzer was perhaps the single exception, and he made it painfully clear that previous questers for the historical Jesus had merely drawn self-portraits. All unconsciously used the historical Jesus as a ventriloquist dummy. Jesus must have taught the truth, and their own beliefs must have been true, so Jesus must have taught those beliefs. (Of course, *every* Biblicist does the same! "I said it! God believes it! That settles it!").

Today's Politically Correct 'historical Jesuses' are no different, being mere clones of the scholars who design them. C. S. Lewis was right about this in *The Screwtape Letters*: "Each 'historical Jesus' is unhistorical. The documents say what they say and cannot be added to." But, as apologists so often do, he takes fideism as the natural implication when agnosticism would seem called for. What he imagines the gospels so clearly to 'say' is the mythic hero! When, in his essay, "Modern Theology and Biblical Criticism," Lewis pulls rank as a self-declared expert and denies that the gospels are anything like ancient myths, one can only wonder what it was he must have been smoking in that ever-present pipe of his!

My point here is simply that, even if there was a historical Jesus lying back of the gospel Christ, he can never be recovered. If there ever was a historical Jesus, there isn't one any more. All attempts to recover him turn out to be just modern remythologizings of Jesus. Every 'historical Jesus' is a Christ of faith — of *somebody's* faith. So the historical Jesus of modern scholarship is no less a fiction.

A third sense in which Jesus is a fiction: Jesus as the personal savior, with whom people claim, as I used to, to have a "personal relationship" is in the nature of the case a fiction — essentially a psychological projection, an imaginary playmate. It is no different at all from pop-psychological visualization exercises, or John Bradshaw's gimmick of imagining a healing encounter with loved ones of the past, or Jean Houston leading Hillary Clinton in an admittedly imaginary dialogue with Eleanor Roosevelt. I suppose there is nothing wrong with any of this, but one ought to recognize it, as Hillary Clinton and Jean Houston, and John Bradshaw do, as imaginative fiction. And so with the personal savior.

The alternative is something like channeling. You have tuned in to the spirit of an ancient guru, named Jesus, and you are receiving revelations from him, usually pretty trivial stuff, minor conscience proddings and the like — some sort of imaginary telepathy. In fact, I suspect that for most evangelical pietists, "having a personal relationship with Christ" is nothing more than a fancy, overblown name for reading the Bible and saying their prayers. But if they did really refer to some kind of a personal relationship, it would in effect be a case of channeling. I suspect this is why fundamentalists who condemn New Age channelers do not dismiss it as a fraud pure and simple (though obviously it is), but instead think that Ramtha and the others are channeling demons. If they said it was sheer delusion, they know where the other four fingers would wind up pointing!

In view of the fact that the piety of "having a personal relationship with Christ" and "inviting him into your heart" is alien to the New Testament and is never intimated there as far as I can see, it is especially amazing to me that evangelicals elevate it to the shibboleth of salvation! Unless you have a personal relationship with Jesus, buster, one day you will be boiling in hell. Sheesh! Talk about the fury of a personal savior scorned! No one ever heard of this stuff till the German Pietist movement of the Eighteenth Century. To make a maudlin type of devotionalism the password to heaven is like the fringe Pentecostal who tells you you can't get into heaven unless you speak in tongues. "You ask me how I know he lives?" asks the revival chorus. "He lives within my heart." Exactly! A figment.

A fourth sense: Christ is a fiction in that Christ functions, in an unnoticed and equivocal way, as shorthand for a vast system of beliefs and institutions on whose behalf he is invoked. Put simply, this means that when evangelists or apologists invite you to have faith "in Christ," they are in fact smuggling in a great number of other issues — for example, Chalcedonian Christology, the doctrine of the Trinity, the Protestant idea of faith and grace, a particular theory of biblical inspiration and literalism, habits of church attendance, *etc.* These are all distinct and open questions. Theologians have debated them for many centuries and still debate them. Rank and file believers still debate them, as you know if you have ever spent time talking with one of Jehovah's Witnesses or a Seventh Day Adventist. If you hear me say that and your first thought is "Oh no, those folks aren't real Christians," you're just proving my point! Who gave Protestant fundamentalists the copyright on the word *Christian*?

No evangelist ever invites people to accept Christ by faith and then to start examining all these other associated issues for themselves. Not one! The Trinity, biblical inerrancy, for some even anti-Darwinism, are non-negotiable. You cannot be genuinely saved if you don't tow the party line on these points. Thus, for them, "to accept Christ" means to accept Trinitarianism, biblicism, creationism, *etc.* And *this in turn means that 'Christ' is shorthand for this whole raft of doctrines and opinions* — all of which one is to accept by faith on someone else's say-so.

When Christ becomes a fiction in this sense he is an umbrella for an unquestioning acceptance of what some preacher or institution tells us to believe. And this is nothing new, no mutant distortion of Christianity. Paul already requires "the taking of every thought captive to Christ," already insists on "the obedience of faith." Here Christ has already become what he was to Dostoyevsky's Grand Inquisitor, a euphemism for the dogmatic party line of an institution. Dostoyevsky's point, of course, was that the 'real' Jesus stands opposed to this use of his name to sanction religious oppression. But remember, though it is a noble one, Dostoyevsky's Jesus is also a piece of fiction! It is, after all, "The Parable of the Grand Inquisitor."

So, then, Christ may be said to be a fiction in the four senses that (1) it is quite possible that there was no historical Jesus. (2) Even if there was, he is lost to us, the result being that there is no historical Jesus available to us. Moreover, (3) the Jesus who "walks with me and talks with me and tells me I am his own" is an imaginative visualization and in the nature of the case can be nothing more than a fiction. And finally, (4) 'Christ' as a corporate logo for this and that religious institution is a euphemistic fiction, not unlike Ronald McDonald, Mickey Mouse, or Joe Camel, the purpose of which is to get you to swallow a whole raft of beliefs, attitudes, and behaviors by an act of simple faith, short-circuiting the dangerous process of thinking the issues out to your own conclusions.